CW00731206

A Commentary on
GENESIS Chapters 1–25

A Commentary on

GENESIS Chapters 1–25

David Pawson

Anchor Recordings

Copyright © 2019 David Pawson

The right of David Pawson to be identified as author of this
Work has been asserted by him in accordance with the
Copyright, Designs and Patents Act 1988.

First published in Great Britain in 2019 by
Anchor Recordings Ltd
DPTT, Synegis House, 21 Crockhamwell Road,
Woodley, Reading RG5 3LE

No part of this publication may be reproduced or transmitted
in any form or by any means, electronic or mechanical,
including photocopy, recording or any information storage
and retrieval system, without prior permission
in writing from the publisher.

**For more of David Pawson's teaching,
including DVDs and CDs, go to
www.davidpawson.com**

**FOR FREE DOWNLOADS
www.davidpawson.org**

**For further information, email
info@davidpawsonministry.org**

ISBN 978-1-911173-82-3

Printed by Ingram Spark

Contents

This book is based on a series of talks. Originating as it does from the spoken word, its style will be found by many readers to be somewhat different from my usual written style. It is hoped that this will not detract from the substance of the biblical teaching found here.

As always, I ask the reader to compare everything I say or write with what is written in the Bible and, if at any point a conflict is found, always to rely upon the clear teaching of scripture.

David Pawson

INTRODUCTION

The Bible is one book with a single drama right the way through, and it is about the drama of redemption. The early chapters of Genesis give us the stage, the cast and chorus and the plot and open up the whole thing. It is called one of the five books of Moses, though in fact it covers the events that finished about three hundred years before he was born. No doubt he got part of his information from memories passed on, either in written or spoken form, but there are many things in this book that he could not possibly have got from any other man. There are things that are unknowable unless God had directly revealed them to him, and this is particularly true of Genesis 1. There were no reporters present when God made the heavens and the earth. We would not know what we know about Creation unless God had told Moses how he did it and what he did.

So, really, we are considering the beginning not of the words of Moses, but of the Word of God. After the silence of eternity, God speaks ten times. The first ten commandments in the Bible are in Genesis 1 and they were all kept straight away. Ten times God said "Let there be" and the next sentence is "And it was so." Alas, the next ten commandments which God gave have not been kept.

Here are three things by way of introduction and they all begin with "B". I was told that alliteration was the province of poets, Plymouth Brethren, and fools. I don't fit into any of those categories. In fact, the Bible is full of alliteration.

First of all, Genesis is the *beginning*. It is the beginning of the Bible but it has got the beginning of everything else in it. Here is the beginning of the universe; the beginning of history; the beginning of the human race; the beginning of marriage and family life; the beginning of government and civilization; the beginning of the arts; the beginning of music; the beginning of sin and the beginning of death. The book of Genesis begins with the living God and it ends with a dead man, and the last words in this book are "in a coffin". That, in a sense, sums up the message of the book. History began with the living God but it very soon became about a dead man, and the tragic story of Genesis tells us about that.

Here is the book of beginnings and the word "genesis" is a Greek word – "beginning". In the Hebrew Bible the Hebrew title conveys exactly the same meaning; it is simply the first three words of the book: "In the beginning". This is the book in which the beginning of almost everything is to be found. When the book opens, God is already there, and that is the answer to the child's question "Who made God?". The answer is that God was always there. He made everything else.

Now the importance of a book of beginnings is that you will never answer the biggest questions in life unless you can go back to the beginning. It provides the clue to such questions as: "Where did the world come from? Why am I here? What is life all about? Is there any purpose at all?" You have to go back to the beginning to find the answers. Therefore, the book of Genesis is a thrilling book, it gives you the answers to such questions.

Many people tell us that there is no purpose. They say, "Make the most of each fleeting moment; get as much as you can out of it; blow the traditions; get away from the establishment; do what you wish now because there is nothing, no meaning, no answer to these questions." That is because they don't know the book of Genesis. It is because they will not go back to the beginning that they cannot see the end. So life becomes futile and empty; as void and formless as the Creation at first.

My second point is this: if Genesis is the beginning of the Bible it is also, by that very fact, the *basis* of that Bible. It lays the foundation on which every other book builds. If you remove Genesis from the Bible the whole thing will shake and perhaps tumble. It is the basis for everything else. The God who is talked of in the rest of the Old Testament is always described as the God of Abraham, Isaac and Jacob. If we did not have the book of Genesis, we would not know what that means. The God of Abraham, Isaac and Jacob has not changed and therefore he is my God. If I want to know what he is like, I must study the lives of Abraham, Isaac and Jacob. What was true about God for them will be true for me.

The New Testament as a whole is also based on Genesis. Do you know that every one of the first eleven chapters of Genesis is quoted in the New Testament directly? All the rest is – implicitly, if not directly. Let me go through the parts of the New Testament. There are the Gospels, and here I am almost picking at random. When Jesus was asked about divorce, which is a modern topic, he said the answer is in Genesis 2. If you want to know what God thinks about divorce, go back to this book.

Consider the Epistles. When Paul is trying to explain what the cross means, he says, "as by one man's act of disobedience death came into the world, by one man's act of obedience, life came in." In other words, you will never understand the cross without the first three chapters of Genesis.

If you turn to the book of Revelation and compare it with Genesis, you will find that, by a marvellous pattern, these books, which were written hundreds of years apart by two people who had never met each other, contain all the same themes. The themes of Genesis 1–3 are taken up again and completed from Revelation 20 onwards.

What a pattern there is – *Paradise Lost* and *Paradise Regained* as Milton put it. The tree of life disappears, and then pops up in the last few pages of the Bible—the whole thing. Therefore, I say that not only is Genesis the beginning of the Bible, it is the basis. If I had to lose every book of the Old Testament bar one I would say: leave Genesis with me, please, that is the one I cannot do without; it is the one that is fundamental to the rest. However much I love the rest, I would have to say that.

This brings me to my third point: Genesis is therefore the *bulwark* of the Bible, which is why this is the book that people attack more than any other; they know perfectly well that if they could do away with Genesis they would pull out the foundation stone. I want to say that this attack is not just a human attack, it is satanic. The devil hates the book of Genesis, and we may therefore expect him to deceive as he did in the book of Genesis – to deceive men and women today into believing that Genesis is a pack of fairy tales, that you need not take it seriously; that science has utterly disproved it, and all the rest of it.

This is Satan, I believe, using unconscious tools to attack the one book in the Old Testament that exposes his devices – that foretells and predicts his doom and destruction; the one book in the Bible that puts us in the picture about our major enemy in the Christian life—no wonder he hates it. If he can remove Genesis from Christians' thinking he will do so. That is why one would expect more attack on Genesis than on any other book in the Bible.

So it has proved to be, and not just in this modern scientific era. Right through the centuries you will discover that men have attacked Genesis more than any other book. But in our day it has almost become a fashion to attack it. Now I know there are difficulties and I am going to deal with them. There are problems: did God create the world in six days or umpteen million years? These are the questions that science has raised, but I do not believe that there is anything that science has proved that should warrant a Christian disbelieving the book of Genesis.

The questions need careful studies, but I find that misinterpretation of scriptures and misunderstanding of science are the twin causes of the difficulties. Yet science and scriptures are, and can be, partners in truth. If I didn't believe that then I would have to throw Genesis out too, but I believe that it is one of the greatest tricks of Satan so to divert people into discussing the supposed "myths" in Genesis that they no longer take seriously the bulwark of the Bible.

If Genesis goes, then chance becomes our creator and the beasts become our ancestors. But if Genesis stays, God created the world, and man alone, among all the creatures of the world, is made in his image. That is the issue: did we crawl up from the slime or were we made in the image of God? Is man creeping upwards or has he fallen down? Is the world the result of blind chance meetings of atoms in space or is there a mind that said, "Let there be..."? The devil would love us to forget the early chapters of Genesis if he could.

The book of Genesis is the basis of the Bible and everything else builds on it – and Jesus built on it in his teaching.

Now we turn to chapter 1, and there are two words in this chapter which are key words. I hope that you scribble in your Bible; I hope you mark it. The two key words are "God" and "good". It is Genesis 1 that first said "Good God" – only it was really meant then, it was not just a slip of the tongue. It was not an expletive; it was a great phrase: "Good God". To say those two words is to say something tremendous and exciting. The word "God" occurs at least thirty-two times in as many verses. This book is about God and indeed you should read Genesis 1 not only to study the creation but to ask questions about the Creator.

The other word that keeps coming in is "good" – we read that what was created was "good". Of course it was because a good man can only produce a good job and a good God can only produce a good world; this is fundamental. It means the world did not start with evil in it and that is a tremendous insight, which science has never stated. History can't tell you that, but the Bible says the world started "good" – and it can be good again. Man started good and can be good again. That is what gives me hope in preaching. That is why I can say to the worst man on earth: you could be good again. Man started good because God is good.

So we take first of all the word "God". I want you to notice that there is a particular approach of the Bible to truth, which is fundamental to Christians. You can never get any further unless you start like this. It starts with the existence of God and then explains everything else. Our modern thinking starts with the existence of everything else and says: now explain God. One approach says, "I accept that man exists, I accept that the world exists, now prove God to me," and you will never get through to truth that way. Truth doesn't open up to that kind of thinking. The Bible begins the opposite way and says, "God exists, now we will tell you why everything else does" – and this is the way to truth.

The Epistle to the Hebrews says: "Whoever would draw near to God must believe that he exists." You start there. In other words, truth is based on the simple faith of four words: "In the beginning God". It is everything else that needs explaining – it is not God who needs explaining. It is the existence of anything else that is a mystery, not the existence of God. Therefore, the Bible doesn't try to prove the existence of God; it never gives you reasons for believing in God.

It tells us: this is a statement and you can take it or leave it. You can't discuss it; it is not a proposition for debate, it is a statement to be believed: "In the beginning God". That is where the Bible begins, that is where faith begins and no one will ever find God unless they begin there. If a man says, "You prove God to me in my scientific laboratory and then I'll believe," that man will never come in to truth. You will have to say to him: "In the beginning God".

Therefore, the Bible begins like this: we start with God and then we look at everything else. Let me say straight away that the book of Genesis is not a scientific book. Thank God it isn't or it would be no use to the twenty-first century. If God had put it all in geological language, nobody would have been able to make head or tail of it for all the centuries after it was written. It does not concentrate on the questions regarding how everything was made or when; the first date in Genesis is in chapter 5.

If you have a Bible that says 4004 BC at the head of Genesis 1, cut it out. Archbishop Ussher put that in – a naughty man because God didn't write that. There is no date here; it doesn't tell us when the world was made, it doesn't tell us how. It does tell us who made it and why, and these are the more important questions. Science concerns itself with method—*how* and *when*, but the Bible concerns itself with meaning—*who* and *why* and these are the important issues.

It may be very interesting for me to know that a certain piece of rock with fossils was laid down in the Pleistocene epoch, and so forth, but it won't make the slightest difference to me tomorrow morning. But if I am told that I was made in the image of God, for God's good pleasure and for his glory, it is going to make a profound difference tomorrow morning. So I need to know why and who, not how and when – the latter are of interest to those who need to know, but they are not of direct application to me. Genesis concentrates on the who and the why.

We shall look at what Genesis 1 says about God, what it says about the world in which we live, and what it says about people – these are the three important issues.

First, what does this chapter tell me about God? I begin on a negative level by asserting that this chapter rules out most other philosophies (if not all) that man has held. By saying, "In the beginning, God created the heavens and the earth," atheism is ruled right out—there is a God. Agnosticism is ruled right out too. That word means "I don't know whether there is a God or not." There is! Rationalism is ruled right out because that is the philosophy that says, "Only what my reason can grasp, is true." But here are things that are unknowable to human reason.

The mysticism of the Eastern world is ruled out. They say that matter is unreal and spirit is real; that is ruled right out by Genesis 1. The materialism of the Western world – which says, "Spirit is not real and matter is" – is also ruled right out. For in Genesis 1 we have spirit and matter, both real. Pantheism is ruled out. That philosophy means to believe that *everything is God* – that when you look at the mountain you are looking at God. Some people think this way, even in England, but Pantheism is ruled out – that is not God. He made that, but it is not God. Polytheism is ruled out. That is a philosophy that says there are many gods. It is ruled right out by this chapter—there is only one God.

Animism is ruled out too – worshipping weather, trees, or boulders on earth, or the sun, moon and stars in heaven, for these are God's creatures. So Animism is ruled out and Animism still covers a fifth of the world's surface. If you think this is not relevant to our situation, there is hardly a woman's magazine in this country that would dare to exclude its horoscope. Genesis rules that out. A man or woman who believes Genesis 1 would never read a horoscope because we say: "God made the sun and the moon and the stars and I put my future in God's hands; they are just creatures."

Deism is the belief that God exists but has nothing to do with this world; that he can neither speak nor act in this world. But Deism is ruled out by Genesis 1, for God speaks and acts. Existentialism is ruled out by Genesis 1. My New Testament tutor at Cambridge was purveying existentialism, which says that "God" is simply the name you give to your own religious experience. There is a kind of subjective digging around in the ground of our being to find God. But God exists out there.

In the beginning, God created the heavens and the earth, and I don't care if an archbishop or a pope were to say there is no God — there is, and he made the heavens and the earth. I have mentioned a number of "isms" and they are all contradicted by the first ten words of the Bible.

That is just one verse of the Bible. You may study this book for a lifetime and still feel: I am only just beginning to discover what it says. It is the most wonderful book, but you will never get to the end of its meaning.

I have tried to convey what Genesis 1 says we must *not* believe, now let me tell you four things concerning what God *is*.

Here is the first wonderful truth – there on the first page of the Bible: *God is personal*. We need not talk about "it", we talk about "he". Here is a God who talks, here is a God who walks. You will find that in Genesis 3. The God who talks and walks is not "it". Here is a God who thinks; here is a God who speaks; here is a God who acts; here is a God who is a person. That rules out Buddhism. God is a person— *he*. I am a person; he is a person. I think; he thinks. I feel; he feels. I speak; he speaks. I act; he acts. I walk; he walks.

Here is the second truth: God is not only personal, *he is powerful*. It is written in Genesis 1, in the following two descriptions: first of all, the material in which he made the universe and, secondly, the means by which he shaped it. First of all: the material. What did God use to make the Earth? The answer is: nothing. The word used three times in Genesis 1 is the Hebrew word *bara*, which means to take nothing and make something. It is never applied to human activity in the whole Bible, it is kept for God – because I can't do this. The man who discovers how to make something out of nothing will be a millionaire in no time! No man has ever discovered it. We always have to start with raw material but God's power is such that he made it out of nothing.

Three times the word occurs: the creation of matter, the creation of life and the creation of man. Each time God had to step in and do something quite new and make something out of nothing. For matter does not turn into life and life does not turn into people. Now I hope you still can't guess what my views on evolution are, but at these three points I'm going to declare very firmly that nothing science has discovered about biological life can say anything against what I have just affirmed. Matter does not turn into life by itself and life does not turn into man by itself. At each point something quite new (that came out of nothing before) had to be created by God's Almighty hand.

Furthermore, his power is seen in the means by which he did it: he did it by word alone. Now I know something of the power of words, calling something into being by saying it, but only in the case of people. I could say to my children, "Off you go up to bed," and sometimes, occasionally, and I must be truthful here, the word produced the result. Usually it had to be repeated with the volume turned up! But I can't say "Do this" to *things*. The only power of word that I have to produce a happening is in connection with people, but

God's powerful control of things as well as people shines through this chapter and God said, "Let there be light!"

I saw something at a do-it-yourself exhibition that operated lights where you just make a noise by clapping your hands and the light goes off and you clap your hands and it goes on again. It had been developed for invalids and those who are confined to a bed and can't reach out and touch the switch. What a sense of power it gave us to make a noise and see the lights go out. Did you see that? God said, "Let there be light" and the whole universe was switched on.

Think of the power of God. He is powerful and that is why I still believe in preaching. I still believe that God only needs his Word to do things. Many people have lost faith in preaching today and some of my fellow ministers say, "You don't still preach long sermons, do you?" As if nobody has any patience to listen to more than ten or fifteen minutes. But I believe the Word of God is still sharper than any other two-edged sword, and still powerful, and that God doesn't need anything but his Word—he speaks and it is. A life could be changed for all eternity when someone speaks – not because it is the preacher's word but because it is God's Word.

The third thing this chapter tells me about God is that he is *purposeful*. Now this is where I get my alliteration because in the Hebrew it says, "The earth was *tohu* and *bohu*." What does it mean? Shapeless and empty – that is how it all began. The world began shapeless and empty but it didn't stay that way, or we wouldn't be living in a cosmos, there would be chaos. But God took the chaos and made a cosmos. He took the emptiness and he filled it; God took the formless, shapeless mass and he shaped it carefully. He is a God of order, not of confusion and he can take whatever is empty and formless and shape it and fill it.

This is the key to understanding the six days, the outline of Genesis 1. In the first three days, he was dealing with the shapelessness of it and in the second three days he was dealing with the emptiness of it. The shapelessness was dealt with by distinguishing light from darkness—day one. The waters above the heavens from the waters below—day two. The land from the sea—day three. He was bringing order, distinction, out of chaos and formlessness. Having created the shape of things, he now began to fill the emptiness, and in that distinction of light from darkness, he put the sun, moon and stars. Into that distinction of sky and sea, he put the fish and the fowl of the air. Into that distinction of land and sea, he put the animals and, above all, people.

Do you see the order of it? Genesis is saying to you that God is a purposeful God. He works to a plan, he has a design. That is why when you get to know God your life will have purpose in it. I spoke to forty young people, all Christians, and I said, "Tell me, what is the one thing that has come into your life since you began to know Jesus? Write it down on a bit of paper and give it to me afterwards. It is a little experiment I am doing." Thirty-eight out of the forty wrote down "purpose". God can take a shapeless, empty life and he can shape it and then fill it.

The fourth thing that this chapter tells us carefully is that God is *plural*. I am going to give you a little Hebrew lesson, not because I am a Hebrew scholar but because there is something in the Hebrew that you will be interested in. It comes out even in the English. The Hebrew word translated "God" in the very first verse should really have an "s" on the end. It is the word *Elohim*, which means "Gods". Somebody might say, "Now just hold on a moment, you just said earlier there is only one God and now you are telling us: 'In the beginning, Gods created the heavens and the earth.'"

Yes, but isn't it interesting that the word "Gods" is plural, but the word "created" is singular? Later, God said to Israel, "Hear, O Israel, the Lord our Gods [plural] is one." Now here we have the mystery of the Trinity in the very first four words of the Bible. Because in the Hebrew language—and here is something even more interesting, this is how they count: they have a singular word which means one, they have a dual word which means two, and they have a plural word which means three or more. This is not the dual but the plural word, which means three. So in the beginning, three—plural, singular—created the heavens and the earth. Don't you find that fascinating? The Jews can't see it to this day. There is a veil hanging over their minds, but God the Holy Trinity is here.

Now since you might not be convinced by the Hebrew, and I wouldn't blame you, let's go to the English. God is plural—there it is in the English in Genesis 1:26. "God said, 'Let us.'" Has that ever hit you between the eyes? "God said, 'Let us make man in our own image.'" Who is he talking to? He wasn't talking to man because man didn't exist then. He wasn't talking to the creation as he had done up to this point, he was talking to himself. He was saying, "Let us, come on, let's the three of us make man like us."

Who were the three? Well, if you look carefully, there is God. Yes, we have seen God in Genesis 1. There is the Spirit of God like a broody hen. Interestingly enough, the first time the Spirit is mentioned, the figurative language that is used is the adjective "broody", the noun "bird" and the verb "hovering"—a broody bird hovering over the waters. The Holy Spirit came down like a bird on Jesus, hovering over him. We have got God in the Spirit, but where is Jesus in Genesis 1? He is there – did you spot him?

He is mentioned at least ten times in Genesis 1. Where? "And God said...." What did God say? He said a word. How did he create the world? Through the word: "In the beginning was the word." Here we have an echo of Genesis 1: "In the beginning was the word, the word was with God, and the word was God and without him was not anything made that has been made." Genesis, to the Christian, says as plainly as if it were written on a blackboard: Jesus is the word.

When God spoke, Jesus was that Word and without him was not anything made that has been made. So, for the discerning eye of the mind that has been opened, we can see the God who is plural, the God who is three; the God who is Father, Son and Holy Spirit and yet the God who is one; "Hear, O Israel, the Lord our God, the Lord is one"; the grace of the Lord Jesus, and the love of God, and the fellowship of the Holy Spirit spring out of Genesis 1.

What does all this say to me and to you? I think of this: the God who brought everything out of nothing can take nobodies and make them somebodies; take the things that are not and confuse and confound the things that are; take the people that nobody else would look at and make them the most important agents of God in the world. The God who can make something out of nothing can make someone out of no-one. Martin Luther once said: "It is God's nature to make something out of nothing. That is why God cannot make anything out of a man until he is nothing." You have to be down there before he can make anything of you.

The God who brought order out of chaos, whose Spirit brooded over the chaos at the beginning, can bring order out of people's lives. The God who said, "Light shall shine out of darkness" is the God who has shone in our hearts to give the light of the glory of God in the face of Jesus Christ. The God who brings good out of evil can take a murderer and make a saint, can take an adulterer and make a holy man of God, and can take a sinner, just such as you are, and make you what you long to be in your best moments. The God who created it all is the re-Creator today. If any man is in Christ Jesus, there is a new creation; he is a new creature. That is an alternative translation, and you can take either – they are both true: he is a new creature; there is a new creation. The God who said, "Let there be..." has spoken to that man, and his word has made him anew.

READ GENESIS 1:1-23

I have stood at a street corner in the City of London, watching men scurrying to and fro, hoping to grab some little part more of the resources of the earth. Above them, emblazoned in the stone of the Royal Exchange, are these words: "The earth is the Lord's and the fullness thereof." One wants to say to those workers: "Stop and read that!" If we really grasped that text, it would solve a lot of our political problems. It could solve the problem of the Arab-Jewish tension in the Middle East. Who does that land belong to? The answer is that it belongs to God and, therefore, it belongs to whomever he gives the title deeds. Why does it belong to him? Because he made it and if he had not spoken there would not have been a world at all.

We have looked at what Genesis 1 says about God and as long as we stick to that, science doesn't need to be brought into the picture because science cannot say anything about God. Science cannot examine God and so no scientist could quarrel with anything I affirmed in the last chapter except on the grounds of his own opinion. A scientist can neither prove nor disprove anything I explained in the Introduction. But when I come to speak about the world and man, then I am afraid science does come into the picture because science does examine the world and it does examine man, and this is where the tension begins. We have each been given a mind that we might stretch it and love God with all of it, so I make no apology for making you think in this study.

The problem arises when you talk of what the Bible says about the world and about man because science apparently is saying some very different things about the world and about man, and unless we are going to live in compartments and keep our different areas of truth completely separate and believe one thing on Sunday and another thing on Monday, which is impossible for the Christian, we must somehow tackle these problems. I want to deal now with the following problem: "Did God create the world in six days?" I am constantly asked about this. I recall many years ago, Professor A.J. Ayer, one of the most brilliant opponents of the Christian faith in this country, going immediately for the early chapters of Genesis.

Genesis, I have pointed out, is the foundation of the Bible; everything else is built on it, which is why one would expect this book to be attacked more than any other book in the Bible, and so it has been. What is not always realised is that the attack on the early chapters of Genesis is not just confined to the last one hundred years. I read a discussion of where Cain got his wife. The date of the publication of this discussion was about sixteen hundred years ago! Youngsters today come up with this, thinking they have thought of something new, as if nobody had ever seen the problem before. But you will find that most of the questions that are discussed today about the early chapters of Genesis have been discussed, in fact, for at least fifteen hundred years. Nothing new under the sun, but what is new is that the same questions are now being asked in the name of "science". Therefore, we have to tackle the questions. Mind you, I think that Christians have sometimes asked for it. There was an archbishop in Ireland called James Ussher, who said that Creation took place in the year 4004 BC and he managed to get it into some of our Bibles. If you have got a Bible that still has it in, then get another Bible. God never said that; there isn't a single date in Genesis until chapter five. He was a very naughty man to put that in. He was followed a few years later by a man called Lightfoot, who was the Chancellor of Cambridge University, who said that you could pin it down closer than that and, in fact, the world was created between October the 18th and 24th in the year 4004, with Adam coming about nine o'clock on the 23rd. One of his critics said, "Being a careful scholar, he did not commit himself more closely than that."

When individual Christians say things that are not in the Bible as if they are, then quite frankly, they are asking for it and they deserve all they get. I find that the clash (so called) between science and scripture on these initial questions, is often due to a misunderstanding of science and a misinterpretation of scripture. I want to thread my way through these problems. First of all, may I begin by saying something about this planet on which we live and this universe in which we live which Genesis 1 clearly states. We live in an ordered world. That means two things. It means first, that the world is the result of choice and not chance. Somebody decided to put it here. Somebody said, "Let there be" and there was. It is not the result of some chance accident. Our little planet is not the result of some terrific collision that took place between two stellar bodies by accident.

You may wonder what that has to do with daily life and I will tell you. That's why I am studying the Bible and not the bingo card at this moment; because I believe this world is not here by chance and that I am not here by chance. I am not going to pin my life to chance. The choice is simple; it is to live by gad or by God. "Gad" is the Hebrew word for "luck" or "chance". You either live by gad (and so gamble) or you live by God and study your Bible. If this world came by choice, then I am here by choice. My life must be pinned to that choice and not to chance. That is why Christians don't pin their hope on luck. So, you see, this is very relevant to daily life.

The second thing that follows from an ordered world is that this world is a cosmos and not chaos. Let me take one little phrase out of Genesis 1: "after its kind". Now this may sound a silly way of putting it, but pigs produce piglets and not puppies and that means I can breed pigs. Water boils at one hundred degrees Celsius and it doesn't freeze at that temperature, and that is why I can make a cup of tea. We live in a world in which there is wonderful order, and in which the order of Genesis 1 speaks to me of a God who knew what he was doing, who worked to a plan, and who so ordered the world that science became possible.

It seems to me an utter contradiction to say that the world came by chance but somehow it is so ordered you can examine it scientifically – that is a contradiction in terms. If this world is open to mind, it must have come from mind. If I can see order in it, then it cannot have come by chance. So I would say that the very fact that science is possible makes it possible for me to believe in Genesis 1, and that the very ordered world in which we live is the result of God's mind speaking through his mouth and saying, "Let there be light." And there was light.

Now we come to two specific problems, which I am going to deal with. First of all, there is the problem of where this planet is in space. Secondly, there is the problem of when this world began in time. As far as space goes, where are we? Not just where in the world are we, but where in the universe are we? As far as time goes, when did we begin? Was it 4004 BC – whether it was October or not – or when was it?

Look first at the matter of space. As soon as you do this, you find that apparently scripture and science say two quite different things. Scripture tells us this planet is the centre of the universe; it is the middle of everything. Everything else is above us or below us, but we are in the centre. Or to use a word which the philosophers love to use: the Bible is "geocentric", Earth-centred; it regards this Earth as the centre of the universe. On the other hand, science tells us that it is nothing of the sort, but that we are just a tiny little speck of stellar dust, whirling around a sun and its system, which is itself part of a huge galaxy, which you can see on a clear night, the Milky Way, which is only one of many other galaxies which are moving away at such a speed that our radio telescopes can't even catch up with their message and that this Earth is not the centre of the universe. Now who is right? Is scripture right, that the Earth is the centre, or is science right that we are just a little bit of dust whirling around somewhere on the edge of a galaxy?

Well, let us ask what are we to do with scripture if science is right. I want to say straight away that I believe, from their point of view, that scientists are right and that the diagram I saw in an encyclopaedia in which our little earth is almost disappearing off the edge of the picture in a maze of stars, is correct. What, then, are we to do with the Bible which puts the earth in the middle? You can do three things. One way that some have taken has been to say that this language is "mythological" – by which they mean that this is primitive man's ideas and they are false and they are wrong and we can now scrap them. In which case, they are saying that the Bible is not the Word of God and that it contains falsehood. Or, secondly, they may say that this is what is called "phenomenal language", which means it is describing things as they appear to man. Consider, for example, the statement: "The sun rose this morning." Now I know that it didn't, it was the earth that turned around. But why shouldn't I still say, "The sun rose"? That is phenomenal language; it is how it appears to me and there is nothing wrong with that. But that is not the final answer because, you see, that would mean that this was the word of man and not the word of God. Is there a different way? I say there is. I would say that the language of the Bible, which puts the earth in the middle of the universe, is true, but is not mythological truth or phenomenal truth, it is God's truth; it is theological truth. When we use the word "theological" we mean this is how God sees it. Can I put it this way? Coming in on the A3 road to Guildford, you see an AA sign, which says, "To the town centre". One day I took out my map of Guildford and, using some mathematical instruments, I worked out where the centre of Guildford is and it is under the railway bridge in Stoke Road. That is the dead centre of Guildford and not one of the AA road signs points to it. They all point you to somewhere in the High Street and they are all wrong. Or are they?

Can you see that both are true? Scientifically, the centre is under the railway bridge in Stoke Road; personally and socially, the centre is in the High Street because that is where everybody comes, that is where it all happens, that is where the shops are and where the bus station is. Do you see what I am saying? Scientifically it is true that this earth is not the centre of the universe; physically it is true that it is not the centre. Theologically, this little planet of ours is the dead centre of the universe; this is where it all happens. This is where all the attention is. This is the only little planet in the whole universe that God's Son visited; this is where the cross was planted. This is where the future of the whole universe has been settled—everything happened here. The earth is the centre of the universe and it is vital that we should hang on to this truth, especially in a scientific day.

I read the novel 2001: A Space Odyssey which was written in the atmosphere in which man was pushing out into space. What is the overall effect of the novel? That man is nothing; that this planet is nothing. We are vanishing into insignificance in the space age. We are realising how big the universe is and so how small we are, and this world is losing its significance. I want to say, thank God the Bible still says the earth is the centre of the universe – we need that truth, and it is true. It is on this little planet, of all the bodies whirling in space, that God settled the future of the universe and the creation of the new heaven and the new earth that is to come one day.

Can you see what I'm saying? I'm saying that science and scripture are both true. If you are going to get the whole truth, you must have both. In this day, when we are in danger of being bemused by science and all the reports of the infinite space out there, we need above all to get back to the Bible and discover again that when God looks at his universe, the earth is the centre of it. If you go to the church of the Holy Sepulchre in Jerusalem, set into the marble floor there is a silver star. The guide will point to this and say, "That is the centre of the earth." Well, I am sure Galileo would disagree with it, but Jerusalem, from God's point of view, is the centre of the Earth. Do you see what I am saying? I am saying that there are different kinds of truth. The Bible is concerned with much deeper truth than the truth you can measure with instruments. It is concerned with the whole truth about the world in which we live.

Now, you may think I have devoted a lot of attention to this, but I have done so quite deliberately because I believe this is the answer not only to the problem of space, which science raises, but to the problem of time in relation to the six days of Genesis 1. So let me now turn to the problem of time. Once again, we have an apparent contradiction between what scripture says and what science says. Scripture says that the whole job was done in six days, under a week. Science says it took billions of years for the first signs of life to appear on Earth and that animals took hundreds of millions of years.

Now there is a slight discrepancy here: six days, less than a week, and billions of years. Who is right? Where do we find the truth? How can we explain it?

There are four possibilities and I will run through them straight away and then treat each one. Possibility number one: science and scripture are both wrong. Possibility number two: science is wrong and scripture is right. Possibility number three: scripture is wrong and science is right. Possibility number four: both scripture and science are right.

Take the first possibility: that science and scripture are both wrong. I am not going to say anything about that view because I have never yet met anyone who held it. Usually they accept one or the other. If they didn't accept either, I would wonder where on earth they would get any other evidence from, so we will drop that one. Number two I take more seriously because there are many thousands of Christians who maintain that science is wrong and scripture is right. The Seventh Day Adventists hold that to be the case – that all this dating, and all these billions of years, and all the geological evidence is wrong and is another example of perverted human reasoning, and that the Bible is right and that Creation took place in less than a week. How do they line it up at all? Well, in two ways. Some people try what is called the "antique theory". It means quite simply: how old was Adam when he was created? Do you see the problem? If God created a man of thirty, how old was he? He was only a few hours. If God created a tree and you immediately chopped it down and counted the rings in the trunk, how old would it be? Now, the antique theory suggests that God created genuine antiques and that though he made them in only six days, when you examine them they look billions of years old. I think it is ingenious but it is pure speculation. The other more serious charge that has been made against science is this: that in fact, all the geological evidence which science has uncovered can be explained as the after effect of the universal flood in Noah's day which scattered the various fossils, then compressed them into rock and so on. This is why one writer, a hydraulic engineer, has produced a book to show that the pressure of the water of the flood could produce the geological evidence. With the new radioactive methods of dating rocks, I honestly don't think, if I can pun, that this holds water.

So I come to the third possibility: that science is right and scripture is wrong – that in fact the six days are a mistake. How then do we explain this language in the Word of God? Again, some people say they are mythological, primitive ideas; ideas that we now know not to be true and we can cut them out. Still others say that these six days were the days on which God showed this to Moses or that in fact, God showed him Creation in a kind of colour slideshow in which he saw something and then came blackness; saw something else, then came blackness, and he then described it as morning and evening. Now I think these are all devices and must be seen to be such.

So I come to my fourth possibility: that scripture and science are both right. Now how could they be? Well, either because they both deal with the same kind of truth or because they deal with different kinds of truth. Those who believe that they must deal with the same kind of truth, geological truth, have to find more time in Genesis 1 than is there. There are two ways of doing that. One is to make the days into ages. Many Christians have done that and said that the day in scripture can mean a thousand years. After all, "a thousand years is but a day to God" and so on, and that certainly gives you more time. The trouble is that it does not cope with morning and evening and I think that is the most serious objection.

The other way in which Christians have found more time in Genesis 1 is through the Scofield Bible, which was based on the work of Pember. That is to find in verse 2 a very long time in which a catastrophic event took place, and to see in the six days not Creation but reconstruction of an earth that had got into trouble. Now again, ingenious though that is, it is neither true to scripture nor to science and I personally cannot hold it. What then is the answer that satisfies me? It is the same answer as was given to the space problem. It is saying that here are two different kinds of truth, which together make the whole truth. From the scientific point of view, millions of years, yes, but if you only listened to science, what conclusion would you come to? You would come to the conclusion that the history of the human race doesn't matter that much.

Let me put it visually for you. You may have seen Cleopatra's Needle on the Thames Embankment. Did you know that Moses used to look at that every morning? It was one of the gate posts from Pharaoh's university, where Moses went as a student. Now look at Cleopatra's Needle. If the height of that needle represents the age of our earth, the history of the human race would be represented by a penny—not on end, but on its side, the thickness of a penny. Recorded history would be represented by the thickness of a postage stamp on top. Now how big do you feel? In all those millions of years, we are nothing; we have lost significance.

So what does God say? I am assuming that God knew perfectly well how long it took him to make the earth. I am assuming that God cannot lie. I am assuming that Genesis 1 is the Word of God and therefore true. I am assuming that God would know that we would find out how long it took him. Why then did he say six days? The answer is because he wanted to tell us the whole truth. When God looks at the time, it is a week—less than a week. The important time for God is this little bit of history in which we live, so that all those millions of years are dismissed in half a page. The history which we know and in which we live takes up three and a half million letters—three quarters of a million words and hundreds of pages. In other words, God is saying: I want to give you the truth about time as well as about space.

Now lest this approach is strange to you, let me ask you this question: when David met Goliath, which was the bigger man? Well, physically with a ruler, Goliath, but in every other way David. In courage, in character, in spirituality, in every other way, David was head and shoulders above Goliath. You don't object to my using that phrase, do you? I am giving you the whole truth about the situation. The mere physical truth would say Goliath was far bigger than David, but the spiritual truth is that David was far bigger than Goliath, and that is what comes out of the Bible story.

What I am saying is that scientific truth, by itself, would tell you that in space the earth is nothing, and in time our little history is nothing. God comes in and says: that is not the whole truth. The whole truth is that in space you are the centre and all my purposes are being worked out on your planet; in time you are the centre, and the history of man is the most important period. Therefore he wanted us always to go on thinking of creation as less than a week's work and the history of man and the years of an individual man as the most important thing in time to God.

That is why I hope that people will never alter the Bible. I hope they will never try to say, "We'll have to bring it up to date and adapt it to scientific truth and evidence." I hope that we will always keep God's perspective. I hope that we shall realise that, to God, this planet and this period of history is the most important of the whole universe and that this was how he told us this. So when you read Genesis 1, aren't you quickly through it? At college I had to read thick scientific tomes to tell me about how the earth began. God says: if you want to get the whole truth, you had better get through that in a page and get down to real business – that I made man as the crown and summit of my creation and that it is his history that I am interested in. To me, six days' work then I had a weekend's rest; to me, the history of the human race is the important thing.

In other words, we are dealing with different kinds of truth, but you will never get the whole truth unless you get both kinds of truth. I do believe that this approach is easier to believe today for the very simple reason that a Jewish man, called Einstein, who understood God, discovered the most amazing thing. In our era he discovered that time was relative. It is interesting that it took a Jew to discover that it is not absolute. It is relative, and you may look at time from different points of view. I think that makes it much easier for us. I think too, that in our day it is more necessary than ever that we believe this.

The novel *2001: A Space Odyssey* begins with primitive animals fighting each other. It goes through the centuries and it goes through into the future and it whirls you around in space and time until you are lost in it. You don't know where you are in place and when you are in time. If you watch the film, it will have the same effect. It simply finishes up with a psychedelic colour sequence and it loses you in time and space. But the Bible says: you are not lost; you are not insignificant; you belong to the centre of time and space to God. You are the heart of it all so you are necessary.

One final difficulty with talking about the creation of the world is that nobody was there to see it. No scientist was there to examine it. No 24-hour news channel was there to give live coverage and commentary. No historian was there to record it for posterity. Therefore, it behoves us to be humble in our attitude and to say: whatever conclusion

I come to, I still realise my mind may not have grasped the whole truth.

But here is the exciting thing: if you are a Christian, a believer, you will get the chance to see just how long he takes next time. Because the amazing truth which science would never have discovered and, so far as I know, no scientist has ever revealed, is that God is going to make a new heaven and a new earth – a new universe – and you will see it because you will be around. How long will he take? The Bible doesn't say. There is no time mentioned for the new creation, except for one part of it. We are told how long God will take to make one part of the new universe – what part? My new body, because if I am going to live in a new universe I can't take this old body with me. It will die; it is diseased. It is tired; it is weak. I shall need a new body and I am going to have one.

One of the most thrilling things to me is that I will be able to shake hands with you in the new universe. Heaven is as real as that. It is a place, not a state. "I go to prepare a place for you." A new heaven and a new earth will be a place, a new universe. The beauty of this one is marvellous but what will the new one be like? Thrilling. How long will it take God to develop my new body? Six billion years? No. Six thousand years? No. Six hundred years? No. Six years? No. Six months? No. Six weeks? No. Six days? No. Six hours? No. Six minutes? No. Six seconds? No. "I tell you a mystery. We shall not all sleep, but we shall all be changed in a moment, in the twinkling of an eye." That is how long it will take God to make a new body for me.

The real question is not did God create the world in six days but could God create the world in six days? My answer to that is yes, he could have created it in six seconds because God is an Almighty Creator. The God who can make a new body for me in the twinkling of an eye could make a new universe in less than that. So this is the real issue. It is whether you believe in a God who is Almighty. It is not whether we believe God did a thing, it is whether we believe he could. I find so often those who argue with Genesis and the early chapters are really saying, "I don't believe that God could," and that is not what a Christian says.

I believe most firmly that God could have created the whole universe in six days, and in six hours, and in six minutes. One day I will tell you how long he takes to make the next one because it is my Christian hope one day to have a body that will never be diseased, a body that will never die, and to live in a universe in which there are no tornados and no bacteria and no cancer and no leprosy – to live in a world in which there is no sin either, to live in a world in which there is nothing that spoils that universe.

When the world left God's hands, however long it took, God said, "That's very good." Into this world came evil, both human and superhuman, and ruined it. But God says: I am not finished with it yet. I am going to try it all over again. I am going to build it all over again. I am going to dissolve this one in fire and then I am going to take all the energy again and rebuild it and make a new heaven and a new earth. How long will God take? I will tell you when he does it. Hallelujah!

READ GENESIS 1:24–2:7

Now what does Genesis 1 tell us about man, about ourselves? I suppose that one of the deepest questions you can ever ask and one of the most important is: what is man? To give you only one illustration of the importance of asking and answering this question, it was the answer of a German philosopher Nietzsche to that question "What is man?" that led ultimately to the Second World War, for it was the philosophy that the Fascist party of Germany accepted.

In asking this question "What is man?" you are really going to shape your attitude to life, to other people—indeed, if you go back to the original question, "Where did man come from?" you are likely also to answer the question, "Where is he going to?" To ask where man came from is to answer the question "What is he?" Because if you can find where we started, you will find what kind of creature we are. Now this raises, of course, the question of evolution, which to the scientist seems to be a sacred cow and to the Christian a bogey man. In between the two we are often terribly torn.

Hitherto, many have assumed (at least in the West) on the basis of the Bible that man started at the top and has in fact fallen and is heading rapidly for the level of the beasts. It is a completely opposite viewpoint to believe that man started with the beasts and instead of belonging to a fallen race, we do in fact belong to a rising race – a view put forward by Edmund Leach in the Reith lectures: "Men have become like gods and we must now exercise our divinity." Now here are the two views and since they are so diametrically opposed I think you can understand why there was such a very hot debate between Christians and evolutionists during the nineteenth century and into the twentieth.

The Bible puts man in his rightful place. He gives him his right connection, so to speak, and I want to look at man's connections in three directions: first, man's material connections; second, man's animal connections; third, man's eternal connections. I am going to ask under each heading just how closely man is connected – or perhaps he is quite distinct, we shall see.

Take first the *material* connections of man. A famous surgeon once said publicly that as part of his student research he dissected a human body to its last little piece and he found no soul. Well, I am not surprised; I wouldn't have expected him to. I remember when I went on an evangelistic mission with Donald Soper. I remember in one open-air meeting, he was asked two questions and I recall his replies, which I think were quite brilliant, as he could be. The first question was: "What shape is your soul?" He replied, "Oblong." Now that is a very profound answer and in fact, it is the biblical one. The next question was: "Where is the soul in the body?" and he said, "Where the music is in the organ." This again was a profound and scriptural answer. You see, if you took an organ to pieces and said you didn't find any music in it you would be a fool. That is precisely what that surgeon was when he said he took that body to bits and didn't find any soul.

You see, it does not say in Genesis 1 that God made a body and then took a soul and then put them together and put the soul somewhere in the body. He said he took the dust of the earth and he breathed into that dust and man became a living soul. In other words, my soul is oblong. When you look at me you are looking at my oblong soul. I am a living soul and I am oblong: when I am buried it will be in an oblong grave in an oblong box.

When you begin to approach the question like this, you will begin to understand some very profound things about man. I want to pinpoint two phrases in the Genesis account of man—one in chapter one, one in chapter two. Take the second first, the phrase "the dust of the earth". I am sure you have heard of the little girl who asked her mother what it meant in the Bible, "Dust thou art and to dust thou shalt return," and after her mother explained, she said, "Well, there's somebody coming or going under the spare room bed." We are dust and we return to it and it is very important to remember that every particle of your body can be found somewhere in the crust of the earth. It cuts us down to size; it keeps us humble. Our material connections are with the dust of the earth. Do you know what the word Adam means in Hebrew? Mud, that is what it means. Dust that has been stuck together. It is very healthy to remember that every part of my body could be found somewhere on the Earth's surface. It is a truism now, but I think most of us have heard people say that if you were sold on the open market in your constituent chemical parts you would be worth a very small sum – which is yet another way of seeing the difference between looking at someone scientifically and looking at them spiritually.

Scientifically I am worth only as much as the chemicals of my body are worth. That doesn't make me feel terribly important or very valuable. But spiritually, God loved me enough to send his Son to this Earth to die for me. You see the difference again, but the Bible never glosses over the fact that you are dust and to dust you will return. Some day those words will be said over you, "Dust to dust, earth to earth, ashes to ashes...." You go back to where you came from, but that is not the whole story.

The second phrase I want to point out when we are thinking of man's material connections is "a living soul". Unfortunately, we can't get out of our minds some ideas about souls that we got from somewhere other than the Bible—namely from ancient Greece, which still provides the basis of our thinking and our education. In ancient Greece they thought of the soul as something that you popped inside a body and you could pop out again later. There was no real connection between the two—it was like a letter in the envelope and the letter was the important thing and the envelope when it was finished was gone.

Or, to use their own illustration, they thought of the soul in the body as water in a glass. The soul is the water; the glass is your body. One day, said the Greeks, the water will be poured back into the ocean, your soul will be poured back into God, the glass will be smashed, your body will be finished, and never again shall the two meet. That is why the Greeks could not see that you would know anybody in the life after death. That's why they couldn't have any real understanding of people being people on the other side of the grave. Ultimately, if you go around the Greek cemeteries and read the tombstones, you will find that there are depressing inscriptions on all of them.

That was their idea and we cannot get it out of our minds. But Genesis says man became a living soul when God breathed into the dust of the earth. What you may not have realised is that in Genesis 1 animals are called living souls as well. The word "soul" applies as much to my dog as to me, according to Genesis 1 and 2. My dog is a living soul and I am a living soul. The word "soul" in the Bible means life, which is why if I had been on a ship that was going down in the ocean I would have sent out a message "SOS" (Save our souls). That is precisely the biblical meaning of the term. I would not mean send for an evangelist, I would mean send the lifeboat, and by "my soul" I would mean my life. I have a body and when God breathes, that body comes alive; it is now a living soul.

Mind you, I am going to affirm later that men have a spirit, but that is a different thing from what we understand by soul. Animals are living souls, men are living souls – a body that is made of the dust of the earth and made alive by God's activity. This then raises the second question: "What are man's animal connections?" Am I beginning to imply already that man and the animals are closely related because the Bible calls them both living souls? I don't know if this is the first time you ever realised that the Bible calls animals souls. Let us now look at the animal connections and this bogey of evolution.

It is not a new idea. The first man to think of it was Aristotle and he lived many centuries ago. People think Charles Darwin was the first to think of it but he was nothing of the sort. Erasmus Darwin, his grandfather, wrote a book about evolution long before Charles did. Indeed, there were many others before Charles Darwin who in fact spoke of this, but he was the one who really made the idea popular.

I define evolution as the progressive development in forms of life from the simple to the complex. That is what most people understand by it. Now I think you can never think straight about evolution unless you separate it into two questions. Question number one: has there been evolution among the plants and the animals? That is a separate question to the second which is: has there been evolution from the animals to man? I would like to separate these two questions because they need to be tackled in a different way with a different approach—evolution among the plants and the animals as one subject, forgetting all about man for a moment, and then evolution in man. Let me talk first about evolution among the plants and the animals and point out that Charles Darwin worked exclusively in this field. Charles Darwin was the grandson of Josiah Wedgwood of whom you may have heard in other connections. Charles Darwin was destined for the ministry in the church and he went to Cambridge and studied theology.

But for a few strange circumstances Charles Darwin would have been the Reverend Charles Darwin and would have never taught evolution because he would not have had the chance to come to study it. But at the end of his course at Cambridge in theology, his interest in nature became too great for him to proceed with that course, and he began to study biology and natural history. In 1831, he set off on the good ship HMS Beagle to go around the world on that little ship studying plants and animals. On islands off South America he noticed certain species of plants and animals which he had also noticed on the mainland, and he naturally began to ask: how did they get there? He spent twenty years studying plants and animals, not man, and finally wrote the book, which we now know as *On the Origin of Species*.

He came to the conclusion that the various species of plants and animals were not independently created but descended from other species. Before he wrote that book, nearly everybody thought that God created the daisies and the lilies separately, and that he created the pigs, the horses and the cows quite distinct from each other. What he was saying was that these could have come from other types of animal, and indeed two different kinds of animal could have come from the same kind originally. That was his basic idea and he took it no further than that.

Now I want to point out that this idea was and still is only a theory. It is not yet a proven fact. Any scientist worth his salt will tell you this. I did have the privilege of studying under Professor Harrison, who was the leading evolutionist in this country, and he was most careful to drum into us students: this is only a theory. So we are not having to cope with facts, we are having to cope with a theory. It has a lot of facts behind it, but it is still just a theory. Furthermore, it is many theories because nowadays I find that evolutionists don't agree with Darwin, they have their own approach. So if somebody says to me, "What do you think about evolution?" I say, "Do you mean the theory of evolution?" If they say, "Yes, what do you think about the theory of evolution," I say, "Well, there isn't one, do you mean the theories of evolution?" In this way, we sort of move the battle from my court into theirs.

It is very important to realise that this is only a theory. Mind you, there are many amazing facts to support it, one of which I have been personally involved in myself. In the mining villages of County Durham where the general landscape tends to be black to grey, there has appeared a new species of moth, which is black to grey. This I have observed with my own eyes. It wasn't there before; it is there now. There are other examples that I could give from other people's experience in which new species have appeared within our lifetime of plants and animals, and this raises the question.

So far, this has been a science lecture. Let me get back to the Bible. What does the Bible say about plants and animals? Does it allow such evolution, or does it exclude it? There are two phrases, which seem to me key ones in Genesis chapter 1. Here is the first: Let the earth bring forth plants, herbs, animals. It does not say that God made them all at that point but that the earth did. Now that is a very important phrase. If you grasped its significance you would realise, and I put it quite bluntly, that since there is no mention whatever of how the Earth did it, I see no difficulty whatsoever in allowing from Genesis 1 that plants and animals evolved.

"Let the earth bring forth of itself," and the earth did

and here we are, and the wonderful variety of plants and animals is around us. So on that phrase I see no difficulty, but the other phrase is: "according to their kinds". Many have felt that this phrase does imply that God created each one separately. I want to say that a careful study of the phrase does not imply that at all. What it does mean is this: that God decided before the process began what the end product should be. The expression "according to its kind" is not a phrase describing the process but the product. It is not a phrase describing how things came but what came as the result.

Therefore, what I am affirming is that the two things which Genesis 1 does say are as follows: God started the process of plant and animal life and God decided where it should end. But not a word is said about anything in between. If science comes up with absolute proof (which it hasn't yet) that plant and animal life evolved to its present state, I would have no difficulty at all with the Bible. There would be no contradiction here and I would be perfectly happy to go on worshipping God, probably with a deeper sense of the amazing wonder of God's creative power to cause a process like that to proceed.

The interesting thing is that Charles Darwin remained all his life a believer in God. In the last chapter of Darwin's *Origin of Species* we read:

I see no good reason why the views given in this volume should shock the religious feelings of anyone. There is grandeur in this view of life with its several powers having been originally breathed by the creator into a few forms or even one.

That is a magnificent statement but Charles Darwin died of a broken heart. Why? Because within his lifetime he saw atheists and agnostics hail his book as an attack on the biblical doctrine of creation. The idea which he had formed purely in relation to the study of plant and animal life was taken and applied to man – and in such a way that man did not need God any more. Men were saying: we are evolving, we are on the up and up, we are on the escalator that is moving on to Utopia; man has come all the way from the slime; he is going to be god very soon. When people said that, Charles Darwin was heartbroken, and he died of a broken heart.

I don't know if you knew all that, but it puts the whole thing in a rather different perspective. You see, so far I have been looking at the question: was there evolution among the plants and the animals, and I have said two things. I have said that scientifically it looks as if there might have been, although it is not yet proved. Scripturally it is possible and there is nothing in the Bible to deny it. I think it is wrong for either the interpreter of scripture or the expounder of science to be dogmatic until we have further knowledge.

Now I come to a very different question. The question is: if evolution is true of plants and animals, is it also true of man? A little boy walking around London Zoo looked in at the chimpanzee cage, turned to his mother and said, "Don't those men look like monkeys?" Now that was his very simple impression and it was that observation that first caused people to wonder. There were other factors that made them wonder. There is the factor of what are called "vestigial organs", the parts of your body that are of no use to you—your appendix, your little toe – where did you get these from? So far, scientists have listed one hundred parts of your body that you could do without. Where did you get them from?

There is the whole study of embryology, which means that now we know how the baby forms inside a mother's womb. During the various stages of that development during pregnancy it does seem that there are some extraordinary resemblances to animal development, which we leave behind before we are born. The tail is much more prominent in the embryo than in the born and grown and adult human being. These things have all helped lead to the question: did they come separately or have they perhaps come from some common stock? Now let me say straight away that no evolutionist that I know dares to say that man came from the monkeys. What they do say, which is very different and very importantly different, is that man and monkeys may have come from something else. Nobody ever suggested that man came from the apes, but there are the similarities. This has been emphasised by the fact that there have been discovered traces of beings almost identical in appearance to man who cooked, who buried, who drew pictures, and who made tools, just as man does.

Neanderthal man is the outstanding example—I know that one or two were found to be hoaxes, the Piltdown man and the Nebraska man were found to be frauds but it was science that found that, not scripture. If you accept that those are frauds, you have got to accept that science says the others are genuine. Now all this has helped to create in people's minds a strong impression that the animals went on developing until one day what we call Homo sapiens developed and men were on the earth. Now I have got to ask if this is true. This is the heart of the question. This is why as late as the 1920s there was the famous Scopes Trial in America, which has now been made into a film with Spencer Tracy as the lawyer who tried to defend the school teacher who was teaching evolution in a school in the Bible belt in the southern states of America.

Why is it that this is the focal question? Well, as I have suggested already, so much hangs on it. Is man rising or falling? Did he start at the bottom, and is he working to the top, or did he start at the top and will he finish at the bottom? This is the big issue and your whole philosophy of life will hang on this question. I comment on science first, very briefly: far, far more than the views on plants and animals, the theory of evolution as applied to man is a theory. One scientist who is not a Christian said in my hearing that three thousand more missing links would have to be found before science could begin to say this was looking like fact. Now that is a pretty big item of evidence to find.

The *Reader's Digest World Atlas* is interesting here. They have a picture called "The Tree of Man" and it looks just like an ordinary tree with a trunk growing into two main branches. On this tree they put little red and blue and green spots for prehistoric man. Then they divide the tree and follow one through to the monkeys and the apes and so on and the other through to man. The interesting thing is that from the division right up to the man there is nothing. There are plenty of prehistoric creatures, plenty up the left-hand side to the monkeys but nothing else. I am intrigued that at the head of it they put a text: "And God made man of the dust of the earth." I wouldn't have thought their illustration just illustrated the text but then some of my illustrations don't either and I mustn't throw bricks! But this is very striking— one side of the tree is blank. It is an act of faith to believe it exists, but I point out that it is faith and not evidence that has caused that diagram to be drawn, and that until they can fill in those three thousand down that side, nobody has the right to say that man came from the same stock as animals. That is my comment on science and I have tried to be fair. Furthermore, something else was discovered in the twentieth century which throws a disastrous light on this whole theory and it's this: a lady went to live with chimpanzees for a year and a half in Africa. You may have seen the publication that she produced when she came out. She found this and it has quite shattered the scientific world. She discovered that chimpanzees make tools. Now I don't know if you realise what an incredible thing that is, but hitherto whenever a skeleton was dug up that had tools near it: man. Animals don't make tools. Now suddenly we find that is all wrong and what we have said was prehistoric man may have been animals and probably were. Now you see the whole flux into which this has thrown us and therefore I would think that for the next few years scientists will be perhaps a little less dogmatic on this issue because of this discovery.

What does scripture say? If you don't remember anything else about this, do remember: there is no natural bridge between animals and man according to the Bible. That means animals could never have developed into man by the natural process of evolution. Now I will stand by that to Doomsday because I think it is absolutely fundamental to the Bible, but I have to face very squarely the following: suppose science did discover the three thousand missing links and I had to look at this, what then?

I look at two possible viewpoints, both of which are now being taught by Christians who believe the Bible to be the Word of God. One is this: that in fact God not only took the dust of the earth to make man but he took the dust of the earth in the form of a developed physical frame. Then with that, he created man in his own image. In other words, he didn't start from nothing, he started from the dust of the earth. But this view states: why should not God at a certain stage in the process have taken the most developed animal and then so acted on that animal and so recreated it, that while keeping the physical form so like the animals, this was a quite new and distinct creation?

Now that is the view taken by such scholars as Banner, Professor of Botany in London University, a wonderful Christian, and others like him. I think that is a possibility

– there is nothing in the scripture to exclude it – but quite frankly I would say that while scripture cannot exclude that view, I don't think it encourages it. My own view on the balance of scientific evidence and scriptural statement is that I still do believe that God made man separately and I have various reasons for saying that. The main one is that God could do it.

I recall seeing the film *The Bible*, in which an Italian director set out to put the whole Bible in a film. I think that was really asking something. He managed to get the first twenty-two chapters into two-and-a-half hours. I was intrigued and I thought, "How are they going to film Genesis chapter 1?" Do you know, after trying many different ways and talking to all the scientists, he decided the best way was simply to play it as it was written and simply to present it as Genesis 1 presents it.

One of the most memorable scenes is looking through the mist at a desert of dust. Through the mist you see dust coagulate into an oblong lump and gradually transform until lying there is an inert corpse into which God breathes. The corpse sits up, stands up and looks up. It is a very dramatic and moving moment. I know it is trick photography, but God would not have needed trick photography if God is Almighty. My reaction to seeing that was, "Why could God not have done that?" I began to wonder if people's difficulties are that they don't think God *could*. How long will it take God to develop my next body? The twinkling of an eye, from nothing. So I see no scientific or scriptural difficulty whatsoever in holding to the simple belief that God developed the animal world and the plant world by evolution if that becomes proved, but on balance I still hold to the special creation of man – something that God did. He may have made our bodies like the higher animals, which is a good thing because they were very well adapted and developed for this environment. Why shouldn't he copy that body? The point is when God made man, something new came, something that could not have come without supernatural intervention.

I would personally not feel free to be so dogmatic on this that I would have to say to someone who held the view that God took an ape's body and re-created that into a man that I would hold that that was the wrong view; I think the Bible could allow it but I still think on balance that both scripture and science allow me to believe that God took the dust of the earth and from the material (not the animal but straight from the material) created man in his own image.

I want to give you seven reasons from the Bible which set man quite apart from all the animals, which say to the question "What is man?" — that he has come from God, that he has come from down there not from up here, even though he is made of the dust of the earth; that man belongs to a fallen race, not to a rising one; that man is quite a different category from every other living thing. However intelligent my dog may be, however much I can have an elementary conversation with my dog, my dog and I are completely different creatures.

Here are the seven reasons. Number one: man is the climax of creation. Even science agrees that the climax and crown and peak of creation is man. Reason number two: the word "created" is used of man and not of the plants and animals. The word "created", as I have shown, has this notion of something new entering into the scene. It is only used three times in Genesis 1—matter, life and man, and therefore I think the Word of God indicates something new at each stage—matter, life and man. Third reason: before man is created, God talks to himself, which he never did before any of the other things. The Divine Trinity had a conference and they discussed what they were going to do before they made man. They didn't discuss any other part of creation. That sets man apart. "Let us make man...."

Fourth reason: God said "Let us make man in our own image, after our likeness...." I have seen volumes three inches thick in theological libraries discussing one thing: what does the word "image" mean in Genesis 1? I think many writers go much too deeply into it, but it means two things: not only do we bear something of the image of God which no other part of creation has, but it also means that I can have a relationship with him.

My dog doesn't pray—I am not ashamed of that because I don't think I could have got the animal to do so. In fact, whenever we do pray she seems to think that licking faces is the correct response. She has no liturgical sense at all. Dogs don't pray; no animal prays. There is no image of God in them and therefore there can be no relationship. But I wonder if you realise that when God said, "Let us make man in our own image," he was not just saying let us make each individual in our own image. He was saying: let us make them dependent on each other. Did you see that important message? Father, Son, and Holy Spirit have relationships with each other, and God was saying: let us make people interdependent. Now do you see why it immediately goes on to say, "And God made man in his own image, male and female, created he them"? You know, it is an extraordinary fact that half the people in the world are men and half are women. Did that ever strike you as strange? It should do. It is an extraordinary fact that God created male and female, making people need each other.

Reason number five: God spoke to man after creating him. He never spoke to the plants; he never spoke to the animals. But when he made man he said, "Now I can talk to you," and he talked to him. Reason number six: man was given dominion over everything else. I've given you the plants,

I've given you the animals, you are to boss them as I am to boss you. You are to lord it over them. That is the meaning of the word "dominion" – you are to lord it over them. To no other part of his creation did God say that.

Reason seven: God wrote the pattern of his own work into human nature and into no other part of his creation. The pattern of God's work is six to one. This is clearly written into Genesis and God rests in that ratio. The amazing thing is that of all nature there is only one part of nature that has a seven-day week built in, and that in fact is man. I have searched everywhere in nature and I have not yet found a seven-day cycle in nature of work and rest. But, you know, they discovered during the French Revolution when they tried to abolish the Christian Sunday and went for an eight-day week that it didn't work.

During both world wars they discovered in munition factories that the same thing applied. It applies to human nature too. Ministers only work one day of our seven by the way—but you need one day a week off. You need that because your nature is built according to God's pattern. My dog doesn't need a Sunday. No other part of nature needs a Sunday, and when I worked on the farm and had to get up at four in the morning to milk cows before breakfast, and before getting along to church, I profoundly wished that he had built Sunday into every other part of creation, but he didn't.

Man alone reflects God's work and is related to God's approach to creative activity. So for all these reasons I say that man is supernaturally made, he comes from God. If you want to answer the question, "What is man?" you must answer the question, "Where did he come from?" If you want to answer that question, you will not get the right answer from the scientist, you will need to go to scripture and you will need to see where he is coming from. There is a text in Ecclesiastes which talks of our dust returning to the earth as it was, and the spirit returning to God who gave it.

Science can confirm the first part but has nothing to say about the second. If I forget that second part then, "Let us eat, drink, and be merry for tomorrow we die." But if I came from God, I am going back to God and that gives me a responsibility one day to face my maker and to render my account for how I have used the life of a human being which he created in his own image. No other part of creation has this responsibility.

"When I consider the heavens, the moon, and the stars, the work of your fingers, What is man..." [There is the question; see Psalm 8:3] "... that you are mindful of him....?" We are well above the animals and a little lower than the angels. If you know your Bible well, you will know that it is your destiny one day to be above the angels—the peak of God's creation.

READ GENESIS 2:4–end

When we lived in Guildford, Surrey, I got hold of a guide book with a map and discovered that our church was in a little box in the middle of a park! That was no fault of the mapmakers, it was simply the most convenient way for them to tell me how to get around. The centre of the town was blown up to a larger scale in a box showing me the centre of town in much greater detail. Now I would be very foolish if I criticised that map because it didn't put the church where it ought to have been. The map, in fact, is much more useful because it gives on one sheet two different viewpoints. In the same way, when you turn from Genesis 1 to Genesis 2, you find that a tiny part of Genesis 1 is now blown up to the size of a whole chapter. Those who have criticised the Bible for doing this and say, "There you are – contradictory accounts," have just not studied it sufficiently. Genesis 2 takes that little bit of the Creation story which concerns man and blows that up to let you see in much greater detail the significance of our human existence.

I could put it another way. Nowadays we can talk about zoom lenses, which from a wide view can suddenly focus right into a very small view and a very narrow view. God had a zoom lens, as it were, and at the beginning of the Bible he held it right back and looked at the whole Creation in Genesis 1 and then zooms in not just to the Earth but to a little area on it, to a locality which we can now put on a map. Within that small area, he focuses his attention on just one person—zooming right in, we are meant to see much more clearly the place of man in the created order.

I could put it yet another way and say that in Genesis 1 you are looking down on Earth from heaven. You get a sense of being out in space and looking down at Creation from the heavenly throne, but in Genesis 2 your feet are firmly on the Earth and you are looking up to God. There is a sense of coming down to earth with a bump when you get into verses 4–5 of chapter 2. There are many other differences.

The most striking difference is that all the way through chapter one it is, "God" – thirty-five times. But as soon as you start reading from 2:4 onwards, you notice that it never says "God" again. It only says now, "the LORD God" and in capital letters LORD stands for the actual Hebrew name of God by which they knew him. Somebody has pointed out, very helpfully, that "God" is a faraway name, but "LORD" is a nearby name. The vague title "God" doesn't tell you anything, but the name "LORD" and the one for whom it stands – Yahweh, YHWH, I AM – makes him knowable.

So now you have a name applied to God. Why? Because if man is going to look up now at God, he has got to know God's name. From now on God is not only the Creator, he is the one who wants to have relationships and to talk to people, and so he has got to have a name by which he is known.

Therefore we are now looking at the Creation through the eyes of man (and not through the eyes of God as we did in chapter 1) and this will give us a different perspective. Now somebody who may have read this chapter carefully might well say at this point: but hold on a moment, there are contradictions. In Genesis 1, the plants are created first, then the animals, then man. But in Genesis 2, man seems to be created first and then the plants and the animals. How do you account for this? I account for it very simply—the order in Genesis 2 and to a degree in Genesis 1 is not chronological but logical. Let me explain what I mean by that. I once bought a book on building. I had ideas of building a house for myself. It never became more than a castle in the air and it certainly did not become a bungalow on the ground. It told me all about bricklaying and English bond and Flemish bond (bricklayers know what I'm talking about). I looked through this book and it said: Chapter 1, Foundations; Chapter 2, Brickwork; Chapter 3, Woodwork, Chapter 4, Plaster Work, Chapter 5, Electrical Work. That is a logical order, it is certainly not chronological, and if you know anything about building you will know that you can't do all the plastering and then stop and then do all the electrical work and then stop and then do all the joinery – you find that these overlap.

But to present the meaning of a house clearly you must follow a logical pattern in the book. So I point out that in Genesis 1 it may well be that some of these things that are described in separate days overlapped. That does not alter the fact that it is well presented to us logically. In Genesis 2 likewise, the writer is not concerned with the exact chronological order. He is saying: let's look at things logically from man's point of view. When you do that, man is the first person you look at and you see everything else as related to him. That is how I get around (if you call it getting around) the problem of the apparent discrepancies. But I don't think it is getting around. It helps me to look at creation from man's point of view and see another side to the truth.

I divide this chapter into two halves—*man in his environment* and *man in his relationships* and I can divide each half into three. We can review the first half quickly. Do you notice that man is placed firmly within nature? In Genesis 1 man is supernatural; in Genesis 2 he is natural. In Genesis 1, man is made in the image of God in highest heaven; in Genesis 2 he is made of mud, of the lowest dust of the earth. Now which is right? Is man a supernatural heavenly being or is he a natural earthly being? The answer is that he is both. You need the two chapters to get the whole truth. If you treat a human being as simply mud, you are not being true to that man. But if you treat him as an angel and nothing less, you are not being true to him either.

The strange fact is that I am a mixture of heaven and earth – at one and the same time a supernatural being in the image of God and a very natural being that will finish up going back to the dust from which I came. Only as you hold these two truths about man will you be able to see him as he really is. We are the only living beings in the whole universe of whom this is true. The animals are natural beings made of the dust of the earth but that is all they are. The angels are supernatural beings made in heaven and that is all they are.

The human being combines earth and heaven—a kind of Jacob's Ladder within myself, a link between two different worlds. That is why I can never be finally satisfied with this one. That is why there is that within me which nothing on earth can fulfil because I am not just natural, I am supernatural. When I am ready for a good sleep, this reminds me I am not an angel – I am very natural.

So here we are, poised between two worlds, linking them both, and Genesis 1 tells you this part of the truth and Genesis 2 tells you the other. Genesis 2 roots me firmly in the natural order by telling me that God used exactly the same process to make me as he used to make the plants and the animals. What was that process? To take the raw material, to provide the necessary stimulus to life, and produce the being. He took the field, he watered it and the plants appeared. He took the dust, he breathed into it, and man appeared. He took the garden, he put rivers into it, and the trees appeared – same process. God made me the same way as he made everything else. I am a creature, part of nature.

Now by the way let me just explain that the word "field"

in scripture doesn't mean what we mean by it. It means "wild nature as it is before man gets his hands on it." The field in scripture is the unenclosed place, and the lilies of the field are not the cultivated product of the market gardener, they are the wild flowers. So the field is the wild part of nature and there was the wild part of nature without a blade of grass in it. God caused a mist to go up and moisture began to penetrate that soil and up came the plants.

I lived in Aden for a little over two years, and the most striking feature there is the old extinct volcano. You can get through a tunnel into the crater and we lived right inside there. You can imagine what it was like in the humidity and the heat of Aden. Around us were what were called "the barren rocks of Aden" – volcanic lava, blistering in the heat, barren of all sign of life, but about two or three times a year it rained and we used to run out in all our clothes and get soaked. It was glorious, great fun. We loved rain there. We did not grumble at it. The amazing thing was that the next day, when we looked out at the barren rocks, they had a green colour. Just one shower and the moisture on that barren rock was enough to turn it into a garden. A few days later the sun had scorched it all up. As I looked at that, I thought: "That's just how it happened at the beginning." The whole Earth looked like those barren rocks and God caused the moisture to come and then the herbs and the flowers came. It is a wonderful world in which we live.

Similarly, it says, "God took of the dust of the Earth". It looked so barren, so dead; of course you didn't use water this time. What did God do? He breathed. You see the one thing that keeps me alive is breath, and when I stop breathing I stop living. The one thing I needed was not moisture – not at first. The thing that man needed was breath. So God took again the raw material, gave that material what it needed—breath. If I could put it this way, God gave that lump of dirt the kiss of life except that he did not use the mouth, he used the nostrils. There is something very tender and touching that God got as close as that and breathed his own life into that mud. The word "Adam". as we have seen, means mud. That is the name which means dust brought together. So God made man, and I think the language implies that God made man as a special act of creation. I still have not read or heard of anything in science that prevents me from believing this and so I go on believing it. I will face the problem when science raises it, but I still believe that God took one step from the material to the human without going through the animal. I find no more difficulty in thinking of that than I do of thinking of the virgin birth or of my future resurrection body. The real question is whether or not you believe that God is Creator.

He then took part of the field, wild nature. Before man got his hands on nature, God made a garden. Now the word means an enclosed, cultivated, and planned place, but the best translation of "garden" is really park land.

One day, my wife and I spent half an hour walking around Wisley Royal Horticultural Society. It is a garden; it clearly bears the stamp of a mind on it – someone planned and developed it. God took a bit of rough country and he made a garden. Now let me again be quite frank and say I believe we are dealing here not with fiction but with fact. History and geography begin in Genesis 2, not later. We are told precisely where that plot was. Why should God tell us where Eden was if it didn't exist? There is again no scientific or philosophical reason why you should not believe that Eden was an actual place, just as there is no reason why you should not believe that Adam was an actual person.

We are told where the rivers were, and a cultivated garden needs far more water than wild country, and therefore there needs to be a steady supply of water. I noticed plenty of that in Wisley. All the hoses and all the taps were needed. So God caused four rivers to develop. Now we can identify two of them on the atlas today, the Tigris and the Euphrates, and the other two we have lost. This means that the events of which we now read took place in the Mesopotamia valley in ancient Babylonia, or possibly around Armenia. We know roughly where it was.

The interesting thing to me is that modern research into the origins of human civilisation are beginning to centre right there. Secular scientists are now saying that this is where it began. They are catching up with Genesis 2, which tells us: here is the geographical situation. It is as if to say: we want to tie you down to fact; this is not to be treated as fiction. We are considering real people, real places, real events and real truth. It tells us a great deal. Now at this point again somebody may well say: "Now hold on a moment. What about these two trees? If you ate from one tree you lived forever and if you ate from another tree you died. Show us where these trees are." Well, I could show you a few plants that if you ate them you would die, but that is not the question.

This may be a helpful thought: if instead of thinking of these trees as magical we could think of them as sacramental, I think we would get around the difficulty. The bread and the wine that we use in church are not magical, but you could eat it and drink it and die as a result. 1 Corinthians 11 tells you that if any man eats and drinks unworthily he eats and drinks the judgment of God. Paul goes on to say to the Christians at Corinth, "That is why some of your church members are ill in bed, and some have even died as a result of taking Holy Communion." There is nothing magic about Holy Communion, the bread and the wine. It is ordinary bread and ordinary wine, but to those physical things God has linked his own grace. He has not changed the bread or the wine, but he said that if you eat in faith, you will have communion with the body and blood of Jesus; if you eat unworthily, you die.

What is difficult about that? Similarly, if I could put it like this: in this garden are two sacramental trees. They may be ordinary trees but to those two trees was attached a sacramental significance. If you eat from one you live and your normal span is extended indefinitely, which seems to imply very clearly that man was not by nature immortal – only God has immortality. But if you eat from the other one then your normal span will be shortened and you die. Can you see the meaning?

So here was Adam placed not in wild territory but in a carefully planted garden. He was given a tremendous start. I want you to notice another very important thing. The trees were not just for food. They were pleasant to the sight, which tells me that man has aesthetic as well as utilitarian needs. He needs beautiful things around him as well as useful things. He is more than just an animal. An animal doesn't look at a sunset and say, "Isn't that beautiful?" An animal doesn't look at a tree and say, "What a magnificent tree," but man does, and a man has a cultural need within him; he doesn't just need food, he needs culture. He doesn't just need something to eat, he needs something beautiful to look at. From the very beginning man has been like this.

We don't just want a house in which we can eat our food and sleep. We want a house that we can create as something that is attractive and beautiful. We want our favourite picture above the mantlepiece – of course we do. Man was made with greater needs than merely physical; he has mental needs. So the garden was helpful mentally as well as physically, and walking around Wisley Gardens I noticed the vegetable plots and the tomato trials and so on, and then the dahlias, which you can't eat. We need both. So if you have a well-balanced garden, you have got your vegetable plot and your rose bed.

What a wonderful situation, what a start man had. Now

I come to the other side of the story. Man is not only put in his environment in this chapter, he is put in the right relationships—a relationship above him, a relationship below him, and a relationship beside him. You need to get all these three right if you are going to know paradise.

Do you know what the word "Eden" means? It means delight. The Arabs used to try and tell me that Aden was in fact the original Eden. Well, they were a few thousand miles out but nevertheless the name Aden means the same. I don't know how it ever got landed with that name. It means "delightful place; paradise". I remember the first time I stepped off the plane and looked at it. My pal in the next seat looked out at another officer and he said, "What a God-forsaken place." I remember saying to him, "I hope it won't be for long", and it wasn't and God was there too. Eden is a place where you would love to stay and spend the rest of your life.

But it wouldn't be paradise just to be in the ideal environment. Just suppose you could go and sit on a seat in Wisley Gardens for the rest of your life, that you never came to church any more, that you never worshipped God. Just suppose that you never spoke to anyone else again. You just sat there – allowed to stay there in a lovely garden and watch the changing seasons. Do you think you would be happy? Real life is not just your environment, it is your relationships. Indeed I would go further and say that your relationships are more important than your environment.

Let us look at these three relationships. The first is the relationship with God above. Notice that we start with this. Before you get rightly related to anyone or anything else, get rightly related to God—that is where it starts. The relationship is to be one of obedience. That is not a very popular word today but it is a word that runs right through the Bible. Here we must now go back to the significance of two things that God now says in vv. 15–17. There are two ways in which people obey God which are mentioned here. The first is labour and the second is loyalty.

Work seems to be an unmentionable word today. Man was made to work, to cooperate with God. He had to till that garden and keep it. God didn't say, "I hand your food to you on a plate". You must till the soil; you must keep it; you are to be God's co-worker. This is the beginning of the biblical view of work and I suppose that we are reluctant to face this simple down-to-earth significance of God's command: six days you shall labour. Man is made to work and a man who is out of work is an unhappy man. Of course he will be. God is a worker, Christ was a worker, we are meant to work and in paradise we work.

Do you realise in heaven you will be on a twenty-four hour shift? We shall serve him day and night in his holy temple — direct quote from the future. Do you look forward to that? We are also promised that we won't get tired, but this is a wonderful thought that – we should be able to work as much as we want to for God. If you are an integrated personality, you don't run away from work. The other side to obedience to God and relating rightly to him is loyalty. I have been asked many times, "Why did God put one tree in the garden that they hadn't to touch. Why didn't he leave it out?" It would have been better, much easier. We would have had none of this trouble. We would have had no undertakers, no doctors. We would have been living in paradise for evermore.

The Bible doesn't exactly say why, but I can guess. You cannot offer loyalty to anyone unless there is also the opportunity not to. Loyalty doesn't just happen, it is something that you develop against the background of the possibility of not being loyal. Here was this one tree in the garden and it is as if God was saying: "You can have all the other trees. You have enough to look at, enough to live on, everything you could ask, but I have to include in your environment the possibility of being disloyal so that I may have your loving loyalty. Now I can go even further and say that this tree stood for something, and this is what it stood for. In a way which man would understand – a pictorial, simple, sacramental way – the teaching was that as far as good and evil go, leave God to decide which is which. You do not want to try everything yourself and then decide what is good for you and what is evil for you.

As far as moral questions go, God wanted loyalty, and the tree was a reminder that *he* decided what is good and what is evil, that he had the knowledge of evil. It is a thing you are not to have. But alas, I have met young people who say, "I think I've got to try everything before I decide what's right and wrong. I feel I must taste this before I label it as sin." I say to that young person, "You are eating of the fruit of the tree of knowledge. You don't need a tree now to tell you, I can tell you straight. You don't need to try everything before you find out whether it is good or evil. Leave that knowledge to God. Take his word for it. Accept his dominion over your conscience. Accept his lordship in your life." That makes sense to me.

So the first relationship that we need to get right is with God and it is a relationship of obedience in which we offer him our labour and our loyalty and leave him to decide what is good and what is evil and offer our conscience for his guidance. The second relationship is to the creatures below us – in this case the animals.

It is interesting that the Hebrew names for animals always pick out their most distinguishing feature whereas modern names for animals are not very descriptive. But it looks as if Adam looked at those animals and said, "I will decide on what is its most distinguishing feature." This shows a great intelligence and a capacity for language right at the beginning of the human race, though that is another story. But what is the significance of God telling Adam to name the animals? The answer is very simple. God has dominion over the sun, moon and stars, but man was given dominion over the animals. I have the authority to name my three children because I have the dominion over them under God. I can't name your children, except behind your back, but I have to name my own. I have authority in the family and that is what naming someone implies. Jesus has the authority to give you a new name – he gave Simon the name Peter.

Adam was given the animals and his relationship to them was to have dominion over them, naming them because they were under him. Now I think this gives a very important responsibility to man in relation to the animal world and in relation to the creatures that God has made. The one thing that I think must have struck Adam was that every creature that came to him came in pairs and he hadn't got a pair. Here was a male and female lion, a male and a female ox, and so on. Those animals in that locality he named and they were clearly partners; they were clearly mated and Adam felt lonely. A man may be in right relationship with God and he may be in a right relationship with the creatures below him and still be desperately lonely.

I was talking to a man who was in a particular job in industry and he said, "You know, it's a very lonely job. I'm in an office on my own. I have plenty of people under me and I can tell them what to do. I have plenty of people over me to tell me what to do, but I have no one beside me. It's a very lonely position. You can't chat over the job with anyone." Man was made in the image of God, a social being; God is a social being—Father, Son, and Holy Spirit.

I think it's rather pathetic when one meets a human being so wrapped up in an animal that they value the animal's companionship more than human beings. You can find this.

Dear old lady and her cat, a man and his dog – you can find this and there is something profoundly wrong. Now I have got a dog and I like going for walks with my dog but it would be terribly wrong if I would prefer to go for walks with my dog than my children, or if I was so wrapped up in God that I didn't want to meet any other human beings.

Man was made for fellowship and so we come to the third relationship. Man had got God above him, a relationship of obedience. He got the animals below him, a relationship of dominion, but what he needed was someone beside him for companionship and God met that need too. The first case in history of surgery with anaesthetic now took place. Adam fell asleep and was operated on. It is a lovely and tender story. It is a story of the first wedding.

Christian views on marriage and sex are based on the next few verses that we are going to look at and I find them very profound. Here is a remarkable sentence from a commentator many centuries ago, on the phrase, "And God took a rib" – and I am prepared to believe that is how a woman was created:

> When God made woman he did not take her out of man's head to lord it over him, nor out of his feet to be trampled on by him, but out of his side to be equal with him, from under his arm to be protected by him, and from near his heart to be loved by him.

Isn't that a lovely sentence? That is Christian marriage, that is the relationship. Now let me say straightaway that I realise that not everybody in the human race is married or will be. The complementary nature of the two sexes is not confined to the relationship of marriage. Within human society there are many other ways of men and women complementing each other. That is why I like to see a church well balanced between the two because in a church we are complementing one another.

The first poetry in the Bible is here (see v. 23 — Adam started writing poetry as soon as she appeared). Now here are the deductions from the passage. First of all, I have four deductions about sex and then secondly, I have seven deductions about marriage, and I just list them.

Sex: here are four deductions: first, it is a good thing; it is not a dirty word. God made sex, he saw that it was very good, and it is blasphemy to say that it's anything else. Basically sex is good. It is not a thing to be embarrassed or ashamed about. They were naked and were not ashamed. Secondly, sex was given first for partnership rather than reproduction in the case of the human species. Now that has profound implications, I just indicate one. It will teach you to think rightly about contraception if you realise that God gave sex not just to have babies but for complementary partnership between two people. Thirdly, man is prior to woman. I did not say superior, I said prior and that is a very important insight. Fourthly, woman is part of man, and that rib says to me man is incomplete without her. He cannot live a self-contained life and a woman hater is a contradiction in terms. He is not truly man unless he thinks rightly of woman.

Now I come to the seven insights of marriage and let me underline again that I am not saying that marriage is the only or even the best relationship between the sexes, it will be the average relationship. Jesus was not married, Paul was not married. Many wonderful people have not been married, but many have been. So let me give you seven insights. First, the fact that the word "wife" is in the singular means monogamy, which is God's rule for marriage. God's plan is monogamy; one husband, one wife. In some areas of the world there is polygamy, many wives to one man. In others polyandry, many husbands to one wife. But God's pattern is: one husband, one wife. Second insight into marriage, a man leaves before he cleaves. In very simple language, marriage comes before intercourse.

Third insight: the phrase "cleave" means no divorce, and when Jesus was asked about divorce he quoted Genesis 2 and said, "A man shall cleave..." and that means he hangs on till death us do part. It was on this story that Jesus based his attitude to divorce, which is the Christian one.

Fourth insight: it is becoming one flesh that makes a marriage, and therefore a marriage can be declared legally null and void if intercourse has not happened.

Fifthly, to leave mother and father means setting up a new home. Somebody once said to me, "One thing the good Lord never intended was two women to share the same kitchen." I have always said to young couples, "If you can get an old caravan, do so." Leave and cleave—you are creating something new, how practical this is.

Next: he called his wife by his name. That means that in a marriage, the husband is the head. He is the leader and in all the happy marriages I have known this has been true. Not the dictator, the leader on whom the wife may rely. So still to this day, as in the very first wedding in which God was the Father who gave the bride away, he brought her to have her name changed to his name. So we still apply the name of the husband to the wife. It is his leadership.

Seven: the ideal of marriage is complete freedom and ease of relationship in which there is nothing you want to hide from the other. They were both naked and not ashamed. We shall find that as soon as they had something to hide, they started getting fig leaves. It is a tragedy if you have got something in your side of the marriage that you have to hide from your partner. It is one reason I could never be a freemason, but there are many other things. If you have got something that you cannot share with your partner and cannot share completely then you should ask whether you should have it. The ideal of marriage is to share everything so there is nothing hidden between the two. Would that sex and marriage had stayed this way, but neither did. We shall see what went wrong. I have described man in his ideal relationship to God: obedience. His ideal relationship to the creatures below him: dominion. His ideal relationship to his wife beside him: companionship. Paradise depends on getting those three right, and when any one of them goes wrong we cease to be truly human. At the lightest level, a hen-pecked husband is wrong.

In conclusion: at the deepest level, a man who says, "God, I will try evil for myself and decide what is good and evil; I don't accept your rule; I don't obey you, I obey myself" will soon find he becomes a slave to his own passions and nature, like an animal.

In this passage we have been learning about God's order – the ordered peace and quiet of God. God's order for human life in paradise has been revealed.

READ GENESIS 3

You don't hear of the tree of life again until the last page in the Bible.

The first question we have to settle right at the beginning of this chapter is this: are we dealing with fact or fiction? It has become almost universal today to treat the early chapters of Genesis as fiction, calling them parable, myth, fable, or what have you, suggesting that they are simply stories like Aesop's Fables that are very poor historically but very good morally. In other words, there is a moral in the story that we need to get but it doesn't really matter whether they are factual. Somebody has recently called Genesis 3 a "just so" story entitled *How the Serpent Lost its Legs* but it is not a "just so" story.

Eden is presented to us as a real place, but why does the Word of God contain specific geographical directions as to where the garden of Eden was; directions, which enable us to put it roughly on the map even today? If it is just fiction, what is the point of doing this? But even more important, when we come to Adam himself it is vital that we answer this question correctly.

Is Adam just a picture of every man? Is he just a fictional character to show us ourselves? Is he just a mirror to modern man or is this story a window into ancient man? Now again, there are many who say this is simply every man – our nature embodied in the form of a myth or a parable or a story, but the New Testament does not take that view. Throughout the

New Testament, Adam is everywhere assumed to be one man, a real man, and the first man at the beginning of the history of our human race.

As I will show you at the end of this study, our understanding of the cross depends upon whether we believe that Adam was a real historical person. Suffice it for me to observe here that there is one profound difference between the story of Genesis 3 and my temptations today, proving to me that it is not just a story of every man. The difference is this: Adam started from a position from which I do not start. Adam started in complete innocence; I do not. Adam started with no human evil influence upon him; I do not. Adam started with no history of sin; I do not. Therefore, it cannot just be my experience because we do not start at the same place. So I give you my own position very frankly: Adam may reflect every man in some degree insofar as I am a son of Adam, but Adam is one man first of all.

So we are dealing here with a real place, a real person, and real events, which leads to the next question: with the serpent are we dealing with an animal or an angel? Certainly the serpent is presented in the chapter as an animal, but as a very remarkable animal, a creature who talks – but I am not so much troubled by the mouth of this animal as by its mind, because animals have mouths and vocal chords and to a greater or a lesser degree, most creatures talk. Even fish talk as we now know. But it is what the animal says that is the problem because here is the revelation of a most subtle and most clever mind that certainly you cannot find anywhere in the animal creation today. Let me underline again that the problem is not that the animal talks. Balaam's ass talked, but when Balaam's ass talked and I take it when this animal talked, there is a supernatural power enabling a natural creature to do this. If you ask me, "Is the serpent an animal or an angel?" my answer would be: both. I think those are right who see – in the supernatural power enabling this creature to talk – Satan himself, that fallen angel, and so I don't have any difficulty here.

What I am pointing out is that if Genesis 3 is not history, some of the greatest mysteries of this world remain insoluble. Why is it that everywhere you go in the world, men have a tendency to do evil? Why is it that every child learns the word "no" before they learn the word "yes"? Why is sin universal, nobody has escaped from it, nobody has got rid of this self-centredness? Why is the world in the mess it is in? Why are we not able to get rid of the evil that is blighting it for our children and grandchildren? These questions would remain unanswered and unanswerable if Genesis 3 was not real, because Genesis 3 gives you the answer to these questions. So I am starting with that assumption. I am afraid that if you don't share that assumption with me, you will find some of my conclusions a bit shaky as well, but I am assuming that we are dealing here with a real place, a real person, real events, and real moral issues that have affected the world ever since.

I divided the chapter into five here, and the first section is concerned with God's Word: whether men and women are going to accept God's Word as it stands or not.

There are three rules for dealing with God's Word and here they are. Rule number one: remove nothing from it. Rule number two: add nothing to it. Rule number three: change nothing in it. These are the three fundamental rules of all Bible study and all approach to the Word of God. I have seen as I study these first five verses that both Satan and Eve broke all three rules separately. The real issue was whether God's Word was going to be seen as the truth, or whether both angels and human beings were going to twist it and distort it. Once I saw this, I realised how subtle Satan was, how clever he is. He doesn't say, "Deny the Word of

God, get away from the Word of God," he just twists it; takes a little bit away there, adds a little bit here, modifies another bit in another place. Before you know where you are, you have come to a wrong view of God and you are no longer in touch with reality. Let me see how he did it and how she did it.

Now you may think I am going to quibble over words but I am doing so precisely because I believe that God spoke in words and that therefore, every word matters and that when God says something, every word of what he says is important and true. Now first of all, see how they both subtracted from God's Word and took away from it. In 2:16–17, and it is only in that sentence that Satan and Eve discuss, and in a conversation which cannot have lasted more than one minute, each of them broke the three rules.

Here is what God had said:

And the Lord God commanded the man saying, "You may freely eat of every tree of the garden but of the tree of the knowledge of good and evil you shall not eat for in the day you eat of it, you shall die."

Now you would not have thought that could be misquoted. It is plain, simple, straightforward. Now the very first thing I notice is that Satan refused to call God "Lord". Do you notice that? It was the Lord God who said this and Satan said, "Did God say...?" He takes away from God his name. He makes God an impersonal unknown power. As Satan uses it, it ought to be rendered with a small "g". No longer the Lord God—that was the name by which human beings knew him and you notice that Eve follows, dropping the word "Lord". It is a very significant subtraction this, because it is still being made today and you can notice it when people will not call him Lord, whether it is God the Father or Jesus to whom they are referring. "Lord" is a very significant name and Satan subtracts it and Eve follows him, but Eve does more than that—Eve misses out a most crucial word. She corrects Satan but she misses out the word "freely". God had said you may eat *freely*—what a lovely word. It has the word "freedom" in it. Satan is going to try to convince Eve that she has no freedom and you notice that she omits that word, a very significant omission. She did say, "God has said we can eat any tree of the garden" but she didn't say freely. Already she is beginning to get a different view of God. Soon she will be convinced in her mind that she is not free. So the first rule they both broke was to take away from God's Word. Satan took the word "Lord" away and Eve took the word "freely" away. It is not a quibble because you will see that in a profound way, by overlooking just one word each, they had already stepped away from the truth.

Now look at the second step—they both added to the Word of God and they both did so in such a way that it turned God into a hard master. Listen to what Satan added: has God said you shall not eat any tree in the garden? God had not said that, "any" is an exaggeration. He is trying to get Eve away from the permission she has, and the privileges, to the prohibitions. You hear people say today, "Oh you can't do anything if you're a Christian." God never said that. God wants us freely to take of what he has made. But as soon as the devil gets hold of your mind, "Oh those people in church won't let you do anything." Notice how the word "any" comes in.

Now Satan had put a word into God's mouth at that point. Where did Eve add to the Word of God? Eve said, "Now that's not right Satan. He told us we could eat every tree in the garden except one." Then she said a most extraordinary thing, "But he has forbidden us even to touch it." Did God say that? Never. Once again here is a mind twisting what

God had said. God never forbade them to touch it, he said, "Don't eat it" – that is all. Now you may think this is a quibble again but you see how her mind is being taken away from the idea of a God who gives all things freely to us and created that garden for them and for their benefit, to the idea of a God who is always hedging you around and telling you don't touch this, don't touch that—can you see?

So Satan and Eve have taken away from God's Word, they have both added to it now let us see them both alter it. We will start with Eve. God said, "If you eat it you shall die." Eve said, "Don't touch it lest you die." Now that is a very subtle watering down of the text "lest you die". It reduces a certainty to almost a probability. It takes the edge off the definite "you shall" and it becomes a "lest". It waters it down.

But, Eve having modified that word, Satan modified much more. He proposed an amended text. He was the first commentator on the Word of God to propose that, but alas not the last. He slipped in the word "not" – it will make more sense: you shall not surely die. What a modification of the Word of God, and it says much for the way he got hold of Eve's mind that she accepted it. It was an absolute contradiction of the Word of God and if a commentator today says there is no hell, that is exactly the same contradiction. Do you see what they were doing with the Word of God? They were subtracting words from it, they were adding words to it, and they were changing words in it. The result was that they finished up with a view of God that was not true. It was now a view of God as one whom you could not know well enough to call by his name, a view of God as a hard taskmaster who was always telling you "you shall not", and a view of God who was a lenient judge and would not punish sin. In all three ways, in just two minutes of conversation, Satan had distorted a woman's view of God.

Now I hope you won't be offended by what I am going

to say now, but I think it is highly significant that he did this with a woman. We are made differently and we must face this. Men tend to think with their heads and women with their hearts. That can make a man too intellectual and a woman too sentimental. Alas, Satan has got hold of women ever since and distorted their thinking of the Word of God – and men too, but he got hold of Mary Baker Eddy; he got hold of Ellen White. He got hold of Amy McPherson and many another.

I think there is a profound reason why there is a prohibition in the New Testament about women preachers. Now I say that in all love but I think it is there. You see, Satan was reversing the divine order. Satan knew perfectly well that the husband was the head of the marriage, and so he attacked the weaker vessel first. Having said that, let me hasten to put men (including myself) back in our place by saying that if Eve fell first then Adam fell worst. He didn't even put up a fight; he didn't even argue; he didn't even try to stop himself doing it. You notice this subtle change now. Eve is now the tempter. Adam didn't meet Satan but he met Eve and Satan had Eve.

You may never have met the devil face to face but you have met people who were the devil's means of tempting you. It could be your best friend; it could be someone in your own family. Jesus said to Simon Peter, "Get behind me Satan." The devil can come at you in different ways.

So we come to the second step: God's will disobeyed. Now you notice the appeal now to Eve? The appeal was physical, aesthetic and intellectual. The devil has a lovely way of dressing the forbidden thing up in these garbs. So sin comes to us as a physical attraction, an aesthetic pleasure, and as an intellectual dream. Eve saw that it was good for food (the physical approach), that it was pleasant to look upon (the aesthetic approach) and that it was to be desired to make her wise (the intellectual approach). In the name of physical satisfaction, aesthetic pleasure, and intellectual satisfaction she took what was forbidden and still to this day Satan is able to say to a young person, "This is physically desirable, aesthetically pleasurable and intellectually satisfying. Take it." It is exactly what the New Testament means by "the lust of the flesh, the lust of the eyes, and the pride of life" – physical, aesthetic, intellectual.

Now let us leave Eve and go to Adam. Three steps down for Adam—the first was that he accepted and ate. The words "take and eat" are amazing words. They are the first words of the sacrament of sin and Eve said, "Take and eat," and Adam did. They are now blessed words of salvation and we use them at Communion – "Take and eat." They are now words of salvation; they were words of sin.

I want you to notice that God had given Adam the leadership of his wife and he is now being led by her and history is strewn with the wreckage of men who have been led by women and allowed themselves to be so. Time and again I have tried to help in a broken marriage where the husband seems just to be putty in the hands of the woman. This is a reversal of the divine order and Adam accepted and ate.

Secondly, he saw and he sewed. You know that the amazing thing is that the blackest lie of all is a half-truth – a lie that has enough truth in it to be convincing – and the devil is a liar from the beginning and he tells convincing half-truths. The devil's line was: you know, if you took this and ate it, your eyes would be open and you would know good and evil – don't you want that? You can be like God. Step out of this human bracket into the divine.

It was true that as soon as they ate it their eyes were opened and they did know evil for the first time. The half of his statement that was not true is that he said, "You will not die". They did. I wonder if I could distinguish between two different kinds of knowledge. You can know a thing firsthand or secondhand, and human beings were meant to know evil secondhand not firsthand. Let me illustrate: there are two ways in which I personally could come to a knowledge of a deadly disease. One would be to become a doctor and study it and study patients with it and get to know it and study it for years until I could get to the point where I could say, "I know this disease." The other way is for me to get it and I would know it firsthand. But that second way is a deadly way to know anything.

God knows evil, yes, but he knows it secondhand not firsthand and he means us to know it secondhand, not firsthand.

Let me illustrate it another way: here is a girl who knows purity and chastity – she knows it. She knows about unchastity secondhand. She may have read about it, heard about it, in some way come to a secondhand knowledge. Then one day she gets into trouble herself. She knows it firsthand now. What happens? Shall I tell you? She only now knows goodness secondhand. You can't know them both firsthand at the same time. She no longer knows chastity and purity firsthand. She only knows it secondhand. Do you see what has happened? It is true she now has the knowledge of good and evil but it is precisely the opposite way to God's knowledge of good and evil. His knowledge of good and evil is this: he knows good firsthand and evil secondhand because the goodness is in himself and the evil is outside himself. But when they ate from that tree, they knew knowledge of good and evil but they knew goodness secondhand now. It had gone from them—they forfeited it and lost it. They now knew evil firsthand, so the eyes of both were opened.

Now they couldn't even look at each other without evil thoughts. Do you remember the last verse of the previous chapter? They were both naked and not ashamed. They had known goodness and innocence firsthand, now they did not know that, so they are busy sewing fig leaves together; they can't even have innocent thoughts about each other now. The third step for Adam was that the relationship with God went wrong: he heard and he hid. No longer did he want to face God, no longer did he eagerly look forward to running out to meet his heavenly Father, no longer did he look forward to worship, no longer did he desire prayer and fellowship. He heard the sound of God and he hid in those bushes. Do you realise that Adam had seen God for the last time? He never comes out of those bushes until an angel pushes him out of the garden and the rest of the chapter is a conversation which he has with God, but now Adam is behind the bushes and there is only a voice. God is there but God is only a voice and from now on there is only a word between them. There is no sight, no vision of God, only words passed to and fro from the cowering figure in the bushes to his Creator.

So we come to the third section: God's warrant denied. Make no mistake about it, Genesis 3 is the story of the first trial and the first courtroom in history. God, alas, appears in Genesis 3 in a function, which he has not yet shown in Genesis 1 and 2. God is now the judge, and as at every trial, it is filled with questions. The man is asked two questions, the woman is asked one question, and Satan is asked none. But look at the questions.

You see every trial opens with a question: guilty or not guilty? Don't approach this chapter too simply and think that God wants an answer to these questions. He knows the answer to the questions; he knows where Adam is, he knows what the woman has done – he knows that. God knows everything. What he is seeking is an admission, a confession. He is wanting them to say they are sorry – that is all.

Why are questions asked in a courtroom? To establish guilt. There may be people in that courtroom who know perfectly well the person is guilty before they have come in but you must have the questions and you must ask, "Guilty or not guilty?" – whatever you know. Adam is concerned about clothing. What a feeble excuse, blaming his circumstances as we try to do. When he realises that he can't blame his circumstance (an empty wardrobe) he blames someone else. Well, it was Eve actually – and then he moves even further and commits the blasphemy: "Well God, it was really your fault. You gave me the woman and she gave me the fruit." He will not admit, he will not say "guilty"; he will not confess. So God turns to the other person in the dock, the woman. Of course, God knew what she had done. Adam had just told him, but he knew even before that. Yet he is asking Eve. Will she admit what she has done and say sorry? That is what God says to every one of us. He is saying, "Will you just admit you sinned this last week? I want to forgive you." Will you just say, "Guilty, my Lord," and then God can deal with us. But there's a cast iron muscle in the middle of my neck that makes me like ancient Israel – a stiff-necked people who would not bow the head and say "guilty". We say: "not guilty, it's my circumstances, it's my pals; it's you God, you made this world like it is," and we won't admit.

The woman blamed the serpent so God turned to the serpent. No question to ask of Satan. There are some beings of whom God has nothing to say. One day Jesus stood before Herod and Herod was such a degraded man it says this, "Jesus said nothing." It is terrible when you get to the position where God has nothing to say to you or where Jesus has nothing to say. God had nothing to ask Satan and God knew Satan much better than Adam and Eve in that sense because Satan was an angel in heaven. Do you know where the devil is tonight? He is in heaven according to my Bible, not in hell. Don't think of the devil as down under, not yet. He is in heaven. The principalities and powers and spiritual hosts of wickedness are in heaven, and God was here dealing with someone from heaven.

So he turns now to the punishment, the sentence at the end of the trial. Have you ever noticed that even Jesus not only said, "Blessed..." he said, "Woe..."? To say, "blessed" is to pronounce a blessing and to say "woe" is to pronounce a curse and Jesus said, "Blessed are you poor, woe to you rich. Blessed are you who mourn, woe to you who laugh now." He was pronouncing a curse, and right the way through the Bible you have the blessings and the curses of God the Judge. Now look at the sentences that are pronounced. Incidentally, from v. 14 God breaks into poetry.

One of the most amazing things in the Bible is that God puts blessings and curses into poetry. Did you know that Handel's Hallelujah Chorus is based on a curse of God? If you look up the passage where it comes from you will find what I mean. Milton burst into poetry when he wrote *Paradise Lost* and we are talking about paradise lost now, and this poetry of doom comes home to us with great power. To the serpent God said, "You shall be humbled and hated." How the serpent lost its legs — I knew somebody who had a couple of pet boa constrictors. I was told by that same person that the snake does have residual legs and a pelvic bone to hold them, but it doesn't use them now – they have gone, shrunk and vanished.

Now we talk about someone who is wily, subtle and too clever by half. He is a snake in the grass and the snake has become the symbol of all that is horrible. One day someone came to tea with us and he brought some of his pets to show us. He gave a lovely little Chinchilla to my children and they were thrilled. They loved this little furry thing. Then he handed a bag to my wife and said, "My real pets are in there – have a look." Without thinking, she sat the bag on the floor, opened it up and looked in. I have only once in my life seen my wife petrified. She was absolutely rigid and couldn't move, and out of the sack came two huge snakes, five or six feet long, rearing their heads up, and she just sat speechless. There will be enmity between you and the woman. Women still hate the snake. It becomes the symbol of all that worms its way into your household, of those who in a slimy, slithery way edge themselves in; and subtle methods where they are not wanted – snakes in the grass. But here there is a spark of light. It is a dark chapter but there is a spark of light because God says, "And this enmity between you and the woman will come to a head, will come to a climax, with one male descendant of this woman". One male descendant will deal you a fatal blow. "You may bruise him but he is going to strike you on the head," which is a fatal blow. It's the beginning of the gospel. It is the beginning of the struggle between the seed of the woman and Satan that came to a climax when Jesus said, "Now is the prince of this world cast out."

The devil was a goner, and so there's a spark of light already even in the darkest chapter. To the woman he said, "Your parenthood and your partnership will both be affected by this." Whatever it means I take it that it does mean that having children will not be an unmixed happiness and joy from now on. That there will be pain associated with bringing new life into the world, and there has been ever since. As far as her partnership with her husband went, because sin was now in the world there was all the possibility of the dehumanising and the brutalising of human sexual relationships. Instead of, "To love and to cherish," there was now the possibility of a man saying, "To desire and to dominate," and that has happened ever since.

To the man he said exactly the same Hebrew word as to the woman. To the woman he said, "You will travail in childbearing," and to the man he said, "You will travail in bread winning." In other words, in your separate spheres you will both have struggles. If I could put that into modern English, I can think of one word that gets across the meaning of both man and woman. It is the word "labour" and isn't it interesting that childbirth is described as labour? We use the word now for man's toil and struggle to keep alive.

From now on he was going to struggle with thorns and thistles. Now you have never seen thorns and thistles until you have been to Palestine. I have seen thistles growing five or six feet high in a thicket you could not get through, worse than barbed wire. I have seen thorns with spikes of two to two-and-a-half inches. Those thorns and thistles of Palestine are terrible things.

In other words, instead of just tending trees, pruning them and gathering the fruit, now you have got to struggle against thorns and thistles. You are going to have a hard time keeping alive. Furthermore, Adam you are going to lose the battle, that very ground which is cursed now for your sake, that very ground will win the battle and you'll go back to the ground you came from and you'll go back where you belong. You may work all your life digging that garden but there will come a time when you are too old to dig it, and when you see the weeds win the battle. There will come a time when you will be buried in the earth. Here we have the explanation as to why we lose the battle against the dust of the earth.

I realise that I have raised many questions but let me remind you that, in all this, God's sovereignty is clear. All that human beings can do, all the freewill they have, does not alter the fact that God is on the throne and that he is still in charge and that he will still do his will. Even though Adam and Eve refused to do his will, God's will must be done in their life. If they will not choose to do it his way then he will do it his way. God's sovereignty and man's responsibility are both clearly in this chapter. If ever a chapter in the Bible said that man is responsible for what he does, it is Genesis 3. You must never use God's sovereignty to deny human responsibility, or vice-versa.

Now we come to the fifth and last main point. God had to defend the world that he made very good – he had to prevent it from being made evil for ever. How did he do it? Very simply by saying that as soon as a man is evil his life must be limited and death must come. Can you see the alternative? If God had allowed man to go on living for ever, evil would have spoiled this universe forever. But God, in his wisdom, said that if you choose the evil path then he will limit your life – you must die. But this word "die" involves more than physical death. It involved three kinds of death all in one. The first is physical. Physical death does come but I want you to notice how at each point God does something in this. He is declaring that Adam and Eve are now in the state where they will die. Death has already begun to grip their bodies. But Eve and Adam both knew that until they died they still had the power to pass on life. This was part of their hope for the future. There have been many women through history who in dying have given life to a new baby. So Adam said to his wife, "I'm going to give you a new name. I've called you woman until now but now I'm going to call you Eve because the only life we can look forward to now is a life that we can pass on to our children." So they faced physical death and placed their hope in their children and she was called Eve, the mother of all living. The word Eve means mother of living.

Now the second kind of death was spiritual. When you have come to know evil firsthand you can only know good secondhand now. That produces a spiritual death in which you are dead in trespasses and sins even before you die physically. So that you become spiritually dead to God—you can't get through to God, you don't know what to do with your sin and shame.

Now let me look at the skins and the clothes, which God made for them. First thing I want to say may shock you but I think it is meant here, I think it is perhaps the main meaning of these skins. There is no way back to Eden as it was; there is no way back to nudity. Now it has become a craze in our day — back to nature, back to the golden age, back to the original freedom that men had when they lived without clothes. There is quite a boom in nudism just now. But when God made clothes for them, he said there was no way back.

Even in heaven we shall wear clothes – we shall never get back to Eden as it was. Those fig leaves of theirs would wither and die within a day or two, so God made them some permanent clothes. To this day we have had to wear clothes and we shall have to go on wearing clothes, and in heaven we shall wear robes. The other, deeper, meaning, as many Christians have of course pointed out, is that if God had to make clothes of skin, then he had to shed blood. Here is a little glimmer of light that will get bigger and bigger – that if our sin and shame are adequately to be covered then the principle of sacrifice must be observed. "Without the shedding of blood there is no remission of sin."

Eternal death follows — it was now impossible for Adam to enjoy that eternal life which is fellowship with God. The tree from which he had been able to eat freely, the tree which kept him alive and would have kept him alive forever, must now be taken away. So a sword of God shuts him out and has shut man out ever since.

Scientists are spending time, money, and energy, trying to find the elixir of life that will keep man alive. But I want to tell the scientists: the tree of life has been barred, you cannot find it. God said that we can't have it, and he shut us off from this. So Adam finished where he began. He was made not in the garden; he was made out in the desert, and he finishes back in the desert and his body is dust.

Why is the world as it is? Why is it such an evil place? Why are people so selfish? What has gone wrong and how can it be put right? I finish by a quotation from Romans 5. Two things are to be found in Romans 5 and here they are, "Through one man," notice this, "Through one man sin came into the world and with sin came death. But, through one man, salvation came into the world and life." Will paradise ever be regained? Yes, it will. Will the gates that were shut ever be open again? Yes, they will be open and they have been opened.

This is where I get excited, where I must take you to the New Testament and show you the clear link between Genesis 3 and the rest – if only to show you that if you drop Genesis 3 you must drop the New Testament; that if you don't believe that one man's act brought death into the world, how will you ever see that one man's act brought life into the world? The first Adam created a humanity that suffered and died, whereas the second Adam to the rescue came and brought into being a new humanity that will live. If you don't see the connection, you will never understand the cross in its deepest meaning. When Adam sinned, not only did it affect himself and his wife, it affected his children, his grandchildren, his great-grandchildren and their children, and it came right down to John David Pawson and to mankind, and we all have to die because of this. You can rebel against this and say that it is not fair – I just state that it is a fact. It is a fact that one man's act could do this. If it couldn't, then I say that Jesus' act cannot give you life either. The two are bound together.

Notice the words – the vocabulary of sin. There are certain words, which come in Genesis 3, which have never been mentioned in the Bible up to this point. Here they are: fear, sorrow, pain, shame, grief, death. This is the vocabulary of sin. But now let me turn to the seed of the woman, the second Adam, Jesus Christ. Adam wanted to be like God so he ate, Jesus was God but humbled himself.

Adam was disobedient, Jesus became obedient, and in another garden Jesus said, "Not my will but yours be done." Adam had said, in effect: not your will but mine be done. Then, as Adam was clothed by God, Jesus was stripped by man, stark naked and hung up on the cross for all to stare at. The very thorns mentioned in Genesis 3 were crammed on his brow and the sweat of his face became drops of blood. To a dying thief he said, "Today you shall be in paradise with me." Do you see why the blind poet Milton, living in Chalfont St. Giles, a mile and a half from my former home, had to write another poem, *Paradise Regained*? Do you see why the second Adam came? Do you see that as one man's act brought sin and death into the world, one man's act brought salvation and life? Do you see the connection?

READ GENESIS 4–5

I am taking chapters four and five of Genesis together because there is a remarkable similarity between them, and the message goes straight through from one to the other. Yet there is a very marked contrast between the two.

Now the word "genesis" means "beginnings" and the book of Genesis is full of beginnings. In these two chapters we have the first birth and the first death recorded, and that death was a violent one. We have the first murder and the first martyr, and a lot of other things happened for the first time. Perhaps the most important point is that the word "blood" appears in the Bible for the very first time. From its meaning here the rest of the Bible will take its cue.

Already we can begin to see that at the beginning of the human race there is a great division taking place. One of the reasons people don't like this book is because it is always dividing people into two groups. In a day when so many are enamoured of the idea of unity – politics united; finance united; one world; one government, one everything – the Bible is a very awkward book because it persists in dividing people up into two.

From the very beginning you have the line of Cain and the line of Seth. Those two lines go right through the Bible. Later you will find the line of Jew and Gentile. But behind it all is the line lost and saved, which finishes up at the climax at the end of history with the division between sheep and goats. This is how the Bible treats the human race and we must face the facts.

Now these two chapters give us the beginning of the two lines. If I can put it this way, here are the two fountain springs from which the two rivers come, which ultimately empty into heaven and hell. Here is the beginning of that great dividing line right through the human race, and blood is the dividing line. We take then, first of all, chapter four, the line of Cain. It is an evil line, and it leads to death—not just natural death, but violent death.

One word is that Adam "knew" Eve, and she conceived and bore a son. In this the Bible is saying absolutely clearly that this relationship between male and female is a totally personal thing. You cannot separate the physical from the emotional and the mental, and the total self-giving. This is what it is meant to be: a means of knowing someone else at the deepest level.

Whenever this relationship is made other than a knowledge of people and is made a relationship between things, it has lost what God meant it to be. So Adam "knew", and this word "know" goes all the way through the Bible. This is life eternal – to know God, and that doesn't mean to know *about* him, it means to have the most intimate relationship with him. The word "know" is a wonderful word and that is why it states later that God foreknew us. He had a deep relationship with us even before we realised it.

But that is a digression. The real theme of the early chapters of Genesis is this: just as when you drop a stone into a pond, the ripples spread out in ever-increasing circles, when sin was dropped into human history it affected the individual, then the family, then the society, then the nation, then the world. By Genesis 11 you come across a whole world that is spoiled. I might put it this way: the sin that ruined the first man caused the second man to kill the third man—that is what sin does. Once it has been set in motion it seems to spread and go on in ever-increasing intensity.

Look at this terrible situation. Adam and Eve got two boys. Eve had no midwife except the Lord and she got this baby with the help of God, so she called him "gotten". Then she got a second boy; I don't know if he was a little wisp of a baby looking like a breath that would be carried away easily, but she called him "breath", or Abel, meaning breath of wind, really just a slight thing. It maybe tells us something about these two boys.

At any rate they grew up happily and no doubt Adam and Eve hoped and prayed that their boys would be different from themselves, as so many parents have prayed and hoped ever since. But if anybody ever wants to be convinced of the truth of original sin – that sin is passed on – let him have a child. Somebody wrote to me recently and said, "The trouble with having children is that you see your own faults coming out in them." You realise that you have passed something on to your children, and Adam and Eve must have watched rather sadly to discover that they had passed on what they had now become. This is one of the truths of the human race. We may dislike it; we may argue about it. But it is a fact that we do pass things on, not just physical likeness, not just temperamental characteristics, but alas, spiritual fallen-ness. We pass it on, and it has come all the way down to me and through me to my children—we are a fallen race.

The name "gotten" simply referred to the birth. It is the nature of Cain that occupies our attention in this chapter – what kind of a chap did he turn out to be? We don't know much about Abel. What we know is rather lovely, but here are two boys from the same stable, as it were, and yet so different. We get the same in families today. You can have two children from the same parents, so different from each other.

Cain and Abel were different, but the difference wasn't temperament, it wasn't physical appearance; the biggest difference was that one boy had faith, and the other did not. That was the ultimate difference. We are told this and the New Testament sheds a bit of light even on this chapter. That will be the biggest difference in any family—the children who believe in God in his way, and those who don't. Cain believed that God existed, but that does not make faith. Faith is very much deeper. Faith is coming to God in God's way.

How do I know that there was a way to come to God? We have to read between the lines here. It is quite obvious that that family had a *place* of worship to which they brought their offering. I don't know where it was – it was not in Eden. But somewhere this family had a place they went to, to pray. We know they had a *time* to worship because, in fact, where it says "in the course of time" the literal phrase would be better translated "at the end of the days". In other words, they had a set time when they came to worship.

More than that, they had a proper *way* to worship, which God had revealed to them – they knew already that the way to worship God was the way of sacrifice for sin. It was the way of death, the way of bloodshed, and Adam and Eve no doubt taught the two boys this.

But now we come to a certain occasion when, as working men, those two came to God. They both came to the same God, but they were not both accepted. Now lest you think it was terribly unfair of God to say, "I'll have yours, but I won't have yours," let me say that God is not arbitrary. He has principles on which he accepts a person and the principles are twofold: first, the *offerer* must be right and second, the *offering* must be right. Which comes first? The offerer comes first. You notice it says that God accepted Abel, the offerer and his offering but he would not accept Cain, the offerer and his offering. Why not? Let us look first at Cain's heart and attitude. Cain did not believe that he needed to come God's way. He was prepared to patronise God. He was prepared to bring his gifts. He was prepared to give God something of his income. But he was not prepared to come God's way. His arrogance is revealed in his anger when God would not accept him for that reason. There is something wrong with his attitude right at the heart. You can tell immediately by his reaction to God's action that in fact this man was not in a fit state to be worshiping. He had a wrong attitude to his God; he had a wrong attitude to his brother, and both come out later. But God saw them before they came out, and God knew what Cain's heart was like.

Furthermore, Cain brought an offering, but it wasn't the offering that God wanted. You realise that to get the offering God needed, Cain would have had to ask Abel for it, and that would have been a rather humbling thing to do. Cain wanted to bring the fruit of his own work: *I* have done this; this is *my* work – *I* bring my contribution. This was Cain. He knew perfectly well that God wanted slain lambs. Abel knew that, so why didn't Cain know it? Because Abel didn't just bring live lambs, he brought the fat portions thereof.

I defy you to bring a fat portion thereof without bringing the whole lamb unless you bring it in death. Quite clearly, Abel had slain his lamb, but Cain—he wasn't going to go and ask his brother for an offering. Cain was the proud man. Cain was the natural man. Cain was the man who comes to God on his own terms, not God's. Cain was the man who was prepared to worship but on his own terms. Cain came and God said: I can't accept you, Cain, and I can't accept your offering either – and he was very angry.

Here are two kinds of worship, and still to this day we have the man who worships on his own terms, the man who will come and give his money, give his time, give his talents, but give only what he wants to give; the man who will not come on the ground of the blood of Jesus Christ. It seems to him too crude. It seems to him too offensive to do so. Can I be very blunt? Cain would come to the harvest festival, but Abel would go to the Holy Communion—that is the difference. The one would bring the fruit of his own toil; the other recognises the need for the blood of a slain lamb.

It is humbling to recognise that. It requires faith to recognise it. Abel had the faith, Cain hadn't. The tragedy is that today we still have all over the world and in Britain those who will come to God on their own terms, who will bring their own labour to God on their own terms, but they will not humble themselves and say, "God, I see that your way is a way of the blood of the lamb slain."

Cain was terribly angry and resentful about this and God said: Cain, if you do well, I'll accept you. You've no need to be angry. Just put right what's wrong. Come in the right way and in the right attitude, I'll accept you. But Cain, if you don't, sin (and here God uses almost personal or animal terms) is crouching at the door of your heart and will spring in and seize you. Cain, you must master this. You must master this resentment, this anger. You must come my way. It was a desperate appeal.

The tragedy is that we know that sin (and elsewhere in the Bible the devil is described as a prowling lion) sin jumped into Cain's heart and sprang on him and mastered him. The next step was that Cain sprang on Abel and killed him. It is a tragic story. If we will not come to God on his terms, and therefore resent not being accepted, and will try to come on our terms, then sooner or later sin will get a hold of us and spoil our relationship with others. Why? Because if you don't get right with God, how can you be right with someone else?

That is the malice that there is in the heart of this man and the malice becomes murder. The first family in history, and one brother kills another. Think what Adam and Eve felt like when this happened. We turn then to the murder. They go into the field and Cain kills Abel. You realise that he had never seen murders on the television. You realise he had never heard of a murder. You realise he was the first to think of it. This was a new act, for one man to kill another, and it was a terrible moment. God comes as he came to his mother and father before him with a question, not because God wanted to know—God knew perfectly well where Abel was. His blood was shouting out from the very soil—but God said, "Cain, I want you to tell me where – where is Abel? Own up, what have you done?"

Cain said, "I've nothing to do with my brother—not my responsibility. You go and find him." It was the most incredible impudence but sin is impudent. Once we have got wrong with God, we will say the most incredibly blasphemous things to God. You can be cheeky to God when you are in a wrong relationship. God was saying: Cain, there may have been no human witness to what you did, but I saw it. Blood speaks to me. It cries out to me for one thing or another.

Then God sentenced Cain. You notice that though God had cursed the ground for Adam, now God curses Cain from the ground and said, "You're going to be a fugitive—no home, no help—you'll wander the face of the earth. You'll be a misfit; you'll be a man on the run." It is not very nice being a fugitive—not being able to face people, not being able to settle down, not being able to integrate into society.

Notice that Cain did not say, "My sin is more than I can bear." He still did not confess his sin. There was only one thing that Cain was sorry about and it was that he had been found out. He was not sorry about the crime but about the punishment. He was not sorry for what he had done; he was sorry for the consequences.

There are many of us who must confess that we have

often been more troubled about the consequences of our sin than the sin itself. This is human. Is it not true that we pray harder when something wrong we have done has been found out and we have to pay the bill – much harder than we did when we had just done it and nobody knew? Cain said, "My punishment is more than I can bear." God, in his amazing mercy, put a limit to that punishment and said, "I will give you a measure of protection. You will still be a wanderer in the land of Nod" – and the word "nod" means "wandering". What a dreadful place to live. But God put a limit and he gave Cain a sign so that he would not be hounded to death.

I want to take this much further. There are two amazing ways in which this story of Cain and Abel foreshadows something millennia in the future. The first is this: this relationship between Cain and Abel goes straight through history to the relationship between Jesus and Israel, who believed in God. When Jesus came to the people of God, Israel believed in God but were coming to him in the wrong way, with their own works, with their own good deeds, with their own righteousness, Jesus came with *his* way, which is the way of shed blood. Jesus said, "You have killed the blood of the righteous ever since Abel, and now I am here, and you will kill me for the same reason," and they did.

What happened? The Jews said, "Let his blood be upon us," and for two thousand years they have been in the land of Nod. They have wandered the face of the earth and been hounded by people. Can you see that this is history linked together in the most amazing way with the insights of God? You read Genesis chapter 4, and you can read the history of the last two thousand years. Cain and Abel became Jesus and Israel. Can I remind you of that wonderful hymn:

> Abel's blood for vengeance pleaded to the skies,
> but the blood of Jesus for our pardon cries.

That is the contrast.

The other foreshadowing in this amazing story is this: Cain and Abel become two groups in the human race who try to get to God in different ways and there will always be enmity between them. You see, in Genesis chapter 3, God said, "There will be enmity between your seed, Eve, and the devil's seed." We are told in 1 John 3 that Cain is of the devil's seed. The real difference between them was that Cain and Abel represented the way of the flesh and the way of the Spirit, the way of men and the way of God, the way of coming on the ground of what you have done and saying, "God, you must accept what I have done," and the way of coming to God on the ground of a sacrifice of something else—there will always be this enmity and it goes right through history.

Now I am going to turn away from Cain and Abel, to the succession. The death of Abel is carried on and is multiplied and intensified. Now I know there are certain problems in these two chapters, and I am going to deal with them, but hope that you don't get bogged down in the problems. Problem number one is this: where did Cain get his wife? Open air preacher Dr Soper was once asked by a man in the crowd: "Where did Cain get his wife?" He replied, "Why are you so interested in other men's wives?" Well, I think that is about the best way to deal with it – he didn't answer the question. I am not sure that it keeps anyone out of faith, but since it is a question that many people raise, let me deal with it very briefly. There are three possibilities, and I honestly don't know which is right. Neither science nor scripture gives you any guidance here, so take your pick. Possibility number one: God created her for Cain as he created Eve for Adam, whether in the same way or not.

The second possibility: Adam and Eve had a large family and many sons and daughters, and at the beginning of the race, when it was pure, God allowed Cain to marry his sister. Of course, this would be one step away from Adam, who married his own flesh, his own actual body, and it would be the next step away from that towards the marriage relationship as we know it today.

Possibility number three, which is pure speculation, is that by now God had created other men. Some have seen in some of the remarks at the beginning of chapter 5 an indication of this. The problem with that third possibility is that we have got to hold to the unity of the human race, that God made of one all people, and we must also hold to the universality of sin – so that there would have to be some crosslinks between Adam and other men if others were created. Now those are three possibilities. If it were an important question, God would have told us the answer. The fact that he hasn't I would think means: don't bother your head about it.

We go on to the succession. Enoch, Irad, Mehujael, Methushael, Lamech, Jubal, Tubal, and Tubal Cain. You notice a pattern—the line goes down and ends with three children. That pattern we shall see in the next chapter just as clearly. But what we notice is that from Cain comes a developing civilisation which is urbanised—he built a city and they began to trade in cattle. Culture develops: the arts and music, and incidentally two forms of music – string and wind. Society becomes industrialised—the forging of metals, bronze, and iron develop. This civilisation develops from Cain. What is the significance of this? Two things: first of all, civilisation developed apart from God—that is the teaching here. Therefore, civilisation is secular rather than sacred. But I want to add straightaway that I am not saying it is sinful; I am saying it is secular, which is a different thing. Art and science and music can be redeemed by Christian activity and can become a sacred thing. But the Bible teaches very clearly that these things developed in a secular setting, and music is not a sacred thing in itself; it needs to be made sacred music. Art is not a sacred thing in itself—art for art's sake —it needs to be made a sacred thing. That doesn't mean by just drawing pictures of the Bible; it means making it a wholesome and a godly thing. Science is a secular thing, but it can be made a godly thing by Christians redeeming it.

In other words, the Bible is saying quite clearly that human civilisation is secular. Until you make it sacred, it doesn't start being godly. This is what the word "world" means in the Bible; it means "secular society that developed in this way". But the other side of it is this: secular civilisation may be redeemed for God or it may be dragged down by the devil. Every scientific discovery there has been could either be used for God or for Satan.

I remember going to an amazing exhibition of atomic energy, and it started with the work of Rutherford and the others in Cambridge who split the atom. Then as you left there were two massive photographs on the wall at the exit. One showed atomic energy being used in industry, agriculture, medicine and so on, and the other just showed Hiroshima after it had fallen. Above the two it just had one word, "Which?" That is what the Bible is saying in Genesis 4. This is secular power of man. It can either be used for God or the opposite.

Lamech, the seventh in the line from Adam, used power for the opposite. We are told that Lamech didn't care for God's instructions. He knew what they were; he knew all about his great-great-grandfather Cain. But Lamech, first of all, took two wives—the first man to step out of God's marriage order and to become a polygamist. Then he began to boast to his wives: Do you know what? My son's invention of weapons of bronze and iron – I can kill a man who strikes me. I just killed a young child for striking me. The bravado of this bully!

Then he says, "I can be avenged seventy times seven." He is saying that he has the weapons of mass murder, the potential of killing in his hands and could obliterate a city with those weapons. That secular civilisation in the line of Cain, ever-increasing destruction, weapons of mass destruction—is Cain's line. It is the line that we still have to cope with today. When Peter said to Jesus, "How often do I have to forgive?" Jesus quoted Lamech and said, "You forgive seventy-times seven."

Now let us turn more briefly to the next chapter. It is such a lovely chapter and such a contrast. I want to go on into some wonderful news. There is another line in the human race. There isn't just the line of Cain—the line of mass destruction, the line of killing, the line of departing from God's marriage standards, there is another line: Adam knew Eve again; she got another boy. Of course we are going back; we are overlapping in time a bit. We have followed one line right down; now we go back and we follow the other one down: Seth.

Eve saw in Seth's birth more of the hand of God than she had seen in either Cain's or Abel's, so she called him "Appointed". She felt that God meant her to have this boy to replace Abel. She felt that this boy had some special purpose in God's sight, and he had, because this boy was going to be an ancestor of Jesus Christ. So Seth was born. It says, "At that time, men began to call on the name of the Lord." Here is a new beginning in the human race, when people are going to pray and to praise God. There is a new line coming into being—not people who are going to forge weapons of war, not men who are going to boast to all their wives about their bullying, but men who are going to pray to God. This is the hope of our human race – that all down the years through history there have been two groups of people and that one of them has prayed and praised. This is the hope of the future.

Now we have another line and it is a very interesting list of people. Here they are: Enosh, Cainan, Mahalalel, Jared, Enoch, Methuselah, Lamech, Noah, and Noah again has three children. So the single line comes to three children: Shem, Ham, and Japheth – just as Jabel, Tubal, and Tubal Cain, but it is a different sort of line.

Now there are two more problems here, and I deal with them briefly but I am going to be very frank – I don't know the answer to either of them. One is that the total period of years from Adam to Noah is too short, and the other is that the lives of individuals are much too long. Here are the two problems: if you add up the chapter, there are 1556 years from Adam to Noah in this chapter, which just doesn't fit because we know that Jericho was inhabited in 7000 BC. The other problem is: what about old Methuselah? But never mind Methuselah, he only beat the others by a decade or so, nearly everybody lives into the nine hundreds, and this is a very real problem. First, as regards the total period, most genealogies in the scriptures have gaps in them. For example, in the genealogy of Christ in Matthew chapter 1, a man called Jared begets his own great, great-grandson. In fact, instead of giving us all the links, these genealogies give us the landmarks in the line, the really important people. So it may well be that we have some pretty huge gaps in this genealogy and it is not consecutive. I just leave that as a possible answer to the problem. I don't think it is the final answer but it is a possible one.

The other problem – as to how they managed to live to 900 odd – is a real one. There are three possible answers to the problem; once again, you can take your choice. The first possible answer might be that the years then were more equivalent to our months. If they were, then this would make them all between seventy and eighty when they died. The problem is, they all started having children when they were nine or ten. I don't think honestly that solves it.

The second possibility which has been mentioned, and many Old Testament scholars have accepted this, is that the name doesn't stand for an individual but for his tribe – as long as his tribe existed and bore his name. In other words, the tribe lasted nine hundred years. That, I am afraid, is not the answer because you just can't get around Enoch and Noah who are clearly individuals and who do things as individuals many hundreds of years after they are born.

The third possibility is that it is literally true. Now I know that scientists digging up upper Paleolithic, Neolithic and Neanderthal skeletons have discovered that they died between twenty and sixty years of age. Is there no possibility that with this line (though he didn't do it with Cain's line, nobody on Cain's line lived long) God might be saying: down this road lies life? Whether he is saying that or not, the chapter says it. I know it says eight times: "and he died", but the real emphasis of the chapter is: "he lived" so long.

It is as if it is saying: Cain—his line is death, death, death. But this line is life, life, life, even here on earth. There is something even more wonderful. There is one man in this line who doesn't even die. And we come to this wonderful man Enoch. Enoch never died. Did you notice the gap? All the way down the line: Enosh, he died; Cainan, he died; Mahalalel, he died; Jared, he died; Enoch walked with God. He went for a walk with God and never came back; he walked right into heaven.

I am absolutely certain that that is fact, and that here, right in the earliest days of the human race, one man's life said in the name of God that death is not the last word and does not have complete control of the human race. So we turn to look at Enoch. Isn't it interesting that Lamech was the seventh in the other line? Lamech was seventh—the man who murdered and killed. Enoch is the seventh man here, as if to say: look at the contrast – same generation, one preoccupied with murder, war and death, and the other who doesn't even die.

There are three things about Enoch that we are told, and I would wish to die and have people say these three things about me. First of all, notice when he began to walk with God. Secondly, notice that he continued to walk with God, and thirdly, notice that he never stopped walking with God. When did he begin walking with God? When his first son was born and very often when you have looked into the cradle of your own firstborn and looked at that act of creation, something deep is stirred within you, something that made you feel a bit like God, sharing in his creative activity, and yet something that humbled you, made you feel the need of God.

So when my wife and I dedicated our three children, we felt the need of God in a deep way, the extra responsibility. There is something more wonderful about this boy here. Enoch had a boy called Methuselah. Do you know what that name means? Here is a translation of it in English; it is quite a long name and it is a long sentence. Methuselah means, "When he dies, it shall be sent". What does that mean? Who gave him that name and why? I'll tell you this: I don't think Enoch would have give him that name unless God had told him to, because it is a name of extraordinary meaning.

We are told Methuselah lived altogether 969 years. What was sent 969 years after his birthday? The Flood. Enoch must have been told by God: the world will last as long as this child; when this baby dies, the world will be destroyed. Enoch had to call his boy Methuselah – when he dies it shall be sent. Can you imagine what it is like to have a baby and to know that the world will last as long as your baby and no longer? Every time that baby falls sick, the world's end stares you in the face, and you wonder how long your baby's going to live, knowing that when that baby dies the world will end. Can you see now how Enoch began to walk with God? He began to see the future; he began to see God's judgment coming, and he walked with God.

We notice secondly that he continued walking with God for three hundred years more. It is great when somebody is converted, but when fifty years later they are still walking with God—that is wonderful. It is wonderful to see young people full of zeal and enthusiasm for the Lord, but what is wonderful is to see a middle-aged or an elderly person still walking with God.

What is walking? Walking is *one step at a time in a forward direction*; that is all we are told to do in the Bible. We are told to walk in love, to walk worthy of our high calling, to walk in the light. We are told to walk with God. It says for hundreds of years, "Enoch walked with God." Wouldn't it be wonderful if when you died somebody suggested putting on your tombstone "...walked with God all their life"? When Enoch died, he was still walking and still going strong, still keeping in step with God, still keeping up with God, still keeping in the centre of God's path. So we come to the day – not when his walk with God ended but something happened which was so wonderful that you can hardly imagine it. Enoch must have wondered how long he was going to live. He lived 365 years, one year for every day of our year. Then one day he went out walking and he just went. What a wonderful way to go. Can you imagine the glory of just going out for a walk and finding yourself in glory? That is what Enoch did. He just went for a walk with God and he stepped straight into heaven. Do you know there is a real possibility that some of us will do that? The Bible tells me that it is a possibility because Enoch's "translation", as it is called, means "to be carried across". Instead of having to go through the river of death, God just carried him across, as later he did Elijah; as one day he will do for millions of Christians. I tell you a secret: we shall not all sleep; we shall not all die. Some of us will still be around when Jesus comes back, and if we are, no funeral for us. No undertaker will be called, no doctor will sign a death certificate—we'll go for a walk with the Lord and land in glory. You will do what Enoch did. This is to say: down this line is eternal life—death conquered; death banished. This is the glory of this chapter – "and Enoch walked with God, and he was not, for God took him." There are only two people in the Bible who are said to have pleased God with their lives. One is Jesus, and the other is Enoch.

In the words of Moses, "I have set before you death and life – choose". I have set before you the two groups of the human race, the lost and the saved, the sheep and the goats. I have set before you those two groups, and the dividing line is blood: those who take the blood of others and those who take the blood of Jesus for themselves; those who try to get to God their way, and those who come to God *his* way; those who bring a lamb – the Lamb slain from the foundation of the world – get written in the Lamb's book of life, and like Enoch, they can look forward to walking with God in heaven.

I have presented you with two lines – Cain and Abel. Did you think that was history? It is reality. Did you think you were just going to dig back into the dim past for some obscure interest? Were you looking forward to hearing where Cain got his wife or are you more concerned to ask, "Do I belong to Cain or to Seth? Do I belong to God or not? Did he accept my offering of praise today, or did he not? Does he look into my heart and say, "You do well. I accept your faith in the blood of Jesus Christ"? Or does he say, "You came with a proud heart. You came prepared to do me good instead of to have me do you good"? This is the question.

I divide these two chapters not quite by chapters into two
sections. The first is the description of a world of evil, and
the key word is flesh which occurs time and time again. The
second section describes a way of escape from that world,
and the key word is
READ GENESIS 6–7
which occurs a number
of times. Now why do I put it like this? Because unless you
get the background to the story, clear, you will be tempted
to think the flood was an extreme act of injustice. It is vital

During the Puritan days in England and Scotland, the only
toy that children were allowed to play with on Sundays
was a Noah's ark. Maybe in your childhood you got those
little animals lined up two-by-two. At any rate, from your
childhood you may have known the basic story of Noah
and the Flood. At this stage I am not going to address any
geological questions except to declare straight away that I
believe that we are dealing with fact and not fiction. Jesus
treated this as fact, and that would be good enough for me,
but I know of no reason, scriptural or scientific, why anyone
should treat this as fiction. The way it is presented to us is
so factual, so real, the vivid details and the actual dating of
when they went in, and all the rest of it, comes across as a
most vivid narrative remembered and passed down through
the generations.

But the thing that I want to convey to you now is this: in
this story of Noah and the flood, there is a perfect balance
between God's justice and his mercy. Where sin abounded,
grace abounded. Where men did wrong and deserved to be
punished, God not only did that but at the same time offered
them a way of escape in his love and mercy. The emphasis in
this story is on the ark; the emphasis is on the eight people
who were saved rather than the thousands (perhaps millions)
who were not. Because it is God's desire to draw to your
attention not the destruction of the wicked but the salvation
of those who believe, and this is the whole thrust of the story.

I divide these two chapters not quite by chapters, into two sections. The first is the description of a world of evil, and the key word is *flesh* which occurs time and time again. The second section describes a way of escape from that world, and the key word there is the *flood*, which occurs a number of times. Now why do I put it like this? Because unless you get the background to the story clear, you will be tempted to think the flood was an extreme act of injustice. It is vital to see what was happening *before* God sent the flood. Why did he do it? It was the only time in history God has ever done such a thing, and the only time in history he ever will do such a thing. What was so terrible about that society that caused God to do it?

The answer is that evil had taken a perverted form that had stepped beyond all previous bounds and right beyond the limits that God has set to human behaviour. There is something so evil, so appalling, happening in the first few verses of this chapter that it makes you shudder. Verses 1–4 describe the expression of the evil that had invaded society by this time. We started in Genesis 3 with sin in an individual, then in a marriage, then in a family, then in a society, and now we see sin on a world scale.

What form was it taking? How was it being expressed? The answer is that certain marriages were taking place of a particularly horrible kind, and we must ask, "What was so horrible about them?" We are told, first of all, that they were marriages based on physical attraction alone. That in itself is an inadequate marriage in God's sight, and to marry on the grounds of physical attraction alone is not what God intended. But that is not what is horrible about these marriages. The horrible thing is that the sons of God were entering into unions with the daughters of men. What is horrible about that? What does it mean? You will find that many people have given different interpretations to this.

First of all, there are those who say that the people of God were marrying people who didn't belong to God, or to put it in Genesis terms, that the sons of Seth – God's line – were marrying the daughters of Cain, the evil line.

Now while there is a truth here, I don't think this expresses the horror of the situation. I know perfectly well that God's people must marry within God's people. You must not destroy the boundary of God's people in your marriage. A believer must marry a believer. That is laid down in the New Testament; it is our Lord's Word. I lay it down very strongly, but I add with full sympathy that our prayers are needed for young Christian girls because there is a shortage of young Christian men and they need our prayers for that very reason. It takes grace and courage for a girl today to say, "I'm sorry, I cannot marry because I could not marry you in Christ."

But that is not what made God feel as he did here. I have heard an intriguing question: was this a marriage between people, made in the image of God, and anthropoid species – in other words, animals. Certainly the Bible condemns as obscene and vile unions between men and animals in which men have engaged from time to time, but that is not quite horrible enough yet.

I am going to suggest – and I ask you to check up in the rest of the Bible whether this doesn't make sense – that the phrase "sons of God" refers to angels. Everywhere else in the Bible that phrase, when it is not defined, refers to angels. Read the early chapters in the book of Job, for example. Now if that is what it means, we have a most extraordinary departure from God's ordered world in which animals were at one level and were to mate among themselves; people were at another level and were to marry among themselves. Angels were in the heavenly realm and were not to marry at all, for the angels in heaven neither marry nor are they given in marriage. But we are told in the New Testament that angels stepped out of their proper order – that is the literal word – and fell. I take it that this refers to Genesis 6 in which we have the most extraordinary occurrence of union between spirits and women.

At one time I would not have credited that as possible, until I came across a case with which I had enough connection to know the situation of a woman who was regularly having such relationships with a demonic possession, and the horror of it struck my soul. Here were angels who left their proper station and entered into union with women (the daughters of men). Nothing could be more horrible, in a sense, than this confusion between the God-given orders.

You can begin to see now how utterly horrible the result would be in God's sight. Here were women who were now physically possessed by evil spirits, the fallen ones – and the Hebrew for "fallen ones" is "nephilim", wrongly translated in the Authorized Version as "giants". Nephilim, fallen ones, were in the earth in those days, and they were entering into union with women. The result was that they were producing offspring that were extraordinary. This unusual combination was producing supermen physically who were midgets spiritually. Now to bring home the utter horror of it, do you realise that these would be virgin births? One day the Holy Spirit came upon a girl called Mary. Notice that the Spirit caused a girl Mary to conceive and produce a Son called Jesus Christ. But here in Genesis 6 we have got virgin births produced by evil spirits, producing a kind of creature that became famous – men of physical, supernatural strength, men of renown, men who were famous heroes, and men who were spiritually destitute.

That is the kind of horrible situation, and it is interesting that God emphasises the distinction between flesh and spirit. When he looks at this he says: my Spirit is not going to go on living in your flesh forever if you are going to let these spirits take your flesh. You cannot expect to dabble in the occult and have the Holy Spirit at the same time. You can't expect to do both—the Holy Spirit and evil spirits are incompatible. My Spirit is not going to stay in you if you let these spirits take you over—that is what he is saying.

Therefore God set a limit to human existence. He said, "Your days shall be a hundred and twenty years." What did he mean? Some have thought he meant that each person's life would be cut down from Methuselah's 900 to a mere 120—no. He is referring to men collectively, not individually, and 120 years after he said this the Flood came. So he is saying: I will give you a chance – I will give you over a century to get these spirits out of you and to have my Spirit control your flesh. One hundred and twenty years—already we are touching the mercy and the patience of God. Fancy waiting 120 years when this was what he was having to look at on the earth.

Now let us look in verses 5–7 at the extent of this situation. It is a contrast, "The Lord saw...." When did we last read those words? We read them in Genesis 1 again and again and again: "And God saw that it was good." When God finished all his work, he looked at it and said, "That is very good." Now God sees what? That lovely, good world that he had made, that wonderful place; now God looked down and saw that the wickedness of man was in all the earth. Do you realise what a horrible sight that is to God when he had been looking on a good world?

Human imagination is what he points at. You know, only God can tell you what your imagination does; nobody else can tell. I cannot tell what those who listen to me are thinking. I could guess with some maybe. They might be thinking, "Did I leave the gas on?" – or thinking about the football match yesterday. I would think that this passage in

Genesis is stirring enough to be thinking hard about, but I can't tell. But God looked down on man's imagination—that is where he looks. He doesn't look at what you are wearing when you go to church. We may put on Sunday clothes—that doesn't bother God one bit, he doesn't look at that. The Lord sees not as man sees. Man looks on the outward appearance; the Lord looks at the heart. He looked at the imaginations of people, and here are three very strong words, "Every imagination of his heart was only evil continually"—every, only, continually, you couldn't get a stronger statement than that. That human imagination which God had to look at—and just bear in mind that God has to study your thought life all the time.

God looks down from heaven and says, "Is that good?" God's indignation was such that his feelings came in. "And God said, 'I'm sorry I made man. I'm sorry I ever did it'." Is there any sentence in scripture sadder than that? That is the heavenly indignation, and it points to an important truth in scripture, which is this: how does God deal with a world like ours? The answer is: no half measures. He offers two extreme absolutes: punishment for sin or pardon for those who believe. He doesn't do what most of us do, and with half measures put up with a mixed situation. That is, perhaps, why people don't like God because we are prepared to "let bygones be bygones," to try to just keep the thing going and say, "Well, no one's perfect." God says: we have got to get things right; and therefore, I must destroy what is wrong, but I give you a chance; I give you every opportunity to get put right. Isn't that fair? Could God do more? Do we expect God to be as indulgent with a mixed world as we are? No, God must have things right because he is a righteous God.

Now against this horrible, black cloth there is one thing that shines like a star in the night. Out of those thousands of people living at the physical level, dabbling in the occult, becoming involved with evil spirits, in a particularly horrible way against all that, there was an exception, and that man was called Noah. In a corrupt world, one man resisted the pressures of society. In a world in which every marriage seems to be going wrong, there is one man married to one wife in a godly way. Have you ever realised how difficult it must have been for Noah to be alone in this?

There are two things we are told about Noah. The first is that he enjoyed divine favour or grace. The first time the world "grace" occurs in the Bible is here. Where sin abounded, grace abounded. Wherever you find the judgment of God upon sin, somewhere near it you will find the grace of God—God is like this.

Noah found grace in the eyes of the Lord. The phrase, "in the eyes of" means that God loved to look at Noah. Isn't that a lovely contrast? God saw the wickedness of men in all the earth, but God loved to look at Noah. He loved to look down and say, "Look at that man, there is one man who walks with me." We are told not only that he had the divine favour but that he enjoyed a devout *fellowship* with God. His relationship to himself was right, his relationship to his neighbours was right, his relationship to God was right.

As far as he was concerned in himself, he was a just and a righteous man, a man of integrity, a man who was upright. As far as his neighbours were concerned, he was blameless in his generation. Not one of them could find an excuse for their sin in his life. As far as God was concerned, like his great-grandfather before him, Enoch, he walked with God and that means he took a step at a time in the right direction. A lovely man, Noah, and we know one other thing about him: that Noah was a preacher.

Far from being one of those whose only concern was to save his own soul, Noah was desperately concerned to get others saved too and he preached. Alas, hardly anybody listened to him, except his wife and his sons Shem, Ham, Japheth and their wives — a congregation of seven used to gather to listen to Noah preach and only seven people believed.

People say to me, "The Church is getting smaller and smaller, dwindling congregations everywhere." If there's one who will come and believe, it is worth preaching. Noah was content with his congregation of seven and they believed the truth. What a great man Noah is. I know there were physical giants in the world in those days. I know there were these extraordinary monstrosities, the result of these strange unions — men of renown with supernatural strength, heroes. But they were dwarfs beside Noah. He was head and shoulders above them. Noah was a spiritual giant, and all the more so because he had no encouragement.

In vvs. 11-12 we come to the extreme. This evil spread through those 120 years until these verses describe what the world was like at the end of that period. People knew about God — they had had so many godly people telling them — but instead of turning back to him, what happened? First, they violated everything that was sacred. Everything became corrupt; honesty vanished. The whole earth was corrupt. The things that were sacred were no longer sacred, trampled in the mud.

The second thing we are told is that violence filled the earth — rioting, marching, fights in the street, children hitting parents, parents hitting children. Therefore, if you wonder why we study such ancient history, then I say, "Go home and look at today's news again." The society that God destroyed had already destroyed itself.

Now we turn to the end of chapter 6 and to chapter 7, in which God offers a way of escape. An ark that was as large as this could have contained hundreds of people. Many people could have escaped if they had wished. God provided all that was needed for this, and God's mercy waited 120 years and then another seven days – gave them every opportunity he could. But God, because he is righteous, cannot wait forever to put things right. You may think that today – because everything is going on as ever it has done and because God doesn't seem to be putting things right. But let me say that God is going to put things right. He cannot wait forever.

Isn't it strange that unbelievers tell me they want God to put things right! Now, do they? They say, "Why doesn't God intervene? Why doesn't he come and deal with wicked people? Why doesn't he get rid of all this sin? Why doesn't he stop wars? Why doesn't he come and deal with it? My answer must be, "Well are you quite sure that he wouldn't have to come and put you right if he did? And are you willing to be put right, and if you are not, what do you think he will do if he comes to put the world right?" You cannot have it both ways – either God comes to put things right now, in which case if you are not right with him you have had it, or else you should thank God for his patience that he is staving off the day that you might come to repentance. God will not wait forever.

I underline that Noah was an example to his generation of how they could be saved. First of all, notice the extraordinary detailed orders that God gave him. Bear in mind that Noah probably lived about three or four hundred miles from the sea. God told him to build an ark – in the middle of dry land. Now the word "ark" means a "chest" or a "box". It was not the little boat that you played with as a child, it was simply a box or large chest, three hundred cubits long, fifty wide (a sixth of its length), and thirty cubits high – a tenth of its length.

I mention those proportions because until recently no ship was ever built on those proportions, but modern shipbuilding is. John West, who designed SS Canberra and based it on the proportions of Noah's Ark, found that it is the perfect proportion. Indeed, West has said that if he had been asked as a ship's designer today to design a craft not for travelling but for floating, to cope with the swell of floods, this is the size and shape and proportion that he would have designed. I find that very interesting.

Noah was told to build it of a wood that is so durable that the Vatican doors in Rome are built of this material, and they have lasted a thousand years so far. He was told to use a flexible caulking of bitumen, which was available. You can still find traces of it in that area, which would be just right for keeping it watertight. It would not need launching, of course, so it didn't need to have any shipyard, and it was just built right there. But can you imagine what the neighbours thought about it? If there had been newspapers, there would had been cartoons: "Old Noah there, have you seen his ark lately? It's getting quite big now," and they would laugh their heads off at this man – as today people laugh at those who still believe the gospel of Christ and say it is the most irrelevant thing you can do, to preach. Don't listen to them; we are preparing for the future, and we don't mind who laughs at us.

Noah built this great big thing and it got bigger. It was properly braced because there were three decks. In the decks there were partitions, which were here called "nests" – cabins, if you like, which would brace it further. This was unsinkable, a modern ship's designer tells us that. The amazing thing to me is this: God planned every detail. God didn't say, "Noah, I'm going to send a flood. You get out of it as best you may." God said, "Noah, I will tell you exactly what to do if you'll do it."

One of the most thrilling phrases in this chapter, which occurs three times again: "Noah did all that God commanded him." That is faith. It was the silliest thing to do; it was the most irrelevant thing to do; it was the most incredible thing to do, and Noah did all that God commanded him. It says, "Because he did, he condemned the world." Now how did he condemn the world? Quite simply this: that not one of them would ever be in the position to say to God, "I didn't know there was a flood coming."

In other words, do you see that Noah's action not only saved him, it condemned others? Alas, this is one of the tragedies of preaching, that in saving some, you are condemning others because they will not be able to say to God one day: "I never heard the truth, I never knew how to get ready for all this. I never knew the way of escape." So Noah building his ark in the middle of dry land was an example to others.

Now 7:1–5 describes how God explained to Noah exactly what he was going to do. God took Noah into his confidence, and God has taken his people into his confidence and said: I'm not going to leave you in doubt. I'll tell you exactly what I'm going to do and why I'm going to do it. First of all: why? Why am I going to save you? The answer is: because you are righteous in your generation.

In other words, God gives a reasoned verdict on his action. God is not an arbitrary God who simply chooses to damn some and save others. That is the kind of wrong deduction that some have made from his sovereignty. God told Noah why he had invited him into that ark. It was because he was going to send rain – and my, how it rained. So God takes Noah into his confidence.

You have a Bible in your hands and God has taken you into his confidence and told you all you need to know about the future, about the end of the world and what lies beyond. You have it there. Have you ever read the Bible right through? Pretty well every other book you ever picked up you probably read right through. I hope that as a Christian you have read the Bible right through. It would seem to me incredible for a Christian to say, "I believe this is the Word of God but I have never read it."

You try reading three chapters a day and five on Sunday and by the end of a year you will have been right through it, and it is a most healthy thing to do. It is God's Word and he has told us as detailed instructions as we need as to how to be saved and how to live the life that he wants us to live and how to be righteous in our generation. Everything you need to know, he has told you. But it is no use leaving a car handbook in the cubbyhole in the dashboard, and it is no use leaving the Bible on the shelf.

Now we come to vv. 6–16. So vivid was the memory of that week that it is dated to the day. Noah was six hundred years old and in the six hundredth year (v. 11) of Noah's life, in the second month and on the seventeenth day of the month.... They remembered that date for evermore. It was passed down from generation to generation. This is the kind of detail that rings with truth – they went in. Now I want you to notice two things about the entry into the ark. By the way, it took about seven days to get them all in. Urgency, but no haste – they had a week to get all the animals into their nests, the birds into their cages. They had a week to do it, they presumably gathered them together already over the 120 years and were keeping animals on the farm. Two things: first of all, Noah took his family with him. I have heard some preachers say that as long as the father has faith, the family will get to heaven. I don't believe it. I wish I could, but I don't, because those six sons and daughters-in-law would not have gone in unless they believed Noah. Do you honestly think that they would have gone in like the sheep just because he said "Come on in", with everybody laughing at them, with all the neighbours standing there – and being ridiculed while they hustled them all in. A cloudless sky, the sun shining down. "See, he's getting into his ark now. He says the rain will be here any day." Do you think they would have gone in if they hadn't shared his faith? Never, Mind you, it is wonderful if a father has faith, but his family must come to share it. Eight people went in and the family was saved. The seven people owed it to one man. You notice they were all monogamous; they all had married one wife only and Noah had managed to pass on a high view of marriage to his children.

Now we notice that representative flesh was also included. Somehow, you know, creation around us is affected by people; nature is affected by our sin and will be affected by our salvation. The whole creation groans in travail, waiting for what? The redemption of the sons of God. Do you realise that nature will be redeemed when man is? So nature is affected and the animals shared not just in the sin and in the destruction of man, but in the salvation of man. So nature came into the ark. The Bible has a lot to say about nature's need for redemption and that is another story.

"God shut them in." What a lovely touch. They didn't have to pull it to, and bolt it hard, and wonder if it would hold out the water. God says, "I'll shut that door tight," and he shut them in. The only window was just a slit, a few cubits high, around the eaves, so that they would not see the water and would not see the destruction but would be able to look up to the heavens.

We come to the final paragraph of this section. It says that water came down from heaven and up from the deeps. I can only take it that there was a disturbance, an upheaval, in the ocean bed, which caused tidal waves to come in, which coupled with the rain from above, caused this flood. Such things are well known, but do you see the point of it? When God made the world good, what did he do? He separated the waters which were above the firmament from the waters which were below the firmament. He kept those waters apart and dry land came in where man could live. Do you see what he is doing? He is saying: "I am going to turn it back again. I am going to reverse the process so that there is no room for man in the earth." He is saying, "I'm sorry I did that, so I am undoing it. I'm sorry I ever separated the waters from the waters and made the dry land, so I'll bring them together again until there is no dry land." These are terrible facts, serious truths and that is what God did.

So the result was that everybody and everything was drowned. I am not going to say anymore than that because God doesn't. God has no pleasure in the death of the wicked and neither must we. There is nothing but a simple, bald statement of fact. No description of their suffering, not a detail of the appalling horrors of the flood, not a word. God had no pleasure in it at all. It is simply stated as a bald fact and left.

But Noah was still in the ark, and the animals were and the eight people were. For God, it says in chapter 6, had made a covenant with him. The first time that word appears in the Bible is here, and a covenant is a marriage. A covenant is a promised relationship which one party offers to the other, and God had said, "Noah, I'll make a covenant with you," and God kept that covenant. Just as when I made a covenant with my wife, we exchanged a ring as a token of the covenant made between us, wherever you see a rainbow, you are looking at God's marriage ring with Noah – a sign of his covenant and a promise that he has kept ever since.

I must now apply that to today, and I do so in two ways— first, by quoting Jesus. Jesus once said this, "As it was in the days of Noah, so shall it be in the days of the coming of the Son of man." In other words, expect all this to happen again.

Therefore, I would expect the human race to become increasingly interested in the occult, to begin dabbling in spiritist things and reading horoscopes—studying the stars in astrology, black masses, sexual orgies. It is coming back again. Jesus said it would. He said: "As it was in the days of Noah", I would expect the world to be increasingly filled with violence. He would be a bold man who would say, "That's not coming back again." As it was in the days of Noah, expect it all to happen again. Expect there to be a few people pleading with the rest to get right with God and saying, "Be saved, for there is a way of escape." Expect the world to laugh at them, to take no notice of them.

The other thing I can do is to apply this *personally*. I have applied it universally. I believe our world is heading for a repetition of Noah. The other thing is this: how do we prepare for it? Are you prepared to believe God's Word? Faith is taking God at his word and Noah took God at his word. He believed that if God said it was going to happen, it was going to. How do I get ready?

The answer is twofold. You get ready by believing in Jesus Christ—that is how you get into the ark, because the ark is Jesus Christ. Some have said, "The ark is the Church." No, I don't think that. I think the ark that saves us is Jesus, but here is a very interesting thing—I don't think that belief is the only way of getting ready. I think that baptism is the other half of it. It is Peter, the big fisherman, who makes the extraordinary link between Noah's flood and baptism for the believer.

A passage which I have never heard preached on is 1 Peter 3:18–end. It is a startling passage:

For Christ also died for sins, once for all, the righteous for the unrighteous, that he might bring us to God, being put to death in the flesh but made alive in the Spirit.

Now that is the basic gospel of the death and resurrection

of Christ, but now comes some extraordinary statements:

Being made alive in the Spirit in which he went and preached to the spirits in prison, who formerly did not obey, when God's patience waited in the days of Noah, during the building of the ark in which a few—that is eight persons were saved through water. Baptism, which corresponds to this, now saves you, not as a removal of dirt from the body, but as an appeal to God for a clear conscience through the resurrection of Jesus Christ, who has gone into heaven and is at the right hand of God, with angels, authorities, and powers subject to him.

Let me just tell you in a sentence what it says: that if you really do wish to prepare for the future and wish to be saved, then the right way to express your faith in Christ is to do what Noah did and pass through the waters. That is your flood; that is your appeal to God for a clean conscience. That is your way of saying, "God, take my judgment now and bring me through the waters as you brought Noah through and assure me that I belong to you and that I shall inherit that new world which will come afterwards."

Saved through the waters, as Noah was, not because anything physical happens to you, as if your body has to be washed. It is not an outward washing you need, it is an inward washing of the conscience. But this is the ordained way of the Lord Jesus Christ, for you to appeal for a clear conscience. Just as the Lord's Supper with bread and wine speaks of his death, baptism speaks of his resurrection from the dead and the empty tomb.

READ GENESIS 8–9

In the account of Noah, though it is also true of every other part of the Bible, I am tremendously struck by the complete absence of feelings and the presence of facts. I seem to spend my days trying to persuade people to put their faith in facts and not feelings. If my faith were in feelings I would not know whether I was a Christian one day or the next.

If I only preached when I felt like it, my hearers would get out of church a lot earlier more frequently. But the point is I do not preach to share with others my feelings, and do not intend to stimulate yours. My task is to tell others the facts. If your faith is based on facts, as it ought to be, you don't need to worry about your feelings. You may have wonderful feelings or you may not. Who cares? The facts are still the same.

If I have a "Monday morning" feeling and feel terribly depressed and low, that does not alter the fact that Jesus Christ is alive. My depression doesn't put him back in the grave, and so my faith will not be affected if I feel low one morning. The Bible deliberately doesn't talk about feelings. It could, but it doesn't. Some of the most poignant scenes in the Bible have a complete absence of emotions and tell you the facts. Let me illustrate this from the story of Noah and his ark, though I could illustrate it more forcibly from the account of the cross, where in spite of the stirring things that were happening, there is not a single description of feelings.

But look at this story. I could certainly play on your heartstrings as perhaps some orators of a former day have done. In describing the feelings of the people who were drowned—how did they feel when the rain came and the floods came up? How did they feel when they realised that Noah was right and that they were all wrong? How did they feel when they watched the ark floating off in the distance and realised there was no chance for them to build one? Well, it could be a very emotional kind of sermon but not a word of God. You might be very moved by it but you wouldn't be moved anywhere. I could preach a sermon on the feelings of Noah. How did he feel? He and his family shut up in that great wooden box, that chest as it is called, almost a floating coffin it would appear to some, though it was to lead to life.

How did it feel to be the only family left alive and to know that outside them nobody else was living? They were the only people left. How did he feel? There is not a word about that, so if I preached like that I might move you but it wouldn't produce faith, which is based on the truth and on facts. I could even preach to you about the feelings of God. How do you think God felt when he had to destroy a whole society? I can tell you this for the Bible does say it: that God has no pleasure at all in the death of the wicked. He didn't enjoy it but there is not a word about his feelings either.

What then does it say? Let me go to the facts because your faith must be in facts. Your feelings will go up and down like a yo-yo. If they didn't go up and down you would never have any. Think that through and you will realise what I am saying. Therefore your faith must not be in that kind of thing. Young people must not get the idea that faith is a nice bubbly feeling inside, as one girl described it to me—that is not faith. Faith is to be sure of the truth even when you feel terrible. Faith is to be absolutely certain that God is on the throne when everything is going wrong. Faith is to be sure of the facts. Now look at the facts. Fact number one: God remembered Noah. Well there was nobody else to remember him. Nobody else on earth could remember this man and his three sons and his three daughters-in-law, and his wife – the eight people. Nobody else could remember them because there was nobody else alive who did remember them. It may well be that there were times when Noah in the ark wondered if God had remembered him.

Can you imagine being shut up in a box, tossed about in the waves for a year, and wondering if it would ever come to an end? You might even begin to think: has God forgotten us? Do you think he has done all this and then just left the whole Earth and forgotten us? But it says, "God remembered Noah." Now the word "remembered" in the Bible means something much more than I am afraid it means in most modern English usage. It doesn't just mean to recall, it means to renew. The only illustration of this meaning that I can think of is a very appropriate one. Do you ever say, "Oh we must remember so and so at Christmas"? Now what do you mean when you have said that? Do you mean that you just think about them or do you mean you will renew a relationship with them by sending a card or present or ringing them up or doing something? Now that is the meaning of the Bible word *remember*. God remembered Noah. If I may give you a little aside, Jesus said, "Do this in remembrance of me." He did not mean this is simply a memorial; this is a kind of gravestone so you can look at the bread and wine and just think back two thousand years. He didn't mean that. He meant: renew your relationship with me. Not just remember but renew – that is what remembrance means.

That is why the cup becomes the fellowship of his blood and the communion of his body, the bread. It is far more than a memorial; it is something to be renewed, and those who come to the Lord's Supper in the right way renew their fellowship with him every time they remember. God remembered Noah, which meant he was going to get in touch with him again. He was going to renew the relationship again. He was going to do something about it. His faithful love abated those waters.

God used natural means to bring the Flood, and natural means to take it away again. He stopped the flow from the oceans. He stopped the rain and he sent a wind to dry it all out. This is quite typical of God. He sent a wind to divide the Red Sea and God can use natural means to do something that is supernatural.

As the waters went down, the mountains began to appear. The word "mountain" here is much more the Welsh meaning than the English. The Welsh don't use the word "hill", they use the word "mountain" for hills. That is exactly what the Bible means.

It doesn't say that the ark came to rest on the top of Ararat, which is seventeen thousand feet up. It says, "It came to rest on the mountains," which means the whole range called Ararat, which varies in height and is hundreds of miles long. One of the most interesting things here is this: did you realise that the ark came to rest on exactly the same day that Jesus rose from the dead? It is dated very carefully and so is our Lord's resurrection. The very day that that ark came to rest is the very day on which Jesus rose from the dead and the disciples' faith came to rest, too. I will just leave that thought with you. You can validate in your own way.

We come now to the ingenuity of Noah. He was a very clever man. To try to find out when was the right time, he began to use some of the birds in the ark. Now I suppose we could allegorise or make this into a parable. I am going to try to resist the temptation because that could lead us anywhere, but he took a raven first, a rather wild, rough bird that tends to live in higher altitudes.

So there was a logic in Noah and so he took the raven and sent it out to see if there was any high, rough ground where a raven could live, and it wandered to and fro. He realised there was some higher ground for the raven, so then he thought, "Now I wonder if there was lower ground, so what bird likes lower ground? What bird keeps in the valleys? What bird is not so wild and way up—the dove?" He took a dove and sent that out too. Now it is amazing how the dove has become a symbol of peace. You will find the United Nations has even taken up part of this story—the olive leaf. This seems to speak to people of peace. May I remind you that the only peace that the dove brought evidence of was a peace that was attained by the destruction of millions of people.

So if you are going to see the dove as a symbol of peace, you must take it in context. The dove here is not so much a symbol of peace as a symbol of promise, of renewal; a proof that the world can begin again. It is something that speaks of new beginnings, new life, a new clean world, a world that has had sin washed out of it, a world that is new and clean. That is what the dove speaks to me about and that is why it becomes a perfect symbol of the Holy Spirit. The Holy Spirit brings peace, but the main thing the Holy Spirit brings is the possibility of a new life, a new world in which to live, a world in which sin is cleaned out, in which it has been washed away – a world which, by the power of the Holy Spirit, you can now enter and inhabit.

That is why the Holy Spirit came down on Jesus like a dove – because he was receiving there the power to give new life to others, to bring them into a new world, to give them a new start, to give them a new conscience, to give them a new heart, a new mind, a new beginning. The dove is the symbol of promise.

The third stage is of course where the ark was opened. Notice that the roof was opened before the door. Noah opened upwards before he opened outwards. There is something very profound in this. Month after month, the rain had been beating on the skin covering of the roof or whatever did cover it. I presume it would be skin—that would be the best waterproof thing. The rain had been beating on that roof but one day it stopped. Noah, whether he got an axe or something like that, began to chop that roof up and he began to throw it off, and the sun came streaming in – the drama of it comes in. Here was Noah looking up at last to a bright sky. He had not seen the sun or the sky like that for over a year.

Did he then open the door? No, he waited until God said, "Go out again now." God had said, "Go into the ark," and he had to wait till God said, "Go out." I want to draw a spiritual lesson from that whether it is legitimate or not. It is legitimate from the New Testament and it is this: that when you are saved Jesus says, "Come in. Come into my fold, belong to my sheep," but it is his will that we should not only come in but that we should go out, and coming in and going out we find pasture. The Christian life is both. But I have the feeling that for the first part of the Christian life the Christian should stay in. The Lord calls us out of the world and into himself. For the first part of the Christian life we should concentrate on being in Christ. But there will come a time when it is safe for you to go back into the world from which you came to do God's will there, and God will tell you the right time.

We need to be very sensitive to God to know when to go out as well as to come in, because if you go out before he says go out you can damage your own spiritual life. Noah waited. A world that had been sinful had to be cleansed and Noah had to wait until it was right to get out, and he waited in the sunshine streaming through the rafters and then God said go – and he went out again.

You may have seen the film *The Bible in the Beginning*.

An Italian film director set out to do something rather ambitious – to make one film of the whole Bible for the commercial cinema. He managed in three and a half hours to get to Genesis 21. The first half of it is wonderful. The second half tails off and becomes rather boring. The first five minutes are the most poetic thing I have ever seen on a screen — the creation of the world.

Since so many scientists and theologians argued with this film director as to how it should be done in this modern age, he finally gave up the battle and did it exactly as Genesis 1 says. It is so beautiful, moving and real that I just think it is the best five minutes of film I I have ever seen. But Noah is acted by the producer of the film and it is a whimsical, moving and human presentation of this and a little thing comes out at this point that is not in the Bible but is there between the lines, I think. Noah having lived a year with all these animals now opens the door at God's command and the animals go out. Noah has got to know them well. They are now his pets. He has fed them for a year, and he is losing all his pets. It is a very touching little thing. It is moving in the film and you realise that at the human level he must have become very attached to God's creatures.

The Bible doesn't have it. Why? Because the Bible is not concerned about feelings, it is about fact. The simple fact is stated that he opened the door; the animals went back to the jungle, back to the desert, back to the forest, back to the hill, back to the valley. The world began to recover its character. It is no wonder that the flood is linked to baptism in the New Testament — and, for the individual Christian, baptism is his flood. It is going through the waters and coming out of them to a new life to live and walk in newness of life. It is to go through the flood yourself and it is one of the deepest meanings of baptism that it is your flood, and coming out of the baptistry you should feel as Noah did as he came out of

the ark. You should think as he did. You should realise that
God is calling you to live a new life now, to make a fresh
start, to live altogether differently – you are on the other
side of the Flood.

We now move on to the second half of our study, which
I call *the future assured*. What was Noah's first thought
when he got out of the ark? What would have been your
first thought after a year in a box on the water? What would
have been the first thing you want? Food; shelter? Would
you have tried to build a shelter for your family as soon as
you got out? To me the glory of the story is this—the very
first thing Noah built was an altar. He could have built a
house, he could have looked for food, he could have done
a hundred and one other things. After all, he was going out
into a new world and had to start again from scratch. But
he called his sons, daughters-in-law and wife around him
and said that the first thing was that they were to go into this
new world with God.

Can I give you an up to date version of this? My great-
grandfather was a greengrocer in Wakefield, in a shop under
a railway arch which I think is still there. It was a small shop
and there were only a couple of rooms behind or above the
shop, where he lived with three sons and his wife. It was
cramped and the business was not good. Just around the
corner was a little chapel where the family worshipped and
where they had fellowship and where they praised God.
One day my great-grandfather came back, greatly excited,
to my great-grandmother. He said, "I've had the offer of a
greengrocery shop up on the new estate, the rent is within
our reach. It has a lovely flat above where we will have
more room, and we'll do better business." He was thrilled
to bits. My great-grandmother said, "Henry, how far is it to
the chapel?" He said, "I never looked." Well she said, "Go
back and look." He came back and he said, "There isn't a

chapel." She said, "Henry, we stay here." That is why my grandfather was a minister and his brother was a minister and his brother was a consecrated choirmaster in a church in Blackpool. I wish that people today, when they are constantly looking for another house would say the first thing is the altar — God first. Whatever our family has or hasn't, whether we are cramped or in a big house, the first thing is that our family should have a spiritual home, to be in touch with God. A very great deal of heart searching would be saved if people did this. Mind you, I do not rule out the possibility that God will say to a family, "There's no church there, go and start one." But you need to be called of God to do that and you need to go into it knowing that.

So Noah built an altar and sacrificed some animals. He said, "Don't let all those animals go, keep some of them," and he made a fire and burned them. It was the Old Testament way of making an offering to God without holding anything back. A burnt offering was a complete gift. It is all yours, God — and as the smoke went up, the smell of burning flesh is not very nice. To men it is offensive, but to God such a smell is good. Just as the completion of the offering at the cross of Christ is an offence to people who are offended by it. I heard that George Bernard Shaw and another man went one day to a Christian meeting. At the end of it, the other man said he was going forward and George Bernard Shaw said, "I'm getting out." They both became famous. George Bernard Shaw said later: "Forgiveness is a beggar's refuge. I will be a man and pay my own debts." It was offensive to him that Christ paid his debts. It was offensive that another man should be punished for his sins. I fear that George Bernard Shaw is paying his debts right now. The burnt offering is offensive to man but it is acceptable to God. The cross is an offence to men but it is a sweet smelling savour to God, and I am quoting Ephesians 5:2 when I say that: God smelt that sacrifice and he looked down and he saw that here was a family starting a new world in putting God first. Now we are wonderfully transported into the thought of God.

Without reading this next section carefully enough, you might think that the promise about seedtime and harvest was made to mankind—it was not. It was something God said to himself. It is very important to realise that. It was not a promise to man, it was a resolution within God. He must have revealed it in some way but it was God speaking to himself. You see, the second question of Noah would be: had we better keep the ark? Did that ever strike you?

Supposing that God does it again, this ark would come in handy. Should we stay nearby in case the flood ever returns? Noah must have said, "Do you think God will do it again?"

God was saying to himself, "I'll never do it again," and God looking back on his judgments on Adam and on the society in Noah's day said, "I'll never again curse the ground like I did with Adam. I'll never again flood the earth as I did just now." Here is the amazing thing, God was saying: I will never do it because man's imagination is evil from his youth. Now did you ever get the problem of God saying that? God had said just in chapter 6, "I will destroy the earth because the imagination of man is evil." Now he says, "I won't destroy it because the imagination of man is evil." What is the difference? The answer is this: if God had gone on destroying people because they were evil he would have to destroy every teenager—that is what he is saying. If God destroyed a man as soon as his imagination went wrong then as soon as he became a youth God would have to destroy him. God in his mercy said: I will hold my judgment back because if I was really just I wouldn't let anyone live to adulthood.

Now I wonder if you realise that that is true. Time and again I get people saying to me, why doesn't God do something? Why doesn't he judge these wicked people?

The answer is: because the imagination of man is evil from his youth – that is why he doesn't. If God had been fair and just with me, I would not have seen my twenties. I don't think you would have either because from our youth our imagination runs away with us. So God said: If I am to go on destroying wickedness I shalt do it every generation. No, I am not going to do it again. I have told the human race that I am just, that I am the judge, that I can destroy; I'll leave that one occasion as an object lesson. I won't do it again and just hope they believe this one – that should be enough. So he resolved never to do it again.

You see, the reason why people find it difficult to believe in the Flood is because God has never done it again. If God had done it every ten years, we would believe in it. Simply because it only happened once and never since, people say, "Well you can't expect me to believe that," but it happened once. Jesus believed it happened once. I believe it happened once, I believe it is never going to happen again while the earth remains.

So we come to this lovely promise. God says: Not only will I not destroy, I am going to help men to live. I will make absolutely certain that they have the conditions in which they can grow enough food – seed time and harvest, summer and winter, variations in light and temperature, will always be there. If you are a farmer or gardener, you know that without this promise you would be out of a job and we would all be out of food.

Let me underline two things that are said here. First, you notice, God doesn't promise to give the food. He promises to give the conditions under which man can produce and distribute it. If anybody is starving in the world tonight, it is not God's fault it is man's. The fault is on the production and distribution side.

A world food expert a few years ago stated, and I believe

he was right: "There are enough resources in this world of ours to feed everybody in it if the human race would give its energies and its money and its time to developing those resources and producing the food and distributing it rightly." In spite of the growing population I do believe that if we could spend some of the money that we spend on getting to a moon that has no food on it at all, we would not be blaming God for what is happening in the world today.

The second thing I would point out is that this still allows for localised disaster. It allows for local floods and local famine. Even within the biblical days, the people of God had to help each other with famine. Sometimes there was food in Egypt and famine in Canaan and sometimes the other way around. Even Paul in his missionary journeys was busy collecting for the hunger fund for Jerusalem, which was experiencing shortage of food. This is part of God's will for his people, that they help to get the distribution right. So we can't blame God for what is happening and we take it for granted that the spring will come. We might get cynical about weather and seasons, but the fact is that God has kept his promise another year. We have no guarantee that there will be a spring any more than we have a guarantee that the sun will rise tomorrow. We only have God's word for it and it is enough to help us believe, and God made this promise.

There was a film called *The Day the Earth Caught Fire*. It assumed that two bombs of huge magnitude had been tested by America and Russia unknown to each other simultaneously, and that this had shifted the axis of the earth eleven degrees and altered the seasons, causing, first of all terrible floods in which a newspaper was raising a fund to build an ark – and then the Earth began to orbit nearer to the sun so that the world got hotter and drier and hotter and drier until people were rioting in London for water. It was done very realistically and I watched it in the light of this

Bible study—quite deliberately. It was very real but at the end, you know what my mind said to myself? I don't know if that is scientifically possible. I suspect not, but I know this: it is scripturally impossible. God has said while the earth remains, summer and winter shall not cease. That is where my faith is and I don't believe if man lit nuclear bombs all around the earth simultaneously it could stop God's promise to himself being fulfilled.

Now we come to God's words to Noah at the beginning of chapter 9. God is now going to describe the conditions of life for Noah from now on and I can deal with this quite briefly. There are echoes of Adam here. It begins and ends with the phrase "Be fruitful and multiply in the earth" – exactly what he said to Adam. There is a phrase here: "God blessed Noah", and that is the first time God has blessed man since Genesis 2. There is another phrase here: that man is made in the image of God. That again is an echo of the beginning of Genesis, as if God is saying: we are beginning again. It is almost a repetition.

But there are some very disturbing differences—first in relationship with the animals and secondly in relationships between men. In relation to the animals, three words will give you the difference: fear, food and flesh. Fear – the animals will still be subject to man, though not through trust but through fear. It is sad, isn't it, that when you go for a walk through the woods and you spot some bird, as you go up to it, it flies away in fear. You spot some animal under the undergrowth and instead of running out to you, it runs away from you. There is something very sad about man's relationship with animals. Part of my job on the farm was breaking in horses. Have you ever done that? It is quite a business establishing the will of man over the will of the horse. When you first get that saddle on, the ears flatten, the eyes roll, and there is fear. Yet the man is not harming the horse — not wanting to, and not trying to. This is to be the relationship with the animal world. It will be overcome but it is the basic relationship. It is for the safety of mankind because here are eight people going out into a world of animals and it is for their safety that God ordains it.

Secondly, from now on Noah is no longer a vegetarian. From now on, the animals become food for man. They clearly were not before – before, animals were only killed for sacrifice, now they are killed for food and man becomes a hunter and a killer. Some people have thought that Christians ought to be vegetarians. Well in certain circumstances they ought to. Paul said that he will neither eat meat nor drink wine if doing so causes his brother to stumble. But since eating meat does not cause brothers to stumble for the most part, there is no principle that the Christian should be vegetarian unless it is good for their health.

Thirdly, the word "flesh" – there is an important qualification to eating meat given here. There is a limit to what they can have and they must not eat the blood. This law goes through to the Jews. You can walk through parts of London and see the kosher butchers who will slaughter animals and drain the blood so that those who observe this law may eat the meat. The Jehovah's Witnesses feel this law still applies and they have built upon it a thought about blood transfusion, which I think you know of from the press publicity given to this.

Does this law go through to the Christians? It is mentioned in Acts 15, which you ought to study carefully, where they had mixed churches of Jews and Gentiles – both Christians. In that circumstance, the Gentile Christians were asked not to eat blood, out of thoughtfulness for their Jewish brethren. But it is quite clear that this provision lasted from Noah through the Jews to teach them that blood was sacred, but is not binding on the Christian in my own humble opinion.

Now we come to something very much more important. From the blood of animals we now turn to the blood of men. Something very important is said. Here is the first mention of capital punishment in the Bible. Again we must ask to whom this applies. Does it still apply to us? Let us recognise that Cain killed and was not punished in this way. Lamech killed and did not suffer capital punishment. This is new, and from this point onwards God says that if a man murders he must lose his life. It is to Noah that this is said – it has not applied before.

Now then, why is this law given? Is it given for purposes of reformation? No, because you cannot reform a man by killing him. Is it given to deter others? No, because in fact the capital punishment does not deter others from murder. Is it given for retribution – that a man who has killed deserves to lose his life having taken one? Partly, but it is something much deeper than that: man is sacred, therefore murder is sacrilege.

Now I want you to grasp this point because I think it is terribly important when we discuss capital punishment that we grasp that murder is sacrilege. People are made in the image of God, therefore to slay someone is to attack God, and it is this which lies behind God's law.

The second thing I want you to notice, which is very important, is that God says, "I require that man should take the life of the murderer." Here is the beginning of human government and human law. You notice that the responsibility for taking the life of a murderer is given to man. God doesn't say, "I will do it." He says, "I require it of you," and that law applied all through the Old Testament and it is a law of God. But the question is: is it changed when it comes through Christ? This is the fundamental question.

The law of blood is changed when it applies to eating flesh. Is this one too? The law of circumcision is changed when it comes to Christ; indeed it is abolished. The law of Sabbath observance is abolished in Christ because it was fulfilled – even though some Christians think circumcision goes through to baptism and Sabbath observance goes through to Sunday observance. I don't think it does. In Christ there is a very definite change in these laws. Does this apply to this? No, it doesn't. Some laws of the Old Testament go straight through to the Christian era and the proof that this one does is Romans 13 where we are told that those who bear the sword in the name of the state are ministers of God to punish the evildoer, and you certainly don't use the sword to spank people with.

So here we have a law that God laid down for Noah, which goes straight through to the Christian era and which I certainly believe is still a law of God. I would hope that however horrible it may seem to you that a murderer should lose his life, that this country will get back to God's law on this. I think if you think that is horrible you should think too that it is very horrible that the victim should have lost their life in the first place, and that will balance out your feelings and then you can get on to facts. Now, finally, I come to something lovely. God now says, "Noah I'm going to make a covenant with you."

A covenant is not a contract. A contract is a bargain – two people with equal powers make a contract, "I will give you this if you will give me that. You give me that if I give you this" – and they sign a contract. You cannot bargain with God. People come to God and say, "God if you will do this I will do that," and that is a bargain, a contract. God says, "I make a covenant with you." A covenant is entered into by one party only toward the other; the other accepts it and the party who enters into it lays down the conditions. Now there was a time when I stood in the front of a church with my wife and I gave her a ring and she gave me one. The ring was a token of the vow and covenant made between us.

Because there was a day in which I had initiated a relationship and had said, "Will you marry me?" That is a covenant—one person entering into a relationship with another, quite freely. Not a contract though, alas, marriage is becoming a contract and a contract can be broken – a contract in which we say, "Okay we'll live together. I'll do this for you, you do this for me and we'll see if this works out." That is a contract. A covenant is something you freely enter into and stay in it. It's a thing of love rather than a thing of law. God says, "I establish my covenant," and seven times here in one paragraph he says this word, "covenant" and there are no conditions to it. It is as wide as the whole earth.

"Every living thing I enter into this covenant," says God and it is for all time – it is while the earth remains. It is unlimited in time and space and every animal and every creature on earth can claim this covenant. God says, "I make you this promise: I will never do this again." The reason why we need never fear it is because he made that promise. Now God gave the ring. He said that when you look up into a dark sky, a sky that is full of the threat of a flood, a sky such as the sky that came over Noah's society, you will see in the cloud his covenant ring, his sign—the rainbow he set as his ring.

It does not say that he created it then, he said it was then that he took it and made it the sign of his covenant. You notice that the ring is not for man, it is for God. It is not to remind you of God's covenant, it is to remind him. He doesn't say that when the rainbow comes in the cloud you look at it and remember him. It says, "I'll look at it and I'll remember you" – just as when I look at a ring I remember my wife. He looks at the ring. Mind you, next time you see one you look at it and remember that God is looking at it and is saying, "That reminds me I must stop this rain. I must stop this rain before it rains too much."

God has kept his covenant. There have been local floods, but there has never again been the destruction on the scale of Noah's day, and there never will be. Thank God there won't. It is a sign of his grace and it is a sign of his glory. When we get to heaven, you know, you will see the whole ring. You can only see a bit of it now but according to the last book of the Bible when we get to heaven we will see the whole rainbow right around God. It won't be due to rain then, it will be due to the light of God. Perfect light, God is light and light is red, blue and yellow together. God is a Trinity and God is light – three in one, Father, Son and Holy Spirit. You will see the rainbow – it is mentioned twice in the Book of Revelation. So we finish this study. His mercy is as long as the earth, but I want you to notice that it says, "While the earth remains", and that means it is not going to remain for ever and his promise, his covenant, will end because he will be released from it when the earth goes.

142

READ GENESIS 9:18–11:9

My lowest mark in what was then School Certificate was Scripture. Indeed it was my worst subject all through school and like George Bernard Shaw I can say my education began when I left school – at least in this regard. The only subject I disliked more was the subject of history. Probably there was a good reason why I disliked both. They were just dates and battles and kings and queens and digging back into the past. Who is interested in the past? We have got to live in the present.

Now the mood of today is very similar to this, not just among youngsters but among adults. There is a question mark whenever you deal with things that happened long ago. What is the point of digging back into the days of the tower of Babel? We were finished with that centuries ago. It is now we have got to live. You preachers are always talking about history – why don't you get on with talking about the problems of today?

Well, I answer that by saying that there are two reasons for studying history and therefore two reasons for reading the Bible, for it is a history book. Reason number one: you can learn from history. It has been said that those who forget history are condemned to relive it. What that meant was what is put in the popular proverb that experience is a hard school but fools will learn in no other. In other words, history gives us certain lessons. You can learn from the mistakes and the failures and the successes of the past if you care to learn.

Otherwise you will have to learn these things for yourself, which is a much harder and slower way.

The other reason why you should study history is that we have to live with it. History shapes my life today. I was born and bred in England and I cannot live as if English history has not existed. History is shaping my life every day in some respect and this is particularly true of Bible history. We have to live with this. We don't just learn from it. Take the Garden of Eden; take the story of Adam and Eve. You can learn a lot from that story, you can learn how to beat the devil, how to face temptation, how to be happily married. You can learn a lot from Genesis 3, but the point is not only that you may learn from that but you have to live with it because you got Adam's nature. You have inherited it. Therefore, the account in Genesis 3 will shape your life tomorrow because you have got to live with it. This is your nature and you were born to those two and you have inherited from them certain features.

Now the tower of Babel may seem one of those stories that at first sight has really nothing whatever to do with us. But at a second look it seems to be the most relevant story in the Bible if you are going to have a discussion on world peace, on world government, on the UN, or on current news. I hope you see the point of that.

First, let me pick up the story where we left it. Noah is out of the ark and he has brought out three sons and their wives, and from now on the story centres around those sons. There are three different stories or subjects. It is a kind of sandwich, only the filling in the sandwich is not terribly attractive. Unlike other sandwiches, it is the bread that is going to be interesting. The filling is a genealogy.

So we look first of all at the top layer of bread, the first bit of the sandwich. It is a rather sordid story. I would give the title to this part of the story "Sons and Sins". Noah came out of the ark with three, and one had a son soon afterwards called Canaan, a name that is going to pop up again and again right through the Old Testament. That boy Canaan was born to Ham. There is nothing much else to say about that but we come now to a story which if I had written the Bible I would not have put in. But fortunately God wrote the Bible and so he put it in.

It is the most remarkable story. Here is a man who has brought his family through the flood. He has kept them straight in a generation that was utterly crooked and perverted. The only thing we are told about him in the rest of his life after the Flood is this: that he got drunk and disgraced himself. It is the most incredible anticlimax. Truth is stranger than fiction and the Bible is more honest and real and true to life than any other book. Can you imagine anybody else writing a story of such a man that finished like that?

Now we must look at what happened and why—the story swings our attention from one person to another. It begins with Noah himself. It says he began to till the soil, that he planted a vineyard, that he grew grapes, that he made wine from it. Whether he was the first to do so or not we don't know. He may have been the first to discover how to make wine but at any rate he at least made it and then he drank it. Did Noah go wrong at one point? Did he go wrong in tilling the soil? I don't think anybody would say that. Did he go wrong in planting a vineyard instead of sticking to safer crops? I would not have thought to be so because we are told later in the Bible that God gave wine to gladden the heart of man, so I don't think we can stop there. Was he wrong to drink it? Well what is the point of growing it if you don't drink it? Certainly he went wrong when he got drunk. From cover to cover the Bible condemns drunkenness and says it is wrong. If a man gets drunk he has sinned; certainly against his friends and family but also against God because he has degraded himself. Is this the point at which Noah went wrong? If he was the first to discover wine, it might well be that he had no idea what its effect would be. So we come to the last verb: after he was drunk he lay uncovered in the tent. Whatever we say about the previous steps, here is introduced a note that is most certainly wrong. This is the real situation of this great man. After all his life, all his preaching, his building of the ark, his bringing the family through it.

Now there are three lessons that I want to draw from this before we move on to the family, and the first is this: wine is a tricky substance. Now let me balance the Bible teaching as carefully as I can by saying that although this is the first mention of wine in the Bible and it is in a particularly degrading context and therefore should act as a warning, wine is not condemned through the Bible as bad in itself. I have already quoted Psalm 104 that God gave it to gladden the heart of man. Furthermore, we know that total abstinence was God's calling only for a few people within the people of God and never for the whole people of God. I think it has remained that ever since. The Nazirites and the Rechabites were among those who were total abstainers. John the Baptist was a teetotaler. Jesus was not, which is why they called him a winebibber.

But there is a balance in scripture and while there are texts to which you can appeal, to say that wine is a good gift of God, there are also many that tell you of the dangers of drinking too much or too strong. You find the book of Proverbs mentions wine six times: three times in a good sense and three times in a bad sense, which would seem to me to give the biblical balance of teaching. The only other factor is that Paul said: I will neither eat meat nor drink wine if by doing either I cause a fellow Christian to have a troubled conscience.

Now that is an important factor for the Christian. He says:

I'll be a vegetarian or a teetotaler – not on principle but lest I hurt someone else if it appears that it is going to. So the first lesson is wine is dangerous and the first mention of it in the Bible should tell us this; the second lesson is that because it releases the restraints on our nature, things will come out from our fallen nature that are there in all of us but are normally kept in check. In other words, Noah had this weakness all his life but it had been kept in check by the grace of God. Noah was not a good man by nature but by grace. We all need to learn this: that there is that within every one of us which can do these things. The restraints have been on us by our upbringing, by our environment, by our conscience, by the laws of the state. In a hundred and one ways I am kept under restraint – above all by the grace of our Lord Jesus. But take the restraints off and you will discover what you are really like.

I read a testimony by Dr Alan Redpath describing his serious illness, when he had a stroke. One of the most moving and challenging things in it was this: having been a great preacher all his life he was shattered that when he was mentally and physically weak immediately after this stroke, he said things that shocked himself, his wife and his children. Out of his mouth were coming things that he had never said in his life. This was the worst battle he had in his illness. Where did this come from? God said to him, "Alan Redpath, this is the real Alan Redpath. This is the one who would get out if he could. I have let him get out so that you may learn that I can offer you the grace to keep him in."

You must learn the lesson that Paul learned when Paul said, "I know that in me there dwells no good thing." Sometimes you have to discover this the hard way. But Noah might have got to the point where he felt that he was a good man in himself apart from the grace of God. If you think that way it is the most dangerous condition. But the lesson I would draw is that Noah discovered that when the restraints are off, the real man comes out and this is what happened. The third lesson I would draw is this for myself and for you: let him that thinks he stands take heed lest he fall. You can go through all that Noah went through of God's grace, and fall.

Well now, the point of the story is really not Noah but Ham. As he lay there in disgrace because the restraints of his fallen nature were off, one of his boys came in – his youngest. We are told two things about this boy in strong verbs. I put these in the kind of English that will give you the flavour. Verb number one: he *gazed* at his father. Verb number two, he *gossiped* about him.

He enjoyed looking at the disgrace of his own Dad and then he went and told somebody else about it. You notice he did not do anything about it. He wanted to pass the bad news on, and no doubt got quite a kick about being the first with a story. Now if you think this is unfair to Ham because of the two verbs *saw* and *told*, and if you think I am reading implications into this that are not there, may I point out that, when Noah woke up, he realised what his son Ham had *done to him*—that is a strong phrase. Ham had clearly done something to his father that was wrong.

Now the story shifts to Shem and Japheth, and undoubtedly there is a clear indication that it was Shem who thought of the answer rather than Japheth, but Japheth joined him in it. Shem, when he heard it, said to Japheth, "There's only one thing to do here. We must cover our father's shame straightaway and we must not add to it." It is a vivid picture and I wonder how many children today would have this attitude of respect to their parent or father. They walked backwards with a cloth and threw it over him without looking, and left the room. There is a respect there for a parent which is quite out of the ordinary.

When they brought a woman taken into adultery to Jesus, what did he do? He stooped and he scribbled with his finger in the dust on the ground. Why? What was he writing? It doesn't matter what he was writing, that is not the point. The point is he was going to be the only man who wouldn't look at her. He was not going to add his eyes to all the many that were staring at her, and so he scribbled on the ground. Shem and Japheth did that. So now the story switches back to Noah, who woke up, and when he realised what had happened he did not say something like a bad-tempered old man who was disgraced. He caught in this incident a glimpse of the future years spreading down through history. He saw the weaknesses that are passed on down the line. He saw the awful influence of heredity. He made a statement about the future which all came true in later history. He looked at his three sons and said, "I can see that Ham has a nature that will curse his son and his grandson and his great-grandson." There is a curse going down through there. In fact, Canaan became a country so noted for this kind of thing—gazing and gossiping, that ultimately God had to remove the land and the cities and give them to his own people of Israel. Do you know what one of the worst cities in the world of those days became? It was a city called Jericho – the first city taken by Israel. Archaeologists have now revealed that perhaps the most degraded city the world has ever seen was the city guarding the entrance to Canaan – Jericho.

So if you think God was wrong to tell the Jews to take that land, to take those cities away, and destroy those people, then you should read the full story. From Shem came the people who knew God's name. It is interesting that there is a possible translation which I would prefer which is down at the bottom of your page probably – at least in the Authorized Version it is in the text: "Blessed be the Lord" (or Yahweh) "the God of Shem", which indicates that Shem already knew

God personally and was already in a relationship of faith. Looking down through the years, Noah could see that from this boy's personal faith in God would come a people who would know God, and the Jews have all descended from Shem and they have known Yahweh by name.

Then he looked at Japheth, whom Shem helped to do the right thing, and he said, "Japheth you're going to enlarge," and that is what the name Japheth means – "to be enlarged". You are going to be enlarged but you will benefit from Shem. You will not only share in this good act, you will share in more. You will dwell in his tents. You will come and benefit from his hospitality. If you want to know where Japheth lives today—you are the descendants of Japheth. I will show you that from chapter 10 in a moment because Japheth's family migrated around into Europe. Most of us have Japheth blood in us. How do we get blessing? By dwelling in the tents of Shem. By taking a Jewish Bible, by worshipping a Jewish Saviour, by sharing in the blessings that came to those who knew the name of God.

History has just fulfilled Noah's prediction. This was a prophecy. This was not just a bad tempered curse of an old man who had lost his self-respect. This was of a man who saw himself in his sons as they really were, and saw his grandsons and his great-grandsons and so on. Now you might say this is unjust, but whatever you think of it I am afraid it is fact. I am what I am by heredity. I have got my father's nose—it runs in the family. I nearly got his voice and I have been mistaken for him over the phone. I have got a good deal more from one of my grandfathers.

I can say it is not fair, but do you realise that if God had made us isolated units in time and space so that we neither hurt nor helped each other within this dimension of space, nor could we pass on good things to our children. If we all just lived as isolated units – and that seems to be what people want when they say this isn't fair – I would hate that life. It would not be family life. But when God made us able to help each other in space this way, he made us able to hurt each other. When God made us able to pass things on to our children that were good, he also made it possible to pass things on that were bad. Therefore we are what we are by our heredity, and this is how life is.

We come finally to Noah's death, and the family broke up. There is no record of them staying together after that, and how often this happens. Many times at a funeral and at the meal that follows I have looked around at the relatives and wondered: will you stay together as a family or will you walk your own ways now? Shem, Ham, and Japheth walked their own ways after Noah had died.

So we come to chapter 10, a list of seventy names, and I would call this passage "Names and Nations". The sons of Japheth travelled to the north and west. Gomer is mentioned. Do you know where Gomer is today? Gomer is Cymru – Wales. Greeks and others are mentioned too.

Regarding Ham, I want to single out two people. They went south, to Ethiopia, which is actually what we now know as Upper Egypt or the Sudan, not modern Ethiopia; and Sheba and Arabia. The two people I want to single out are Nimrod and Canaan again. Nimrod was a man of great strength and cleverness. At first I think it indicates that he used these for God and for good because it says he was a mighty man before the Lord and this would seem to indicate that he started right. He gave these physical and mental gifts to God. But there came a time when Nimrod began to use them against others. At first against animals, and he became a great hunter, and then he began to use them against men.

We have the word "kingdom" creeping in, and here is the first king recorded in the Bible. Nimrod got ideas and he began to use his strength and his cunning against men. He began to build cities and he began to build an empire. He was the world's first dictator—the world's first man to try to build a power and a kingdom around himself. This was Nimrod and the first city he had built was Babel and we pick that up in chapter 11.

Canaan settled in the land, which was one day to be the Holy Land but before it was ever the Holy Land it became the unholy land and it became the most degraded land in the whole of the ancient world. It was only when they got so far that God said they had gone too far to do anything with them, that the Jews were allowed to go in and take it from them and that is a very important point in the history of Israel.

Now we come to the people of Shem. I would point out here Eber, which is the beginning of a word Hebrew. Eber means someone who is always passing over or travelling around. It is the equivalent of gypsy in those days. The *habiru* were the people who moved around, always on the move. They were the people who passed over and it is interesting that right from the beginning this people had the name of Passover – *Heba*; Hebrew – people who were always passing over. The other interesting name here is Peleg, which means division, and it was in his days that the earth was divided. Some people think that was the period in which the continent of America drifted off across the Atlantic from Africa. No, the division that it is referring to is of language and people from one another.

Finally, the third passage, Genesis 11:1–9, I call *Dialects and Dictionaries* because it says the people then were of one language and one speech and it means they had one dialect and so they had the same set of words. Because they had the same dialect, they had the same dictionary. Do you see the meaning of these two distinctions? Dialect and dictionary are two different things; language and speech are two different things. If I spoke in my native tongue I don't think many people would understand me. It is not a change of speech but it would be a change of language. In fact, I come from Tyneside and I am a Geordie. There comes a point where dialect changes so much that the words become different and the dictionary alters and you can't speak together without an interpreter. Now this is the story of how that all began.

Let us look at what happened first of all. They built, they blasphemed, they babbled. Look first at the building—here is a group of men migrating around. They are doing so in obedience to God, who had said, "Go out and fill the earth." Don't stay here. Get out and migrate and go all over the earth. I want it repopulated. But this group of people got to a place and said, "You know it's very nice here, we're not going to go any further. We're going to stay right here." They came to the middle of what we now call Mesopotamia and they found a somewhere called Shinar and said, "Let's settle down. Instead of scattering around; instead of spreading out as God told us to, let's stay together. We could be more powerful we could do more. Let us build a city not just stay in tents or rough houses. What are we going to build with? There is nothing here. There are no stones, there is no mortar, no lime, what are we going to do? Well, let's make bricks of clay and there's sticky black stuff to stick them together." You can still see bricks that they used with the black bitumen stuck on. I have seen one. So they began to build and then they said, "Let's not just build a city. Let's be great, let's be powerful." Do you notice that all this was because they could talk together? All this was done through conference and they said, "Come let us do this." They were full of ideas but they had to communicate these ideas to each other to do anything. They had to hold a committee meeting – they had to talk before they could build because this task was way beyond any one of them. They could only do it together. So the idea was: unity means strength.

So they began to build. After talking they built the city and said "Let's build something in the middle of the city, let's have a skyscraper." The phrase "reaching to heaven" is a colloquialism. Why did they build a big tower? Some say it was a military tower for defence, a watchtower to look out for the enemy, but I don't think that is the reason. Some will say it was for prestige—in the plain of Shinar you could have seen that for fifty miles and people would say, "They must be pretty big, powerful people to have buildings like that." I have seen nine and ten storey buildings of mud in Arabia, but they built this tower of brick and it went up and up. I think it had a religious significance. It would have been in what we know to have been their shape – a ziggurat shape, which is almost like a pyramid. When we ask what is the deepest significance of the phrase "reaching to heaven" we come across an unusual interpretation, which I think is the right one. They were saying, "God, we don't need you. We can get into heaven." The modern man says, "We can get out into space, the universe is ours. We're going to get out in the heavens. We're going to get up there. We're going to be where God is. We'll be like God." There is something as old as the Garden of Eden about this. "We will be like God; we'll reach to heaven." But there is an even more subtle meaning that may well be true. The Hebrew could be translated: and the top of the tower will be the dome of heaven. We now know that on top of their ziggurats they would have a huge dome, and painted around the dome would be the signs of the zodiac and it would become a centre of the worship of the stars, astrology and horoscopes. We know that by the time they built the tower of Babel they had the signs of the zodiac.

Here is the beginning of the horoscopes, which are in newspapers and magazines. The top of it will be a dome of heaven. Babylon became a centre of star worship. It was from this area that three wise men came following a star and it led them to the truth—Jesus, and they would never need any more stars after they got to Jesus.

The top of it, the "dome of heaven" – what was it? It was an act of defiance of God. "We don't need you. We can build. We can be strong. We can protect ourselves. We won't be scattered abroad. We'll have the name. We don't need you God." My proof of this would be the name "Nimrod". Do you know what that name means? It means rebel. Now in the next verse, the tower looks very small. Do you know why? When you are standing on the ground it looks pretty big but when you are up in heaven it looks nothing. Have you ever noticed that?

Now we are up in heaven, looking down from God's throne at that little pile of bricks in the middle of Shinar. God says that they are getting so big headed, so proud and so powerful, they will stop at nothing. We must set limits. Now God did not do this because he was jealous, he did it for mankind's own good. Unity outside of God is one of the most dangerous things there can be. I have very mixed feelings about world government because of this. Unity outside of God becomes totalitarian. Unity outside of God is a terrible thing. God said, "We'll have to stop it." The most simple and effective way of stopping them was precisely what God did. He stopped them being able to have committees and conferences.

Sometimes you know how I wish God would come down to the church programme and do the same so that we would just have to get on, each with our work for the Lord. What would we not lose by not being able to confer together? So God came down and he performed a miracle on their speech and while their thoughts were right, when they said what they thought they meant, their mouth said something different. The word, "come" sounded like the word "go" and the word "yes" sounded like the word "no", and before they knew where they were, they were completely at cross purposes. They could not communicate.

God said: if we spoil their dialect, sooner or later their words will change and their speech will go, and that is precisely what has happened to mankind. Concerning the city which Nimrod called, literally, the gateway of God, God changed the phonetic pronunciation of it to "Babel", which means utter confusion. That word has come down to us ever since and it is now "babbling" — these people babbled to each other. They did not understand each other so they separated. The very thing they said they would never do – be scattered abroad – they had to do.

Lest you think that this is a funny sort of God who does this, may I tell you that Jesus Christ was involved and the Holy Spirit was involved because it says, "God said: let us go down and do this." The same God who said, "Let us make man in our own image," said, "Come on let us go down and do this." Jesus Christ was involved as the Son of God. So the people left off building and we have a half finished monument to show that God has set limits to what man is allowed to do.

Adolf Hitler set out to create a Reich that would last a thousand years – God says twenty. Man after man has set out to create a world empire and be mighty and make a name for himself and God says, "There's a limit and I stop you at that point." The tower of Babel was never completed.

Babel was rebuilt and a man called Nebuchadnezzar said: "Is not this great Babylon which I have built for my glory and by my power?" [and Babylon is Babel — same name]. God set a limit to that man. The next thing you see of him he is scrabbling in a field, with long nails and long hair, eating grass – and he is insane. Fortunately, he recovered his sanity and worshipped God. But he rebuilt Babylon and Babylon was the country that came, and in its greed and lust for power and territory took away the Jews from Jerusalem and pulled the temple down to the ground. Babylon did it. Babel was rebuilt in the Old Testament.

But even more relevant to you, according to the New Testament Babel is being rebuilt today. Babylon comes back into the New Testament in a glimpse we have of the final stages of the history of the human race. Are you interested in the future? This is what it says: one day there will be a vast metropolis, which will be the centre of world government. In that city will be the commerce and the centre of all the entertainment world and the centre of everything. In this great metropolis, Babylon will be rebuilt as the centre. It may not be in that place. I don't know, I must wait and see. Into that Babylon will come a man who will say, "I'm going to be the world ruler. I will make a name for myself. No one will scatter me abroad. This is my capital and I'm ruler of the world."

The Bible looks forward to a world ruler. We call him Antichrist because scripture teaches us to do so. In the last book of the Bible we see what happens to the final Babylon, which came from this original Babel. The final metropolis of the world, the capital city with its huge skyscrapers – and they are talking now of blocks of flats two miles high. That will be the ultimate Babylon. But it says in the last book in the Bible that it is not their buildings that reach to heaven. God says, "Your sins reach to heaven", and there is a dramatic description of God coming down to destroy the capital city of the world and of ships out to sea able to see the flames and the smoke from that city. It will be the end of godless civilisation—the end of man's great technological achievements, the end of it all in rubble, ruin and ashes. I honestly believe that is going to happen because God says so.

If that is a bit grim, let me turn it around now. The rest

of the Bible not only talks about Babylon and finishing up like that, it tells us about what God is doing to put it all right. Here is a man who is stark naked (in spite of all the pictures and the sculptures) in front of a gazing crowd. He is a man who is refusing to take wine. It is Jesus on a cross. Something different is happening now. He died for the sins of everyone else.

Just a couple of months later, God comes down and does the second miracle of language in human history. People begin to speak in other languages. God makes his own mighty works known to the nations of the world by a reversal of Babel and by giving the languages to preach the gospel. Pentecost is the only other event in scripture analogous to Babel. Now out goes the word of God in every language, the Bible is translated, missionaries learn the languages, and Babel is being reversed to unite people in Christ – until in him there is neither Jew nor Greek, bond nor freed, barbarian nor Scythian, and all these divisions go down.

Handel's Hallelujah Chorus is based on the hallelujah chorus which the saints will sing when Babylon is destroyed and their capital city is gone and then out of the sky comes a city, not built from earth reaching up to heaven but a city whose builder and maker is God – and it is coming down out of heaven and you have read about it.

It is a metropolitan capital of the universe, fifteen hundred miles across, and it is God's city, and it is a city the saints are going to live in. Now if this seems like a dream to you, well then Babel seems like a dream to me, but I accept them both as true. I accept that the world that I want my children to live in and the world that I dream of is not a world that man is going to build up. You can't build up to heaven, it is a city that God is going to send down. It is the new Jerusalem and into that city the nations of the earth will come. The kings of the earth will bring their glory into it and the nations of the earth will worship in unity. Not until then can you dare to speak of such a thing as the "united nations".

But then you can—centred on God, centred in Christ, Babel will be put right in the day that the new Jerusalem comes down as a bride adorned for her husband and you see the whole sweep of the Bible story.

There is one simple choice before every man and woman. It is the choice between the Bible and Babel, between man's pride and ambition in seeking to build up, and the biblical account of a God whose Son came down; a God who says, "I'm going to send down the city that I want you to live in, a garden city with a river running through the middle of it."

Don't you want to live there? You can by faith in Jesus who was born at Bethlehem, died at Calvary and was raised from the dead – and is coming again to take us to be with him where he is.

READ GENESIS 11:10–12:9

We are going straight into a study of this genealogy. The Bible is full of treasure but it is very much like a mine. Indeed the wisdom of God is likened in the Word of God to gold and silver, which have to be mined. Now frankly that involves a lot of hard work digging. Those who like everything in letters two inches high with plenty of pictures to keep them interested will not get much treasure out of the Bible. It is for those who dig and who work hard.

I remember going into a little cottage in county Durham where there was a retired miner whom everybody called Granddad Harrison. He was about eighty-five on the occasion of which I am thinking. I used to go and see him regularly and I never caught him reading anything but his Bible. I knew he read it straight through from cover to cover. I said, "How many times have you been through it now Granddad?"

He said, "Eighteen times I think."

I asked, "Why do you go through from cover to cover like that?"

"I don't want to miss anything," was his reply.

Here was a man who found this book full of gold, full of silver, full of precious things, but it was because he sat down and dug, and worked at it. A very good example of this would be these chapters full of "begetting"– genealogies which just seem to be lists of one generation after another, full of difficult names that tie your tongue in knots. People say, "Why did God put these chapters in? What possible connection can they have with me? It is not my family tree. If I want that I'll go to Somerset House and look it up. Why should I read a chapter like this?" In fact, most people just skip over it. The answer is, though you may not think so at first sight, that there is wonderful treasure here.

It is as if you were to go down a mine and seams are pointed out which look dull and grey. A man who took me down a mine said, "That's one of the best seams we've hit." At first sight I would have said, "You'd get nothing out of that, just dirty, grey rock." People have treated the genealogies in exactly the same way. These genealogies link Adam to Jesus and there are three lists of relationship that link. The first is in Genesis 5 and we have already covered that – from Adam to Shem. The second is here in Genesis 11, from Shem to Abraham, and the third is in Matthew 1 and is from Abraham to Jesus. That takes us right through to Christmas. Indeed, when Matthew tells the Christmas story he virtually says that you won't understand it unless you read the genealogy of Jesus first. Yet I have not gone to a Christmas service in which the first seventeen verses of Matthew have been read.

Matthew makes it the beginning of the Christmas story, and you need it to get the right perspective. From Adam through to Jesus there is an unbroken line and God was preparing this line right through the centuries. God knew that the Nativity was going to happen because he planned it before he made Adam, and Adam's seed goes right through to Jesus and the promise that God made in Genesis 3 about the seed of the woman comes true in the baby of Bethlehem.

So I am going to take you through these two genealogies. I divide this one into three parts. If I may put it this way, God uses a zoom lens. He starts with a whole tribe, then in the second section our view is narrowed down to a family.

Finally in the third section, one man stands out – this wonderful man Abraham. Verses 10–26 underline for me again the great truth of predestination. Out of all the lines of the Earth – Shem, Ham, and Japheth – God chose one and only one. From that line onwards God blesses in a particular way. Now this is an offence to some. They say, "Why should God have favourites? Why should God choose one line out of all the others to bless? Why should he show this particular regard?" The answer is very simple. I want you to imagine that you want to send a message to six people. There are two ways in which you can send that message. You can either make six separate journeys and go to each one and give them the message, or you can choose to say, "I'll give it to one of them and ask that person to pass it on to the others." Now for his own good reasons (and he has not seen fit to tell us these reasons), God chose the second method to bless the whole human race. Instead of coming to every nation, tribe, kindred and tongue, he said: "I will choose one. I will pour all my blessings into one. I'll take that nation and I'll bless them especially and I'll say now, take that to everybody else," and this was why he chose the Jews.

"How odd of God to choose the Jews. But odder still of those who choose the Jewish God and scorn the Jews" – but this was God's method. He needed a people, a nation of missionaries—a whole people who would go and share this with the rest of the world. From Shem down to Abraham the line comes down. It is God's line and they are his people. It is called the Semitic line after the name Shem. Halfway down the line you find the man called Eber from which we get our word Hebrew, and it means someone who moves around or someone who passes over, someone who will be a pilgrim, someone who will be on the move all the time. God needed people to be on the move; God needed messengers to go and tell.

So he gave them the name, "migrant" or "moving about" from the very beginning – the Hebrew people. This then was predestination at work. He might have chosen Japheth, he might have even chosen Ham, he might have chosen anyone else. Why did God choose the Jews? It is unanswerable. Later in the Bible God says to the Jews, "Do you know why I loved you? – Because you're lovely? No, because you're greater than anybody else? No. I'll tell you why I loved you – I loved you because I loved you." That's as far as you can get. It was his method to get through to everybody else: to get hold of one nation, give them all his love and all his blessing and say: now take it to the rest and share it. That is why we are reading from a Jewish book. That is why I preach about a Jewish Saviour. That is why the baby in Bethlehem was a Jewish baby, circumcised the eighth day like every other Jewish boy. The Jews got the blessing of God for us and to share it with us.

The second thing I notice in this passage is that God not only needed a people to share blessing with the whole world, he needed a particular place where he could bless them and from which they could spread out. He chose the only place in the world really suitable. The three largest continents on which lived the majority of the world's population were Europe, Asia and Africa. God chose a place in the middle of the corridor between those three continents. It is the centre of the earth. It is the one place from which his blessing could spread quickly to the majority of the human race. You can see why God didn't only need a people, he wanted them to go to a place – and he had a very definite place. The people and the place were going to be so tied up for the rest of history that you could never contemplate one without the other.

Traditionally, until a few decades ago, one Jew would greet another with this phrase at Passover time: "Shalom, next year in Jerusalem." For over two thousand years they greeted each other like that. Why? Because they know as a people that they must be in the place where God wants them if they are to be the people that he wants them to be. So we find in this second section, vv. 27–32, that he said: out of there, into here; leave your country, leave where you are, and come into the place where I can use you.

In the Middle East there is an area of land we call the Fertile Crescent in a half-moon shape and that is the area within which the Bible was written and God's purposes worked out. That crescent linked Europe to Africa, Africa to Asia, Asia to Europe. Everybody came through it in some way. There, right down towards one side, God said: that's the place I want you. They left one end and they started going around. Ur of the Chaldees is at the very tip of the half-moon, and halfway down there is a place called Haran. Now I want to describe Ur; it was an amazing place. It was civilized, cultured and comfortable. Let me describe some of the features for you. We now know from archaeology that the houses in Ur had central heating in the bedrooms, not just the living rooms. It had running water in the bedrooms. There were modern type fireplaces and I have a photograph of a fireplace found in Ur which I showed to my wife once and asked, "How do you like that as a fireplace?" She was quite fooled for a moment and replied, "Well, it's a bit old-fashioned but it's quite nice." I said, "It's four thousand years old that one—Ur of the Chaldees." It was the kind of fireplace you would find in a Surrey cottage. Libraries and art galleries have been unearthed. It was a place above all where they worshipped a god called Sin, which is rather intriguing. Interestingly enough, it was the god of the moon and they worshipped the moon. Rather like a South Sea Island where they worshipped the moon and when a missionary who went there asked, "Why do you worship the moon? If you want to worship something in heaven why not the big strong sun?"

They replied, "Well, we worship the moon because the moon comes out when the sun isn't, when it's really of use to us, because the sun only comes out when it's daylight and it's of no help to us, but the moon comes out at night."

Well, they worshipped the moon god in Ur, and they built great big ziggurats, temples to the moon god. It is the origin of the word "lunatic" incidentally, as you probably know but they were lunatic enough to worship the moon.

Well now, here was Ur of the Chaldees, comfortable, civilised, pagan, worshipping God's creature instead of the Creator. God said: you will have to come out of all that. Abraham came out of there at seventy-five years of age and never slept in a bed again. He left his centrally heated home with running water in the bedrooms, and he lived in a tent for the rest of his life. The whole family began to move around this Fertile Crescent, this moon-shaped green area. They got as far as Haran. One of the saddest things we are told in the narrative is that Abraham's father settled there. I want to begin to apply this very personally now. I meet Christian after Christian who got out of "Ur" alright but never got into Canaan— they settled down halfway somewhere; out of the things that would have dragged them away from God but not into the things that bring them close to him.

I remember one of the RAF officers whom I knew. He was the son of a minister. Always remember minister's children in your prayers. It is terribly difficult to be a child of the manse. Because of this he had been brought up "out of Ur of the Chaldees", as it were. He didn't drink, he didn't smoke, he didn't gamble – he didn't do this, that and the other. He had been brought up not to do these things. The trouble was, he had never got into Canaan either and he was the most miserable officer on camp. He didn't enjoy having a good old "do" with the other officers because he had scruples due to his upbringing. Neither did he enjoy the fun that we had as Christians because he hadn't got right into that either. He had "settled down in Haran" – halfway.

As a Christian, you may have got out of your former life but have you got into the best life that the Lord has for you? Terah settled down in Haran. God called him to get on the move and get into Canaan but he never got there. He got out but he never got in. He just stuck halfway and many Christians do this. They get out all right but they don't get *in* all right, so they are not really rejoicing in the Lord. They can't be until they complete the journey.

Now let me point to one of the most awful sentences in this genealogy. So and so begat so and so, and so and so begat so and so – it gets monotonous, doesn't it? At one point in the story it all comes to a full stop: but Sarai was barren; she had no child. Do you realise this is the first time this has happened in the Bible story? What a shock it must have been.

Here was God's line coming right down, and every mother had a child and the line continued. God said it would continue until some boy came who would deal with evil finally, and here we have a mother and no child. That is why all the "begats" are there first. I'm sure that is why God put it in – so that we should realise that suddenly we have come to the end of human possibility. We have come to the end of the road. There is to be no more. The line has stopped – and right there God steps in again. May I draw a lesson from this? When you get to the end of your resources, you have got to the beginning of God's. When you think you can't go a step further, everything has stopped, everything is against you, the world has collapsed, things have come to an end, that is just the point at which God steps in.

Do you remember the woman who spent everything she had, trying to get healed? Finally, when she had spent all that she had, she had no one to go too now. She couldn't afford a doctor, she had come to the end of her resources, so she turned to Jesus and he began where her resources failed. He took over at the end of all she had. Now then we come to 12:1–3 and the most amazing promise. God speaks to one man.

He is an old man and God is saying to him: "Now Abraham listen, you think it has all come to an end. You think you have left Ur and wasted it all. You think there is no future now and that you will just die here somewhere in your wanderings. Abraham go on, get into the place that I've told you. Complete the journey, arrive, and Abraham I'm going to see that you have more children than you can count. Abraham I'm going to bless you more than I've blessed anyone else. If people bless you I'll bless them and if they curse you I'll curse them. Abraham, do you know why I am doing all this? I am doing it so that you can be the means of blessing to every family in the earth."

Now do you see the unfolding of God's purpose? This genealogy is focusing on one old man who left Haran and said, "Alright Lord, I'll go. I believe that you can do it. I believe you can give me a family. I believe that you can get me into that land. I believe that we are just at the beginning, not at the end" – and he and his wife Sarai set off.

That is the message of that genealogy. Let us go right through now to that other genealogy – an even more exciting one – and see how it all came down to Bethlehem.

I must have read this genealogy in Matthew 1 before, but a young French lady who was attending our church in Buckinghamshire gave her testimony from our pulpit and I have never forgotten that testimony. She said, "I was converted by reading the genealogy of Jesus in Matthew chapter 1." Since then I have asked the Lord to forgive me for not taking more notice of it. She read this genealogy just to v. 17 and it converted her. She knew the basic facts of the gospel of Christ before then. She had been brought up a Roman Catholic and she knew the basic facts about Jesus. But they had never come alive for her because she did not really believe that he was a real person. He was a stained-glass window figure to her, or else just a bit of bread sitting on a table.

Then one day somebody gave her a New Testament and she began at the beginning, which is a good place to begin but might daunt many people. She read through the genealogy and she said: "Jesus really lived. He had a family tree just as I have." She got on her knees and gave her life to the Lord Jesus and is now a missionary. So I have held a much greater respect for this part of Matthew 1 since then.

Now we can approach this genealogy in three ways. We can ask: is this the story of one man, is it the story of many people, or is it the story of all people? If of course it is the story of all, then it is your story too.

The first interesting thing about this genealogy is that in the original language the word at the beginning is not *genealogy*. Matthew wrote down, "This is the book of the genesis of Jesus Christ," and I find that a fascinating link. The book of Genesis begins the Old Testament. It was the genesis of the world, the genesis of man, the genesis of sin, the genesis of science, the genesis of language, the genesis of murder, the genesis of so much, the beginning of so much. Now at last we have another book of genesis, the genesis of Jesus Christ, and the whole story takes on a new meaning.

Look first at this chapter assuming that it is the story of one man. Why begin the story of Jesus with his pedigree? After all, if you were going to write an interesting account of someone's life I don't think you would begin like this. Calculated to put people off in the first page. If ever I have given a Gospel to someone to read, someone who is not interested in Christ, I have always given them Luke's Gospel (never John, incidentally, because John was not written for

169

the unbeliever but for the believer and it is a tough Gospel for the unbeliever). The Gospel to give to someone who is not really interested is Luke's. It gets straight into the story, it's dramatic, it's real, and the genealogy doesn't come until the end of chapter 3. But Matthew started right in with this and it seems at first sight to give such a poor start to the New Testament until you begin to dig, until you begin to read what it really says and it becomes so exciting. Why give the pedigree of Jesus? Is it just as a matter of interest? Is it just to prove that he is a Jew and has descended from Abraham – or is there something more in it?

If you wanted to be accepted as a Jew, you had to prove for five generations beforehand that you have Jewish blood in you. If you wanted to be a Jewish priest you had to prove a family line going right back to Aaron, and if you couldn't prove that, you couldn't be a priest even though you were convinced it was true. There are cases in the Old Testament after they came back from Babylon of priests who tried to get back into their job but had lost their family records and therefore could not have the job back. But it is not to prove he is a Jew and it is not to prove that Jesus is a priest, because Aaron doesn't come in the family tree. Why is it given? The answer is that it is the proof that Jesus is heir to the throne of David. The keyword in chapter one is "David". When God sends a message to Joseph through an angel, Joseph is addressed as "son of David". Here is Jesus Christ, the book of genesis of Jesus, "Son of David" – as well as "Son of Abraham." It is to prove his royalty. You cannot inherit a throne unless you can prove that there is royal blood in your veins and that you are in the line of the succession.

David's throne had been vacant for centuries. No one had sat on it for centuries. It was vital to prove from the very beginning, and Matthew was writing for the Jews as Luke wrote for Gentiles. Matthew found it essential to begin here, this is the man who was born to be king.

Now it is that which explains Herod's anger. Why did Herod commit that dreadful massacre of hundreds of babies? The answer is because some people came to his palace and said, "Where is he that is born king of the Jews?" Matthew started here. You can't understand the story of the wise men in chapter 2 unless you have read the genealogy in chapter 1. If Herod's family tree were examined, and Herod was the king of the Jews when Jesus was born, there are only two names in Matthew 1 that he could have put in the family tree, and those names were Abraham and Isaac.

Herod was descended from Abraham and Isaac but from no one else in this family tree. Abraham had his son Isaac. Isaac had two sons, Jacob and Esau, and they split and God's line went down through Jacob whose name became "Israel" and he gave his name to the nation. That was God's line and Jesus' line goes right back there. But down through Abraham, Isaac, then Esau, there went another line that was not blessed, a line of whom it is said in scripture in most blunt language: "Jacob have I loved, Esau have I hated." That line comes down and down through the hated Edomites to Herod.

Herod was sitting on the throne as a puppet king, having paid the Romans for the privilege, and he was saying, "I am the king of the Jews," and the only two names he could claim were Abraham and Isaac, which did not give him any right to the throne of David. Into that situation a baby is born that goes right down: Abraham, Isaac, Jacob, David, Joseph, Jesus. I know that somebody will tell me that in fact Joseph was not the father of Jesus, but for purposes of legal inheritance a foster father was in fact the legal father of a boy. Because he married Mary before the boy was born then the inheritance would pass to Jesus. But if you feel that is not quite right either, Luke's Gospel gives us the genealogy of Mary and shows that by blood relationship she was in the same line, so we are through our problems.

The name "David" is interesting. It is my name and in Hebrew it is made up of the three letters DWD (as near as I get to it when rendering the Hebrew in English). The Hebrew language has no numbers. So they use "A" for one and "B" for two, and so on. If you take the three letters of the word David and add up the numbers for which they stand, it comes to fourteen. This is especially interesting because Matthew seems to press his message home by saying: Abraham to David – fourteen; David to the deportation to Babylon – fourteen, so his name is written into Jewish history; the deportation to Jesus – fourteen. It fits, it is right, there is an underlying plan and timetable being worked out. The message is there: Jesus has the right to the throne of David.

Before we leave this point and leave it simply as a pedigree of Jesus, may I point out first of all some of the wonderful men and extraordinary women in Jesus' family tree? Now if you will take my advice, you will never go to Somerset House and dig up your relatives or their names because you will discover some things that might shatter you. You might discover all kinds of murky history in your family tree. When I was up in Lancashire as a minister, an American came up to Manchester having saved up all his life to come and see his birthplace. There it was on his birth certificate— 1 South Hall Street, Manchester. If you know Manchester at all, you will know that is the address of Strangeways Prison. They put that address on the birth certificate for babies born in prison so that there is no stigma attached to them in later life.

Let us dig back through Jesus' genealogy. We shall discover some surprising things. Take some of the great men striding through this. Abraham, Isaac, and Jacob, isn't it interesting – Abraham had a wife who was barren and there should have been no descendants at all, but Sarah was given Isaac. Isaac fell in love with Rebekah and married her but she was barren and there was no child. There should have been no descendants, but God stepped in. Jacob, too, had a wife who was barren and there should have been no children there either but God stepped in. Isn't it amazing how God steps in when it looks as if the situation is hopeless? The three great patriarchs of faith head up this genealogy. God in heaven called himself by them. He said, "I'm the God of Abraham and the God of Isaac and the God of Jacob" – and they are my ancestors. Fancy being able to say that. There are two great kings — David, a man after God's own heart; and Solomon, the man who built the temple. There was Josiah the boy king, who at the age of twelve was responsible for pulling a nation back into the straight and narrow track. It is a fascinating list.

We come now to Joseph, the spouse of the Virgin Mary. Joseph is a man who has no face, no character, no personality in the pages of the Bible. There is not a single word recorded of anything he ever said. There is no description of him at all – just a name; almost incidental to the story, did you ever notice that? Mary's words are there, but not Joseph's. But it is when we look at the women that we get a shock. Now I am not saying that all men are great and all women are terrible. But let me say first that, in the Jewish family trees, women were never included. The line came down through the father. Why should they be put here? Wherever Christianity has gone, womanhood has been lifted. Women were emancipated by Jesus and here written into his genealogy are the names of women. That in itself is so striking it is worth noting. God thought fit to put women into the genealogy of Jesus. That in itself is something staggering. The second thing: what kind of women did he put in? The first woman mentioned is Tamar and if you read the story about her in Genesis, you will wonder why God put her name in here. She was not a good woman. The second woman mentioned is Rahab a common prostitute in the most degraded city the world has ever seen – Jericho – and she is an ancestor of Jesus.

The next one is the wife of Uriah, not even given her name. You know that Solomon was the child of adultery and she is there, though she was more sinned against than sinning. These are the women in the genealogy of Jesus. What is it saying? It is saying that God is a wonderful God of grace and can fit anybody into his purposes. It is saying that he can use even the things that we would think could not be used in the people we would think could not be used for his purposes. It means that not only does God have a place for women, he has a place for bad women too. The whole life of Jesus underlined this again and again. Haven't we a wonderful God? Isn't this a wonderful beginning to the story of Jesus? When you read the rest of the story, it just all fits in. I missed out a most amazing woman—Ruth. She was a good woman. That balances it up, but nevertheless, she was a foreigner, she was mixed blood, a Moabitess. She is there in the genealogy of Jesus, and if a Jew knew of a single person in his family tree who was not pure Hebrew blood he deliberately crossed them out of the genealogy and said, "No, I'm not a true Jew if that person's in."

Yet here is Jesus in God's own record of his genealogy content to include Ruth. He could have left it out because she was a woman. She is not needed in the family tree but God puts in a foreigner, an alien, a Gentile, as much to say: and there's room for them too in Christ. So when you begin to read what seems to be just a family tree it speaks of a Christ who came for everybody, a Christ who came for good and bad, a Christ who came for men and women, a Christ who came for Jew and Gentile. It is all there in the first seventeen verses so that now we can say, "In Christ there is neither Jew nor Greek, male nor female, bond nor free, all are one in Christ Jesus" – and it was true before his birth as well as after his death.

Finally Mary, that young girl who was given the great privilege of bearing the Son of God—I had a strong letter from a member of my church telling me never again to call her an unmarried mother, but I use that phrase quite deliberately because I think it helps us to understand the whole situation. Nobody but Joseph knew the truth and Nazareth was a small village. I think we need to enter in to some of the amazing faith and trust she must have had in God to face what she did. Mary comes in at the end – this simple girl who was probably about fifteen when all this happened and God made her the mother of his own Son. That then is looking at this genealogy as the story of *one* man, Jesus the Son of God – the Christ.

We now turn to this "family tree" from another angle. In the three sections of the family tree you have the history of *many* people in the history of Israel, God's people. If I made a time chart, right up to the top would be when David sat on the throne. Right down to the bottom would be when they lost the land and were deported to Babylon and taken virtually back to where Abraham started – Ur of the Chaldees. Then up again but middling; back in their own land but not properly back – back in blessing but not much, back with a new temple but not as big a one as the first one.

That is the history of Israel between Abraham and Jesus. Right up because fighting their way into Canaan, overcoming their enemies, they finally extended their frontiers further than ever before, and David sat on his throne and in his day they had peace and plenty so that forever afterwards the Jews would say, "Oh if we had another David; if we had a son of David on the throne – oh that God would send us another king like David." This became their national dream and it still is for many of them. But after David came Solomon, the rot set in during his reign, and idolatry and immorality began to wreck this nation that had defeated enemies outside and now was defeated by enemies inside. Down they went until God said: "You're not fit to have this land. You've sunk to the depths of the people who had it before you. So out you go." Way back around the Fertile Crescent they were taken to where they began.

The history of Israel is the reverse journey. Abraham started at one end of the Fertile Crescent, went to Haran, went to Canaan, and in Genesis 12 went down into Egypt to find food. Israel started in Egypt, came out of Egypt into Canaan, but when they began to depart from their faith and their God, God said, "Right back to where you started," and away they went. They came back for those last fourteen generations but they never had a king again. They were ruled over by the Egyptians, then the Syrians, then the Greeks, and then finally the Romans marched in.

They had their land and yet it didn't belong to them. They had puppet kings who were terrible people and who finished, as they should. Read the end of King Herod in the book of Acts. Into that situation Jesus came as the Son of David to bring them back to what they had called David earlier. They had said of David, "He is the prince of peace," and Jesus came as the Prince of Peace. This genealogy is the history of many people. It is the history of Israel. They were called to the heights, they sank to the depths, and they finished up middling. Jesus came to lift them higher than they had ever been raised before.

Now I come to my final point about this genealogy. I believe it is the story of *all* people. It is your story. God made man from the dust of the earth and made him in his own image and set him in paradise with everything he needed. That was his up and then came his down, and he fell so low. Genesis 3 describes the sin that ruined him and so now the human race is settled down, middling – a mixture of good and bad, a mixture of sin and love, a mixture of the image of God and the image of Adam.

Into that mixed situation in which good and evil struggle with one another, in which men long to get back up to what they once knew, Jesus comes. If this genealogy is the story of the human race, it is your story too. Let me be very personal. I set off in life with dreams and hopes. I set off as an innocent little baby, as a not so innocent little boy, but I had dreams and I had so many castles in the air. Life was very wonderful – it was the up and up. Then in my teen years I discovered that there was sin in my nature that dragged me down. So I began to settle for a middling life, coming to terms with this thing called "sin". Into that situation, Jesus comes to help us out of it.

I would call this part of our study a message for the middle-aged. Did you set off as a Christian hoping to reach the heights of sainthood – hoping to become the best that you could be? Then you had battles with yourself and you were dragged down and you have settled for a middling situation, something about halfway. The perils of middle age are that you settle for a middling spiritual life. The worst handicap the church has is when spiritually we are middling people. We have settled in Haran, we have settled down for half the victory – and Jesus came to sit on the throne of your life. Here is a little doggerel I came across, written by a middle aged man: "When I was young I set my goal as far as I could see, but now I'm nearer to my goal, I've moved it nearer me." Is that where you are? Jesus came to get us out of that and to lift us to heights we never dreamt possible and to make us what we ought to be and what we want to be and to make us his people and his saints, worthy to bear his name. I find all that in these genealogies. I find myself because genealogies are made up of people and people are like me – sinners needing a Saviour, and Jesus comes.

When we pass from Genesis chapter 11 to Genesis chapter 12, there is a big change in atmosphere. I notice three changes. First of all, from talking of the whole human race and many nations and many languages, the book of Genesis now begins to speak of one man and his family. Our attention is focused right down, as if somebody with a zoom lens zoomed from the crowd to the individual, from considering the whole human race suddenly one man stands out alone – a man called Abram.

The second change I notice is that chapters 1–11 deal with thousands of years whereas chapters 12–25 deal with one lifetime. It is as if God says that all that has gone before is a mere preface; this is where the story really begins. It is as if all that is just a summary: the beginning of the world, the beginning of the human race, the beginning of history, the beginning of society, of wars and rumours of wars. The important thing is what happens to individuals now. Out of the whole human race, which must already have numbered hundreds of thousands, God says: I'm a God of the individual, the God of Abraham, and Isaac, and Jacob; Out of the whole crowd, these three men are important to me.

But the biggest change is this: Genesis 1–11 deals with sin and shows how one man's wrong act spread out in ripples to his family, to his community, to his society, and ultimately to the nations until we reach the climax of international sin by the building of the tower of Babel. Now we are going to see the opposite: from Genesis 12 begins the story of salvation. Like sin it begins with one man and it spreads out in ripples from that man to his family, to his community, to his society, and ultimately all the nations in the world are blessed through this one man.

Just as one man, Adam, brought enough sin into the world to contaminate the whole human race, one man, Abraham, brought enough faith into the world to save the whole human race. We see the ripples of salvation spread out from this moment. Since salvation is far more important than sin, God spends far more of the Bible on it. There are plenty of people telling us what is wrong with the world; there are not so many who can tell us how to put it right.

God tells us what is wrong briefly – in eleven chapters you can see what is wrong. Now God spends the whole of the rest of his book on telling you how it can be put right, because that is the important thing. I have read many books diagnosing our present problems, our future needs, and all the rest. Only God can tell us how it can be put right.

It begins with one man, Abram. It is awfully difficult not to call him Abraham before he is called that, but Abram is the one man with whom God started. This man is a father in four ways. First of all, he is the father of the Arabs. If you want to understand the Arab-Israeli conflict you must read Genesis. If you want to understand how it all began, you have to go back four thousand years. Abraham is revered by the Arabs as their father—that is where it all began. His first child, Ishmael, was the father of the Arab races.

Secondly, Abraham is not only the father of the Arabs (and revered by all Muslims, incidentally) but he is the father of all Jews. It was his grandson Jacob whose new name "Israel" was given to the nation—a name that is still there in the atlas today, and it all began here. He is the father of all Jews and they revere him.

Thirdly, Jesus revered him, and if you study the family tree of Jesus in Matthew 1, the first man mentioned in it is Abraham.

Fourthly, Abraham is the father of all Christians. Time and again in the New Testament he is said to be the father of all who share his faith. Both John the Baptist and Jesus said something like this to the Jews: "Don't count yourselves sons of Abraham even if you can trace physical descent. The true sons of Abraham are those who share his faith in God." Therefore Paul, in Romans and Galatians, says to every Christian: if you believe in the God of Abraham then you are Abraham's son, he is your father and you revere him.

Now there are three things about Abraham we are going to notice, which are all important to understand his life – and these are open to you as his son.

First of all: his faith in God. Somebody has called Abraham the "Christopher Columbus of faith". I love that title – the man who pioneered, the man who was first, the man who went out into the unknown as an act of complete faith. His faith appeared at three striking points. First of all, God didn't show him where he was going but he went. Second, God didn't show him how he could have a son but he believed that he would. Thirdly, God didn't tell him why he was to sacrifice that son but he was prepared to do it.

If you want to know what faith is, it is this: to believe in God sufficiently to do what he says even if he does not tell you where, how or why. The trouble is that without faith we want answers to these questions. Why does God do this? How can God do that? Where is God going to lead it all? We want to know the answers before we will trust him. Abraham stands out as a giant of faith: a man who didn't want to know where and didn't want to know how and didn't want to know why, but was ready to do what God told him. That is what faith is. It is ninety-five percent obedience when you don't know where, how, or why it's all going to work out—you do what he tells you. That is the first thing, and one of the most wonderful things, that is said about Abraham.

Perhaps the most wonderful thing that is taken up in the New Testament is this: Abraham believed God and it was reckoned to him as righteousness. In other words, God said to Abraham: you're not a good man but I will accept you on the grounds of your faith; you don't have righteousness to offer me but I'm prepared to accept faith instead. And it was reckoned to him as righteousness. Abraham was not a good man; he was a man of like passions with ourselves.

The Bible is the most honest book you will ever read—it never presents its heroes with flawless characters. Already in the first chapter I read that Abraham is lying about his wife and getting her into dishonour and disgrace. Here is a man of like passions with ourselves, a man who lies, a man who does things to save his own skin that are wrong, a man who is concerned about number one. Abraham is not presented to us as a saint, as a good man free from faults; he is presented to us as a man who believed God – that's all. The Bible tells us about all his weaknesses and all his mistakes.

As a great saint once said when he read the life of Abraham: "I'm very sorry that he sinned, but I'm very glad that his sins were written down because that encourages me." Now that is a profound remark. If the only way to be accepted by God is to be righteous, then I don't stand an earthly chance. If I have got to live an upright, straight life that is honest and pure through and through, in thought, word, and deed, I cannot be accepted by God, but Abraham is the first man who stands out as a man who is accepted for his faith not his goodness. His faith was reckoned to him instead of righteousness and he was accepted on that ground.

That is how you were accepted; that is what makes you a son of Abraham—not because you are good, not because you are perfect, but because you believe. So the second outstanding thing about his life is forgiveness by God.

Abraham is three times in the rest of the Old Testament referred to as "the friend of God", so the third thing is his friendship with God. Once you share Abraham's faith and have found God's forgiveness, you can share his friendship with God, and that is a lovely phrase. Abraham's epitaph written in the rest of the Old Testament is "the friend of God."

I can think of no better epitaph for anyone than that phrase. Wouldn't you like that on your gravestone? Wouldn't you like people to say about you when you've gone, "That person was a friend of God"? It implies an intimate relationship and mutual understanding, a relaxed relationship in which you enjoy being in each other's company.

It also implies, quite clearly from the Bible that Abraham was the only friend God had in the world at that time. He is called "*the* friend of God". Everybody else was an enemy of God, rebelling against him, running away from him, disobeying his laws. Abraham was the only one who got through to God and became a friend. Every son of Abraham who shares the faith and God's forgiveness will share the friendship.

This narrative about Abraham was the beginning of God's bringing peace and it is more relevant than a great deal that is discussed in political circles today. So we return to this story of Abraham and see how it unfolded. Does God approve of war? That is a question, which many people ask and I want to try to answer it.

We go back again to Ur of the Chaldees, where God's peace began with this young man Abraham. Now we have seen his family tree in Genesis 11 and remember that it contains some very interesting people: Shem, the firstborn son of Noah; Eber, from which we get the word "Hebrew," and so we get the Semitic peoples and the Hebrew peoples; they are all bound up together in this tribal family tree. But the family we are concerned about has three generations in it: Terah, the grandfather, who had three sons: Nahor, Abram, and Haran. One of those had a grandson, Lot. These three generations were living together in a house in Ur. Even though some of their forefathers had worshipped the true God, Noah among them, nevertheless as a family they were now worshiping the moon. We are told elsewhere in scripture that "Terah served other gods." He was caught up in the superstitions and religions of the day.

So Abram did not have the benefit of a godly upbringing; he was brought up as everybody else in Ur lived. One day, God spoke to Abram. We don't know where it was, how it was, when it was, but God stepped into this young life of the second generation of this family. So we have been told not only where they lived, we are told that they migrated, and that they migrated round the Fertile Crescent. Three generations set out: Terah set off, Abram his son went—one of his other sons had died, the other preferred to stay in Ur. So he took one son, Abraham, and then there was the nephew Lot, the son of Haran who died, and they decided to take him too. Presumably, Abraham had adopted him because his wife was barren. So they began their long journey through fertile land, in country that they knew, with a language they knew, with customs that they knew, until they got to Haran. I would think that Terah had connections there since he called one of his sons by the same name, but they settled there – and the word used means they lived in a house.

They intended to go to Canaan but they had settled in Haran. Why? First, because they had reached the borders of their country; second, because it was the last centre of moon worship that they knew of, and if they went on further from there they would no longer be able to attend the place of worship as they used to. Thirdly, this was the end of their familiar way of life. Fourthly, they were now on the edge of the desert because in fact, though the green belt continued right round, from Haran the road cut across the desert to Canaan; therefore, it meant leaving a house and living in tents. It meant leaving the green fertile area and living in a desert. It meant leaving what they knew and were familiar with and going into the unknown.

We know from chapter 12 that Abram was willing to do

this, but we also guess from chapter 11 that Terah was not. After all, he was an elderly man. He lived in comfortable, centrally heated homes all his life and to ask an old man to go and live in a tent was quite something. But do you notice from chapter 12 that Abram should never have had Terah with him? Sometimes family ties can hold back from God's will—there are missionaries who have found this. Here was an old man unwilling to leave Haran, and Abram settled in Haran and stayed there until he died.

Now the question comes up: "Why did they ever leave Ur?" This is where chapter 12 comes in. Why should they ever take such a long journey, thousands of miles? Chapter twelve verses 1–3 is a flashback to the beginning; it tells us how it all started. One day God came to Abram and spoke to him. God steps into a life and speaks to that life, and everything hangs on to the response that is made.

God stepped into this young man's life and he says, "I've got something to say to you." What he had to say was negative and positive. Negative, "Get out"; positive, "and I will do something for you." Negative, "Forsake"; positive, "and I will bless." Negative, "Leave behind"; positive, "come to me." This is the call of God as it has always been. When Jesus went to the fisherman of Galilee, he said, "Drop your fishing, drop your nets, forsake that and follow me and I will make you..." – same thing. Time and again God's call comes to a man to drop things that in themselves are perfectly good and yet which are going to handicap his blessing. He says, "Drop that and come and I'm going to make something of you." Follow me and I will make you....

Negative things that Abram was asked to drop were these: "Leave your country," which in fact he didn't; "leave your kindred," which in fact he did—those are his relatives; and "leave your father's house," which doesn't just refer to the building but refers to the relationships, the ties. In other words, "Leave these three things. Leave it all behind and I will bless you, I will make you, I will give you three things in their place. First of all, in place of your country, I will make you a great nation. In place of your relatives who normally would have looked after you, I will bless you. In place of your father's house, I will make you a great name and make you the father of a new house."

This is God's offer, "Drop this and you can have that. Forsake this and you can have the other. Drop that handful of mud and you can have a handful of gold. Leave this behind and you can come into this." Alas, many of us try to have the blessing and hang on to all we have already got. There never was such a person who knew the blessing of God who was not called to give something up. So Abram was called to leave three things behind. What followed was conditional on this. He was to be blessed but now comes God's amazing purpose. God said, "I'm going to bless you in order that you can bless the whole world. Abram, I'm going to bless you. I'm going to make you a nation and a name. Why? Because through you the blessing can be passed on to the whole world, and in you every family on earth will be blessed." Now that is the lovely promise he made to you. He never blessed you for your sake; he blessed you for other people's sake. Therefore, if we pass the blessing on we are fulfilling our high calling. But he also said this, "Because I have chosen you to be the means of blessing to the world, those who curse you will be cursed."

I was in Jerusalem for the trial of Adolf Eichmann. I will never forget seeing him in his bulletproof dock. Six million Jews murdered – that was the accusation. Do you know what Hitler's greatest mistake ever was? It was not his mistake in postponing the invasion of England, though military historians say that it was. It was not the mistake of opening a second front in Russia when he should have concentrated on the west. Writers dug through Hitler's mistakes, telling us where he went wrong, but let me tell you in the name of God where Hitler went wrong. He went wrong in the 1930s; he went wrong when he touched the Jews—that was his crime. That was the point at which things began to go wrong, and anybody who lifts his hand up against this nation, this name, this group of people whom God has chosen, has sealed his own destiny.

That is why the Russian Communist empire could not last. They had already begun to persecute God's people, the Jews. Since God chose these people as a blessing, those who see that will find the blessing of God through them. The Bible is a Jewish book – every author bar one was a Jew. Jesus was a Jew, and without Jews we would not have a church. But if you lift up your hand against these people, crack jokes about them and persecute them, God's curse is upon you—that is the other side of the coin.

Abraham was going to be the means of blessing and cursing. He was going to be the means of bringing life and peace to many; war and death to others. This was Abraham's chosen calling under God and it has been the Jewish calling ever since. I once gave a talk, which was recorded and which seems to have gone further than any other talk I have ever given on the history of Israel. In it I examined the whole period of history from Abraham right through to today and showed again and again that those who bless the Jews have been blessed, and that those who cursed the Jews – including the appalling anti-Semitism of the British nation from the days of King Canute to Cromwell, and things we did in this country were just as bad as Germany did during the 1930s and 40s – has been cursed. One of the first things Christians should be concerned about is missionary work among the Jews. They are God's own people and they always will be. God is not finished with them yet as the New Testament says.

Now that was Abraham's calling and he obeyed finally. I know he stayed in Haran; I know that his old dad didn't want to go any further, and that this can be an awful tug. I have talked to those who feel called to the mission field and whose parents have said, "You're not going, we need you here to look after us." Abram was stuck in Haran for many years until he was seventy-five years old, but he never forgot the call of God, and better late than never.

When his dad died in Haran, Abram said to his nephew Lot, "Come on, we are going. God has called me and I am going," and he came across the desert in his tent into the land of Canaan and was completely surprised when he got there to find it full of people. I suppose he thought that God was going to bring him into a land that he could develop, that he was going out like the cowboys in the middle of America in the middle of the last century, that he was going to open up virgin territory, that God was going to make him a nation in a land that was empty. He got there and it was full of people. The Canaanites were then in the land and he pitched his tent on a hillside and he looked around the land—he had obeyed.

Now I want you to notice this and here is a big lesson. As soon as he had obeyed what God has told him first, God had appeared to him a second time and told him the next thing. If you want to know why God doesn't guide you, give you further direction in your life, ask this question: have you already lived up to the light he has given you already? Have you already obeyed what he told you to do? If you have not done so fully, and are not yet in the place you know you ought to be, then why should you expect him to say any more to you? God never spoke to Abram in Haran because God had said, "Go to a land that I will show you," and he knew it was Canaan.

Many Christian lives get stuck at this point. They get guidance and then somehow God stops speaking and they don't get any more, and the relationship isn't real, and he is not showing them what to do. One of the reasons is likely to be that they have not put into practice what he has already told them. Why should God give us more light if we have not lived up to the light we have had? But the moment that Abram is where God wants him to be, God says, "Now I'm going to tell you the next thing."

The next thing is lovely. God says, "I'm going to give you what I have shown you." He had not told him that before. He had said, "Get out and go to the land I will show you." He did not say what would happen when he got there. He just said, "I'm going to bless you." When he got there and he found it full of people, Abram wondered, "Well, what am I doing here?" Then God said, "It's alright, I'm going to give you this land, all that you can see."

If you want to understand the Arab-Israeli conflict today, then may I say that you must read Genesis 12, the trust deeds of the land. The earth does not belong to the first one who grabs it. I know that human beings operate on that assumption: that the first person there should have it. So the Arabs say, "We were there before the Jews so we should have it." But, in fact, the Turks were there before the Arabs so the Turks should have it; the Jews were there before the Turks so the Jews should have it; the Canaanites were there before the Jews so the Canaanites should have it. But then there aren't any Canaanites now, there are just Turks and Arabs. Who should decide whose land this is?

Human beings will say, "Well, we'll let anyone have it who keeps the peace. As long as the place is kept peaceful, that person can have it." That is how we argue but *the earth is the Lord's and the fullness thereof.* However unpopular it may seem, I must say that Israel has the title deeds to that land. It was God's land; he gave it to them as a possession forever to Abraham's descendants, not through Ishmael but through Isaac. This was their title deed to the land.

Abraham now travels through his inheritance. There is a lovely phrase: "He pitched his tent and he built his altar." I have heard sermons on that text. Let me underline two things. First of all, he pitched a tent. He never tried to build a house. He did not believe he was there forever. He had no continuing city – he looked for a city whose builder and maker was God. He was not going to make the mistake of Babel again. He pitched his tent; he lived under canvas until he died as an elderly man. We may have comfortable, solid homes that will outlast us – never forget that you are just a pilgrim and a sojourner. You are just passing through. "Temporary accommodation" – that is your address.

The second thing is that he built an altar. He didn't pitch a tent to worship in, he got stones and he built to last. The contrast is very clearly there: he pitched and he built. What is of man is fleeting and goes; what is of God will last. Wherever Abraham travelled through his inheritance the only thing he left behind were reminders of God, not reminders of himself. So that anybody who followed him through life would say, "Somebody has worshipped God here." Now there are many great men who have left behind reminders of themselves but only saints leave behind reminders of God. He built an altar, and everywhere in Canaan these little altars appeared, built of stone. They would stay there and people seeing them would say, "Somebody has prayed to God in this place."

I can go further than that and point out there were altars everywhere in that land already. Why didn't he use any of them? Because they were foul altars decorated with blasphemous objects, and because they were pagan altars. He alone believed in the one true God; he was the only friend God had on earth. So there must be altars that were not mixed up with this. Therefore he built an altar everywhere he went and he travelled through that land leaving behind him these lovely reminders of God.

I wish the story could end there: a man calling on God's name; a man pitching his tent and then, as soon as he had settled there, building an altar and worshipping his God everywhere he went. Every time we move house, perhaps one of the first things we should consider is: "Where is our spiritual home going to be?" Time and again I have known Christians move to a place because they liked the house and the district and discover only too late that it is going to handicap their spiritual life to live there. They have not asked first. The house we live in is just a temporary tent; there must be an altar; there must be provision for worship.

We can see why God wanted Abraham there. As we have noted, this little green strip of land is the corridor between three continents: Europe, Asia, and Africa. It is the middle of the junction of the world – the crossroads. Whatever happens there affects the whole world. Why do you think the whole world is interested in what is happening in those borders now? Because that is the hub of the world. What happens in the Middle East is going to decide the future of the world. East and West meet here; North and South meet here; the "haves" and "have nots" meet here.

There is a little Silver Star set in the floor of the Church of the Holy Sepulchre in Jerusalem. The tourist guide will point to the star and say, "This is the centre of the world," and it is. God wanted Abraham at the centre of history, at the hub of the world. He wanted Abraham – who believed in him, who was forgiven for his faith and became a friend of God so that the whole world might hear and might be blessed through this nation – at this crossroads. I can see God's unfolding purpose already.

Now, four thousand years later, I listen to my television news and I hear about the sons of Abraham, both lots, Arabs and Jews, wondering what to do about the future of their history there. It all started four thousand years ago with an ordinary man who said "Yes" to God. He heard the voice of God and he said, "God, I don't know where you're taking me. I don't know how you'll work this all out, I don't know why you're doing it, but I'll go, and I'll go to where you want me to be."

READ GENESIS 12:10–14 end

In much of the Holy Land you are dependent for water from heaven, not from earth. If the rain doesn't come, that's it, there is famine in the land. The wind comes from one of two directions in this whole area. Having lived there, I have seen the wind change from one to the other. When the wind comes from the west, clouds build up and moisture from the Mediterranean drops on the hills and it goes green and fertile. But when the wind swings round to come from the east, it comes across the Arabian Desert—and it is dry. The Arabs call it "the hamsin". This dry, burning wind burns up all the grass and the coastal strip is as dry as the desert.

All God needed to do to discipline his people was to turn the wind around. Again and again in the Old Testament God said, "I'm going to punish you by turning the wind around," and that is all he did. In the days of Elijah, for example, for three and a half years the wind was from the east and there was no rain. When Elijah prayed, God turned the wind around and Elijah saw a cloud no bigger than a man's hand forming over the Mediterranean. If you want to get into the Bible you must realise that rain means life and blessing, and drought is curse and death.

Here was the promised land of Canaan. God told Abram to get out of a land that gets water from earth and come into a land that gets water from heaven. Some places are very worldly – they never look up to heaven; they never pray for rain; they have got enough water without prayer.

So they can live and never think of God and just enjoy the pleasures of whatever life can offer them. This was the great difference between the two ends of the Fertile Crescent and the middle; life was precarious in the middle, it was settled and safe at either end.

So God called Abram out of Ur and we have noted how he got stuck at Haran for a bit with his old dad and was delayed getting into the Promised Land by his natural ties. We are now going to see that his physical hunger drove him out again – south, down to Egypt, and that this was a fundamental mistake. Why did he go? Well, he went because the wind switched from the west to the east, and in the Promised Land there was a famine.

Now there is something very deep here: if you obey the call of God and come into the place where he wants you and find blessing, sooner or later your faith will be tested by a famine in the Promised Land. I have known it again and again. Maybe for two or three months a Christian feels he is in the land of plenty, flowing with milk and honey, everything in the garden is lovely. What a wonderful place to be; what a wonderful life this is. Then suddenly something happens that makes life not terribly easy, that takes away some of the pleasures, takes away some of the security.

God deliberately lets this happen to his pilgrims to strengthen their faith and would say: you've trusted me for the big things; trust me for the little things; you've trusted me for spiritual things; trust me for material things. Abram, you had enough faith to come all the way from Ur around by Haran to Canaan. Can you trust me now enough to stay here? Or as soon as trouble hits, will you be off again back into your old kind of situation?

Time and time again, I have known young Christians fail at this point as Abram did. As soon as the going got tough, as soon as troubles began after they had obeyed the call of

God, they decided to go back into the kind of situation they were in before. Abram didn't go back to Ur—there was a much nearer place than that to which he could go. He set off for Egypt, where the rain was not needed, the river was still flowing, and there was still food. Egypt was the nearest land like the land that he had left in the beginning, Mesopotamia – a well-watered fertile land with no shortage of food – and off he went.

Now you notice a number of things: he never prayed about it, he never asked God if he should go, and after he went he never built a single altar again, he never lived in a tent again, he got into someone's house. We are told that one of the verbs "sojourned" means to go and lodge in a house. He left this tent, he left his altar, he left the Holy Land, he left all that and he never got it back again until he got back to Canaan. In other words, for the sake of some physical need, for the sake of a bit of food, he gave up all his spiritual advantages. Now that was the cost of going.

If he had only prayed, I am quite sure that God would have found some way of feeding him during the famine. But as soon as this material, physical need came he never thought about asking God about it, he just went, and it was common sense. If he had consulted his friends they would have said, "Well, it's only common sense. You're starving here, go down to Egypt there's food there." But then, of course, one could also say that common sense would have told him to never leave Ur.

If we make our decisions by common sense we shall make wrong decisions sooner or later. Because sometimes God's will goes right against common sense and it is right that we should ask him. So he went down to Egypt—it was a step of disobedience and one step of disobedience leads to another and another and another, and gets not only you into trouble but other people. So down into Egypt—that steamy, fertile delta in which affluent people just lived at the fleshly level, enjoying their food, enjoying the plenty – down into that he went, from the clear air of the hills of Judea.

The second thing he did was to involve his wife in the act of disobedience in a particularly horrible way. He was ready to endanger her purity and even her life to save his own skin. Here is a man, no longer a man of faith, a man of fear. Here is a man who used to make all his decisions by faith in God; now he is making his decisions by fear of death. Here is a man who said to his own wife, "I don't mind you being part of Pharaoh's harem if it saves my skin. Will you do this for me because you can lose your husband if you don't?" It is moral blackmail and he forced his wife into Pharaoh's harem that he might save his skin.

Now you notice that he didn't tell a lie, he told a half-lie. Sarai was his half sister and I am quite sure he squared it with his own conscience by having a little chat with himself. "Well, it's not really a lie. She is my half sister after all." This is exactly how we get caught up in the snares of deception. After disobedience comes deception. When you have done the wrong thing, sooner or later you lie, but the worst lies are not the black ones but the grey ones – not the utter outright lies but the half-truths that disguise the real truth. Satan is a master at half-truths. So he lied about Sarai and said, "She's my sister." Well, that was half true but it was half untrue and Sarai was taken into Pharaoh's harem and Abraham prospered materially.

I have known people say that material prosperity is a sign of God's blessing—it could be just the opposite. You notice that everything he touched turned to gold in Egypt. He got menservants, maidservants, she-asses, he-asses. Oh, he got plenty; he became a wealthy man from being a poor man. In Egypt there is wealth. The devil can prosper you as well as God; indeed, it is more likely that it would happen the opposite way if you become one of God's own people. The devil prospered Abram down there. Everything seemed fine materially: he was prosperous; his wife was getting plenty of food, but what a price she had to pay for it and there it was.

The third step is a step of disgrace, "Be sure your sins will find you out." Sooner or later what you do that is wrong gets discovered. This great man of faith is being told that he is a liar by a pagan emperor – Pharaoh discovered what was wrong. Now God in his wisdom decided that the only way to bring Abram and Pharaoh to their senses was to visit that harem with disease. God justifies himself. God, being wise and wonderful, knows the only way to bring some people to their senses. He allowed this rather terrible thing to happen to bring Pharaoh to his senses, to bring Abram to his senses, and to bring Sarai out of that situation.

Notice that Pharaoh says to Abraham: "You would have been perfectly safe if you had been telling the truth. You didn't need to lie. You've got yourself into trouble by lying. If only you'd told me the truth at the beginning, you'd have been all right. I wouldn't have killed you." All that deception had been wasted. It had been worse than wasted; look at the damage it had done to so many different people. There is Abraham with his head hanging, he can't even lift up his face now. He is ashamed, he has lost his time, and Pharaoh says, "Deport him. Go, get out of this land you deceiver." Fancy, a superstitious pagan emperor telling the man of God: you don't even come up to my standards. The disgrace when a child of God can be told by a pagan: you don't even come up to pagan standards – and Abraham went.

He did get back, and you notice at the beginning of chapter 13 it says, "He got back to Bethel as at the beginning. He built an altar as at the first." Who has not done this kind of thing? In some way or another every Christian has been "down to Egypt" at some point – has gone by common sense instead of the guidance of God. The glory of it is that you can get back. You will not be able to have again the time that you wasted. But you can get back as at the beginning; as at the first, you can start again. You can build an altar; you can start all over again where God blessed you.

What has all this got to do with us today? Ur, Haran, Canaan and Egypt are not just places in the ancient world far away and long ago. They are four places in people's lives today. Everybody is living in one of those four places – somewhere on that map.

I am going to tell you a story that is fictional but is made up of bits of people's lives that I've known. I'm going to call a young man Mr. X, and I'm going to describe his life as he passed through these four places.

Mr. X was born in Britain, somewhere we can call Ur. His parents were prosperous; they had a lovely home. They were terribly superstitious—his mother used to read the horoscope every morning. His father drove a sports car with a St Christopher badge on the dashboard and a lucky mascot in the back window. The grandparents had been godly people. They had worshipped God; they had been simple folk who read their Bible and said their prayers. But the parents had been swallowed up in the rat race and they were just living for their own enjoyment and he was born into that home. That could be anywhere in any suburb in England.

But after a bit this young man began to feel that life was more than just a comfortable home and enjoying yourself. So he started going to church and he persuaded his parents to come along to church with him. They all three became regular church members and they attended once every Sunday. If there was anything on at the church which they felt they ought to support, they were there. Every bazaar, they were there. They were living at Haran now—they had come a little way towards God as a family. It was about this time that Mr. X got married. He found a girl who was also a church attender and there they were living together and Haran could be in any suburb in England.

But somehow the young man felt that just going to church, there was more to life than this — much more. He began to feel the call of God to get deeper. But at this stage his parents cooled off and said, "Now, don't get religious mania. Don't get too involved in this." So for their sakes, he stayed that way and didn't go any further. But finally his father had to move house because of change of job, but the young man stayed on in the place. After his parents had left, the young man was converted and came right through to his Canaan. That could be anywhere in England. He became a real believer in God and he began to raise an altar and say his prayers where he lived at home. He began to ask God to guide his life, and so he lived happily with his wife.

Then they got into financial difficulties and they began to wonder what to do. To get out of them, he was offered a job that had certain shady things about it, but nevertheless he was desperate and he had a young family to support by this time. So he took a job, and he prospered in the job. They got more money and they moved to a bigger house in a nicer area and so they prospered. His wife had to join the bridge club to make friends with other businessmen's wives.

He became a freemason so that he could get some of the right contacts and get to know the right people and so they went. They are beginning to live in "Egypt" now and it could be anywhere in suburban England. After a while, the prayer life dropped, and after a bit, churchgoing was squeezed out. After all, he had to do business trips on the weekend – and down to Egypt he went until there was little more religion.

Here is a young man, Mr. X, who's made the whole journey from Ur to Egypt, been through all four places, and I have seen that happen again and again. Who says the Bible is out of date? Who says that we live in such strange circumstances and changed conditions that the story of Abraham has nothing to say to us? Isn't this what is happening today all around us? Is there not Ur of the Chaldees in every town and village? Is there not Haran in churchgoing nominal Christianity in this country? So far – but not far enough for God to bless.

Thank God there are many who get to "Canaan" and they live there in blessing. But it is a place where the blessing has to keep coming down from heaven. It can't flow from earth. Therefore, there is a relationship of dependence on God the Father, who sends the blessings that shower down. Then comes the temptation to get on, to meet the bills by getting involved in certain deceptive things – and down to Egypt we go. There is plenty of prosperity in Egypt—it is an affluent place. But it is not a place where people build altars, it is not a place where people talk about God, it is not a place where people pray. It is a place where they hold cocktail parties and business lunches, but it is not a place where God says, "I will give you....." "I will bless you." That is the end of chapter twelve.

We now look at chapter 13, which is quite brief. I have to begin by saying that when Abraham got back to Canaan he brought certain things with him that were going to prove a handicap to his future. Indeed, you can't go down into Egypt and come back to Canaan and remain unaffected by what you have done. There are bound to be limitations in the future from your past. It isn't as if these are completely blotted out once you get back. God forgives us the penalty of our sins, but he does not remove the consequences.

There were two things that Abraham brought back from Egypt, which were going to be real trouble to him. First of all, he brought an Egyptian female slave called Hagar. She was going to come within a very close distance of wrecking his marriage with Sarai. This would never have happened if he had never been down to Egypt. The other thing he brought back was great wealth and many cattle, and so did Lot, his nephew. The result was that when they got back to the Promised Land there were not enough resources there to cater for both Lot and Abraham and all that they brought back from Egypt. Had they never gone to Egypt the Promised Land would have supported them. But since they went and came back with all that, then they found that there was strife between the two of them, or between their herdsmen.

If you come back from "Egypt", try to get rid of everything from there. Do you understand me? If you have been away from God, come back to him empty-handed. Don't bring things with you that you want to keep from the period in which you were away. Abraham should have left it in Egypt, but he didn't and it caused trouble with Lot.

Now that was the strife and there was disagreement, and the danger of this was that the Canaanites and the Perizzites were also in the land, and if Abraham's retainers and Lot's retainers were fighting with each other, then they certainly couldn't protect their cattle against the Canaanites and the Perizzites—it was a tense situation. Abraham called Lot to him, and now, Abraham having learned his lesson in Egypt, rises to the heights of magnanimity with a generous heart. Abraham says to his young nephew, "You can choose any part of the land." What a big thing to say. He didn't say, "Now look, you're the nephew. You go over there I'm staying here." He said, "Look, the land is before you Lot. We're not going to argue. We don't want to fight. I give way to you. You can have any part of the land."

I have mentioned elsewhere the cynical proverb, "Where there's a will there's relatives." I have been at funerals where people were arguing over furniture in the house of the person we had just buried. Abraham was a bigger man than that.

Does that come home to you? We should not divide a family over things. So: you have what you want and I'll go the opposite way and we'll be at peace. Here is a big man who has learned the lesson not to make decisions by common sense but to let God rule in his decisions.

Lot, you notice, didn't say, "Oh no, Abraham, you're the eldest, you're my uncle, you should have first choice." He immediately looked around and his quick eyes spotted what he wanted. There is no greater test of your character than to be told by someone, "You can take what you want from this lot." Have you ever seen children offered this kind of choice on a children's television programme? A table groaning with toys – "Now, you want a prize, take what you want from here." Have you seen their eyes darting around trying to fasten on the biggest, the best and the most expensive? You say to a man, "You can have anything you like. You have first choice." That is the biggest test of his character, and Abraham lifted up his eyes to the hills and then he looked down again to the valley.

There was one part of Canaan that was not given to Abraham by God. It is the lowest part of the earth's surface and one of the hottest and dirtiest parts, but it is fertile. It is the Jordan Valley going to sixteen hundred feet below sea level. Way down in that valley the River Jordan creates a little model, if you like, of Mesopotamia or of Egypt. There it is – a fertile valley. There were affluent cities down there, everything Lot wanted. He looked at the rather bare hills of Judea and he looked down at the valley and said, "I know, I'm going down there." It reminded him of the Garden of the Lord—Eden, Mesopotamia, and it reminded him of Egypt. These are the places men get rich; these are the easy places to live, and this is where people enjoy themselves. Off he went. He moved his tent nearer and nearer to a city called Sodom.

It was the worst decision he ever made in his life because

not only was there prosperity down there but there was immorality. Lot saw a fertile valley with big cities, lots of people enjoying themselves, but God looked down and he said that there were wicked, great sinners down there. Lot, choosing after his eyes alone, choosing his residence from grounds of temporal advantage rather than spiritual welfare, found himself pitching a tent outside Sodom. Down he went to his "Egypt". Quite frankly, it was a good thing that Abraham and Lot separated. They would never have got on together like this.

For the first time, Abraham is in the condition that God told him to be back in Ur. God said, "Separate yourself from your kindred," and now for the first time Abraham is alone on the hills. God now speaks to him: "You have seen what happened to Lot and his eyes, but now you lift up your eyes. Look as far as you can, in every one of the four directions, to the hills around you. I have promised to give you this land, now I'm going to add something else. I'm going to give you it forever, and I am going to give you such a big family that no one will ever count them and both of these things will be true."

Abraham is now told to appropriate the land, and he walks through the land and every bit he steps on he says, "This is mine." If you were left a large country estate, one of the first things you would do would be to go and walk around it. You would walk around and say, "This wood is mine and this field is mine. All this has been given to me." Abraham walked around the land, but he settled in a place called "Hebron", near a bunch of trees called the oaks of Mamre. Hebron means fellowship. Mamre means fruitfulness or fatness. It is as if God said: Lot thought he could get that by judging with his own eyes; he's made his decision. Abraham, I will now give you what Lot thought he was taking: fellowship, fruitfulness, security, here you are."

I remember hearing a phrase from a little hymn, "He gives the very best to those who leave the choice to him." That is the story of chapter 13.

I want to summarise 14:1–12 in a bit of history. It is full of horrid sounding names, but it is very interesting that there are bricks in the British Museum with the names of the kings from Genesis 14 engraved into them. So if you ever go to the British Museum, you can see Genesis 14 in one of the ancient orient rooms. It is amazing how archaeology has confirmed the Bible. But the situation was this—down in the Jordan Valley there were kings, chieftains – sheikhs we would call them today. A king of a town was just a local clan chief – a bit like the highlands when there were clans there. Four of the kings were ruling the other five. These five rebelled against the four. Among the five was the king of Sodom. They had a pitched battle down in the valley; it was the first war ever recorded in the Bible and Sodom was taken. Lot, who was now living in the city, and his family, his children, were taken off as prisoners of war by the four kings. That was the situation and Lot had found that his security vanished like the morning dew.

At 14:13, once again Abraham is faced with a test of character and he has learned from Egypt how to behave. When the news came to him that his nephew Lot was a prisoner of war, Abraham could have said: "Serves him right. He chose to live down there. He chose the affluence. The war usually comes to affluent places, he made his bed and he must lie on it. I'm not going to risk my people to help him now. It was his choice and he must pay the price," but he didn't say that. He said, "That's Lot my nephew; that's my kinsman. I know he chose to live like that; I know he separated from me, I know all that, but he's my kinsman."

May I apply that? Do you have any relatives living in the "Jordan Valley", who have chosen that kind of life? Are you concerned about them? Would you help them? I know they may be living godless lives and may never think anything about your spirituality at all, but may I suggest that when Lot is in trouble Abraham is to go and help him—that is a big man again. Abraham sets off with all his men; Abraham is a godly man and when it comes to his own safety, he is a lamb; when it comes to someone else's, he is a lion. This is the combination that makes a mature character. A man who doesn't fight for his own rights or his revenge but a man who will fight for others hard. A man who will not see someone innocent suffering.

So Abraham sets off and we notice that in this, the first war mentioned in the Bible, God gives him the victory. By clever strategy, rather reminiscent of Gideon's later, he brings back Lot. Now comes the main point of the story. The biggest battle is after he got back. He is now on his way back up to the Judean hills and he has got a very subdued Lot, his wife, and his children with him. They are passing a valley, which is called the King's Valley, the valley of Shaveh, and there are two men coming to meet Abraham. One is coming up from the valley and one is coming down from the hills. The king of Sodom and the king of Salem, the two chieftains are coming to meet him: the king of Sodom who has been defeated but is now free; the king of Salem who never was in the war. It is in the interchange of these three men that Abraham is faced with a very stark choice.

Let us take first of all the king of Salem. In these verses the most amazing person almost in the whole of the Old Testament strides on to the stage and off into the wings and is never heard of again until the New Testament, with the one exception of Psalm 110: Melchizedek. He has no connections with anyone else in the Bible; there is no family tree, no father or mother, no children. He just literally comes out of the blue and goes into the blue again. I say into the blue advisedly because that is almost a synonym for out of heaven and back into heaven.

The names are interesting. Melchizedek means "the king of righteousness; the king of justice." "Salem", the name of his town, means "peace". It is the town that became God's own city, Jerusalem, the city of peace. Here is a man who is a king of a city of peace and the peace is based on the justice of the king – what a picture. This is the very city that a thousand years later King David is going to capture and it will become the city of the Lord, the city outside which Jesus is to be crucified. Jerusalem: the city of peace.

Furthermore, this man is not only a king, he believes in the same God as Abraham; he believes in the God Most High. How did he ever come to believe in the same God as Abraham? I don't know. It is a mystery. The next thing is that he is a priest; he leads the religion of his city and not just the civil administration. This royal priest of the city of peace, whose name is justice comes striding out to bring bread and wine to Abraham. It is not a coincidence that we think of the Lord's Supper.

He brings Abraham some simple refreshment of bread and wine. He has been fighting a battle; he has been travelling miles – about seventy miles up to Dan. He needs food and refreshment. Then he says: Abram, the Most High God has blessed you; you must bless him. He has given you the victory in the battle; you must bless him. He made heaven and earth and he enabled you to rescue your nephew Lot." So Abram who had all the loot, all the goods and property, which the kings had taken from Sodom and which he was now taking back, he took a tenth of it and he gave it to this priest to give to God. Abram had never met this man before but he recognised his greatness and he bowed before him and rendered blessing to God through this priest.

As soon as the king of Salem had finished, the king of

Sodom came up and said: "Abram, let's make a bargain ... you keep all the wealth, you keep all the goods, you can keep all our property, let me have the people back." If you won the battle it was an unwritten law – you could keep the people, but Abram didn't want to be under any obligation to a godless king. He did not want to be under any obligation to Sodom.

That was a wise and great move. It is a biblical principle that the work of God is to be supported by the people of God, that we must not put ourselves under obligation to godless people. This is why Abram refused to receive anything at the hand of the king of Sodom. He didn't want him to be able to say afterwards: "Well, I gave you that to help you, now you come and help me." He let the king of Sodom take the property, though Abram's allies who came and fought were to have support for their fighting.

Now this is a new Abram. The Abram who once took riches from the Egyptians has now learned that you don't prosper by taking things from godless people; you prosper by relying on God.

So we come to the end of chapter 14. Abraham had learned two lessons in Egypt. It was a bitter experience. He had been down to Egypt and his own son was to make the same mistake. Isaac made the same mistake and lied about his wife too. But Abram had learned in Egypt two profound lessons. First, Abraham had learned to let God run his life and make his decisions. Lesson number two: he had learned to let God reward him. When God did, he gave him only what he needed. Through the king of Salem, Melichizedek, he got bread and wine—and that was all he needed. The king of Sodom offered him all the loot, but Abram didn't want it. He learned to let God guide him, to let God reward him. One almost feels like saying it was worth going to Egypt to learn those two lessons. Abram had learned how to live.

From now on you see Abraham rising to the heights, and in chapter 15 we come to the mountain peak – when he believed God and it was counted to him for righteousness.

READ GENESIS 15–16

I do not know if you have ever been troubled with insomnia, but it can be a wretched experience. I am afraid it is not only a wretched experience because of the physical effects but because of the mental effects. I know that physically you feel rotten the next day, but mentally the worst period of the day to think about your problems is the early hours of the morning because your worries tend to get bigger and bigger.

Everybody else is sleeping peacefully and they are not worrying about things, whereas you are lying awake, you are thinking about the future and you are worrying about this and that. The more you worry about them, the greater the problem becomes until finally you really are in a state, at which time you usually get up and have a walk around the house or make a drink or something like that.

Now Abraham was troubled with insomnia. I know exactly what he thought about when he lay awake because chapter 15 starts in the middle of the night with Abraham wide awake. I can tell you what he is thinking about because the chapter begins, "After these things". After what things? In chapter 14, Abram, to rescue his nephew Lot, after he had gone into battle. By a very subtle and surprising strategy, in the middle of the night he had defeated four powerful kings and their combined army, rescued Lot, and brought him back to his own place. On the way back he had been offered by the King of Sodom all the loot that had been taken in the battle. Abraham refused to take any of it because he did not want to be made rich by ungodly people.

Now these were the things that were preying on his mind, and as he lay awake, this is what he was thinking: first of all: those four kings are likely to come back and take their revenge. After all, I only defeated them because I surprised them by night; they didn't expect anyone to attack them. But they are far stronger than I am; when will they come back and what will happen when they do? They can wipe me off the face of the earth, and my three hundred and eighteen men. He lay awake, afraid of revenge from those four kings.

Sometimes in the night, temptations are much more subtle and real than in the day, and the second thing he found himself thinking about was the loot that he had refused. He began to think: I could have done with some of that and so could my men. Was I right to refuse it? After all, it was offered freely as a reward for winning the battle. Why didn't I take it?

As he began to think around this, another thought struck him: But even if I got all that stuff, I'm an old man, I'm not much longer for this world, who would I pass it on to? I've no son; I've no heir. He lay awake tossing and turning—there was Sarai next to him asleep, all his three hundred men asleep. He is tossing and turning – he is afraid of the kings. He is finding that actually he really did want that loot and that he is sorry now that he did not take it. He is worried about the future because he has not got a son and heir.

My advice to those who are troubled with insomnia, when you get into a state worrying about the future, is this: have a talk with God about it. While you lie awake, talk to him about the things that are worrying you. At this moment, as Abraham lay tossing and turning on his mat in his tent, God spoke to him. Every word God said met the need of one of these worries of his. Now you know why I am able to tell you what he was worried about.

The first thing he was very badly worried about was the fear of the kings. God said, "Abraham, fear not. I am your shield." In other words: I am between you and every enemy you have got. I will be your protection; when they attack you, it is me they will hit first. I am your shield; I am between you and them. For the first time in the Bible, God says to a man, "Fear not." It will not be the last time; it was one of our Lord's favourite phrases, "Fear not."

I once asked a group of men in the RAF to do a little devotional homework—we had a fellowship in which we gave each other homework. I sent them home to find out how many times the phrase, "Fear not" or "Be not afraid" came in the Bible. They searched for a week and they came back. One man said, "I found sixty." Another said, "I found eighty." But one man said, "I've found three hundred and sixty-six. I've come to the conclusion that means one for every day of the year and one for every leap year thrown in."

Fears come to us in the night: fears about the future, fears about what people will do to us – and they loom large in insomnia. God says to Abraham, "Fear not. I am your shield." Then God says, "Now Abraham, you're worried about that loot, aren't you? Were you right to refuse that reward for winning the battle? Your reward will be very great. You don't need to worry that you lost that. I make it up to those who honour me. To those who refuse to take riches from worldly men, I make it up in another way; your reward will be very great."

"Abram, you shouldn't be worried about the kings coming back to fight you, I am your shield. Abram you shouldn't be thinking about what you've lost. Because you were true to me, your reward will be very great." Now, does this help you? You may have lost material things because you were true to God. Maybe you lay awake at night afterwards thinking, "Well, I could have done with that. Why did I turn it down?" God says, "Your reward will be very great."

But Abram now says, "God, there's another worry I have. I have no son, no heir; even if you bless me, who do I pass it on to? I have no son and therefore I lose the inheritance. I have no one to pass your reward on to, so what's the point of giving it to me? What will you give to me seeing that the next of kin is a slave in Damascus?" Now, I don't know Abraham's family tree, but I know that the next person in line to get all his property would have been this slave, Eliezer. Abram says, "What's the point in rewarding me because you haven't given me any offspring? The line comes to a full stop with me." In other words, for Abram lying awake that night, the future looked black. He saw battles in it, he saw poverty in it, and he saw no future in his family tree and that was what caused the insomnia.

So, God got him up out of bed and said, "Abram, come outside, come out of your tent, I'm going to have a word with you out there." On that still night he went out and looked up and the stars were twinkling above the tent. God loves to do this – to speak to you through something he has made. "Noah, look at the rainbow. Every time you see that rainbow, Noah, I want you to think that it's my wedding ring to you; it's my covenant sign that I will never let the earth down." I hope that whenever you see a rainbow you think of that. It is God's wedding ring to the human race. It is his covenant that he has made.

Now God took the stars and said, "Abram, every time you look at those stars I want you to remember this: you're going to have as many descendants as there are stars," and that is a mighty big number. In Abram's day they thought there were only six thousand stars. With the naked eye, that is all you can see. I don't know whether you have ever tried to count them, but if you go out on a clear night and count as many as you can see you can get to six thousand. It will take you most of the night and you will have to chart the sky off into squares to do it—but those who were amateur astronomers in those days counted six thousand.

We now know, and God knew it then, that there are far more stars and that you can't even count them. No astronomer today can count the stars and no astronomer today would even try. God's point was: you will never count the stars and you will never count your descendants. Now we come to v. 6, which is the most important verse in the whole of the Old Testament. We have reached the peak of Abraham's life. He was already eighty-six years of age. He had no son, his wife was way past childbearing age, and God said, "You will have as many descendants as those stars."

Now Abram could have said three things. He could have said, "I don't believe it." He could have said what would be much more human: "I'll believe it when I see it." Or he could have said, "Lord, I believe you," and he said the third thing. Abram believed God. Now that is a most important statement because it is the beginning of faith in the Bible at the deepest level. Everybody who believes God is a son of Abraham because of this. From here runs a thread straight through to the New Testament where in Romans 4, in Galatians 3–4, and in James 2, you will find this incident referred to as the fundamental incident in Abraham's life: he believed God.

Now there is an awful lot of nonsense being talked about today concerning what faith is, so I want to point you to this verse to tell you what it is: it is to believe in a person and a proposition. It is not just to believe there is a God, it is to believe that what God says is true. Faith is not just saying, "I think there is a God up there." It is saying, "I believe what he said he will do, he will do." That is what real faith is. Now I want to underline this because I meet a lot of people today who think you can believe in God without believing in God's Word. To say you don't need the whole Bible, that you don't need to believe God's Word in order to be a Christian, is rubbish. That is not faith as the Bible understands it. There are those who say, "I believe in Jesus, but I don't believe in the virgin birth," or, "I don't believe in the physical resurrection" – that stance is rubbish; it is a contradiction in terms. To believe in God is to believe what God says. It is not just to believe in a person, it is to believe in the proposition. It is not just to believe that he *is*, it is to believe that he *does*.

Therefore, a man who says, "I believe in Jesus but I don't believe some of the things he said," is talking through his hat. He does not believe in Jesus. He may think he does, but he does not; he does not believe in the Lord. He may be a man who says, "I believe in God but I don't believe in the Word of God." That man does not believe in God. He is just accepting part of the facts and that is not what the Bible understands by faith.

When Abram believed God, he was not just believing that there was a God, he was believing that God would give him descendants. If God said it, it must be true and it was going to happen. Therefore, it seems to me that faith in God is quite inseparable from faith in the Bible. Faith in Jesus is quite inseparable from faith in everything Jesus said. You cannot believe God unless you believe the proposition as well as the person.

This is so terribly important because of this division that people are making between God and his Word, between Christ and the Bible, and saying, "You can believe in one without necessarily believing in the other." That is not what makes you a son of Abraham – to be a son of Abraham you must believe not only that God is, but that all his words are true, and everything he says he will do will be done.

For example, one new year I decided that I would go

through the book of Revelation in January and February. It is a wonderful book, telling us what God is going to do in the future; it is one of the most thrilling books in the whole of the Bible. It is a good thing to jump from Genesis to Revelation in your Bible study and see the end as well as the beginning because God is the God of both. Some people find it difficult to believe that God is going to do what he says he is going to do there. But you cannot believe God and not believe that. If you do not believe what God says he will do then you are not believing God. You may think you are believing in God but it is only your own idea about God.

Now Abram was told that he was going to have as many children as there are stars. Abram believed God, which means he did not just believe God was nice, he did not just believe that God would look after him; he believed every word that God said.

Now comes the exciting part of the verse, and the most revolutionary idea in all of religion because there is no other religion in the world that includes the second half of this verse: "God reckoned it to him as righteousness." Many people have an idea that God sits up in heaven with a big book and he writes down on the debit side all your bad deeds and on the credit side, all your good deeds. I want to tell you that that idea is absolutely true and that according to my Bible God does have books that will be opened in the day of reckoning. It is all there in Revelation 19. Everything I do, everything I say, everything I think, everything I feel, goes down in that book. At the time when God calls me to account, books will be opened. So this idea is not a childish idea, it is true. In Abraham's book there was already a big mixture—he had done some good things, he had done some bad things and there was the book: some credits and some debits. The question is, "What is the balance going to be?" That is the question that everyone is going to face.

The word, "reckon" is an accounting word and it means to "add up a sum". It means to settle the accounts, to draw the double line under the figures. The simple truth is that what God requires of a person is righteousness; that is the one thing he requires to settle your account properly. The only thing that will settle your books in God's sight is righteousness. Don't get me wrong, that does not mean doing one good deed every day, it means being holy as he is holy; perfect as he is perfect; clean as he is clean; pure as he is pure. It means being absolutely righteous in thought, word, deed, character—everything. There is no doubt at all that Abraham had already done enough wrong things to spoil the books and that he could not possibly offer God righteousness. Neither can anyone reading this book do that.

I shall never forget reading a book, which said what I found to be a bit of an appalling thought: "If during the last thirty years of your life, you have only done one wrong thing each day, in speech or thought, or word, or deed, then there are ten thousand sins on the debit side of your book." I remember that shook me rigid. Just one a day and I cannot even begin to hope that I have kept it down to one a day, and nor can you. Ten thousand in my book! It is only because we have got short memories about the wrong things that we have any complacency or peace at all.

Abraham, we know, had already lied about his wife and got her into disgrace as well as himself. He had already done wrong things and in the very next chapter he is going to do wrong things again. Abraham had not an earthly hope of ever being righteous in God's sight. Now comes the great news, so pay close attention. God took Abram's book, and he wrote across the whole book: "Faith." He closed the book and said, "Abraham is righteous." Now that is one of the most astonishing statements in the whole Bible. Every other religion says, "You will have to get the books balanced on righteousness," but the Bible here says for the first time that God is prepared to accept you on one other ground as righteousness and that is the ground of believing his Word.

Now this is what opens up the possibility of what we call justification by faith. It opens up the possibility of a person who has never done a good thing in their life getting to heaven. It opens up the possibility for every single person on earth to be accepted as righteous by God. It opens up the possibility of anyone being quite sure that the Kingdom of Heaven is thrown open to them. Quite frankly, if this were not so and if this were not possible, one thing is absolutely certain: I would have no hope of getting to heaven, nor would you. This is the great news. God said that night to Abram: Abram, I've closed your books in heaven. I've written "faith" across your record and I accept you as righteous because you are a believer in me.

Now is that not exciting? Is that not thrilling? I can't think of anything more revolutionary in religion because other religions say: "Do this, and you will get to heaven. Do this and you can have life. Live right and you can be accepted." But that is not good news, it is bad news because I can't do it. It knocks me down, it does not pick me up. But when somebody comes to me and says, "Believe and you will be saved," that is good news.

Now that is what is revolutionary in v. 6. If you have got a Bible that you don't mind underlining, then get your pen out and underline that verse. Put a red ring around it, put a cross in the margin, do anything that will take you back to it.

Abraham is held before us, not as a righteous man but as a believer. Not as a man who never sinned, but as a believer. Not as a man who did not have weaknesses and passions like ourselves, but as a believer. He was reckoned as righteous because he believed God. God, in this book and in Jesus Christ, has made wonderful promises to us, he has told us wonderful things, and everyone who believes God will be reckoned as righteous.

Abraham sees the hills in the dawn and as he looks around the land, God says to him, "Now look at this land, I'm going to give you all this land. I've told you that; you're going to possess it all." You know, Abraham's faith began to fail in the daylight. Isn't it interesting that you can sometimes believe things more clearly at night than you can in broad daylight? In daylight, Abram having believed God for his sons and descendants, could not believe God for the land and said, "How am I to know? How can I be sure that you're going to give me the land?" Abram believed in the middle of the night that his descendants would be as the stars, but when he came down to earth in the morning and looked at the hills around him, he could not believe. Is this not so of us?

There are times when in church on Sunday evening we can believe in heaven and then the following Monday morning we have a little down-to-earth need and we find it difficult to be sure that God is going to give us that. It is so human and when daylight came and Abram saw the hills around he said, "Lord, I'm not sure you're going to give me the hills. I believed you last night for the stars and the sons but not the hills. How can I be sure?"

God did something that is very unusual to us and is very difficult for us to understand but was very common in those days. If two people wanted to make a very solemn promise or if one wanted to make a solemn promise to the other, he would take an animal, kill it, cut it in two, lay the two pieces on both sides of him and stand between them and then swear on an oath that he would be cut asunder rather than break his promise. It was a dramatic and sombre way of saying to someone: "This is how seriously I take my promise."

God came down to Abram's level and said, "I'm going to give you an assurance that I'll keep my word in the same way that anybody else would do it if they were desperately serious to keep their word. You bring me some animals and birds and lay them out for me as you would lay them out for anyone else who promised to give you a land." All day Abram waited and not a thing happened. He got the animals, he cut them in half, he laid the carcasses open, and nothing happened. Mid-day came and nothing happened except that vultures tried to get the carcass and he had to shoo them off all day. Still he waited and nothing happened.

The sun began to go down and still those carcasses lay there. There were flies on them now and nothing was happening. Then as the sun went down, poor Abram, having had a sleepless night, fell asleep. If you have had one sleepless night and you have then managed to sleep the next, you know how deeply you go off and he went into a deep sleep. He had a nightmare, it was all dark and he was filled with foreboding and dread. In the nightmare, God spoke to him and said, "Before I promise to give you the land, before I prove to you that I am going to, I want you to know that there will be a dark and very difficult period for your descendants before they get it. I don't want you to be under any illusions, I want to tell you the truth. For four hundred years they will go through a dark and very difficult experience like your nightmare now. They will be slaves in a foreign land, but they will come out with great possessions and then they will get the land I am going to promise to you. In other words, God did not lead Abraham up the garden path to think the land was going to be theirs tomorrow.

He wanted Abraham to be quite sure that the land would come but he did not want him to feel it would come quickly or immediately and so he had this terrible nightmare. Then God said, "There is one thing holding me up in giving the land to your descendants." These Girgashites and Hittites, and all the other "-ites" that were in the land, were terribly

219

wicked people. They deserved to lose the land—all except one tribe called the Amorites. God said, "I can't give you the land until their wickedness is complete."

God never yet dispossessed a person of anything they owned, unless they deserved to be dispossessed. When the Israelites came in to take the Promised Land, it was only because the people living in it did not deserve to have it—their wickedness was complete. God told Abram, "I will give the land to your descendants but I can't do it immediately. Will you take it on trust?" Abram woke up, as you do after a nightmare . It was pitch black now, the sun had gone right down, and there were the carcasses laid in front of him. As he looked, he saw fire passing through between the halves of the carcass and he knew God had taken the most solemn oath he could to assure him that his descendants would have that land.

Now God often spoke in fire in the days of the Bible: to Moses from the burning bush, to Elijah on Mount Carmel, and on the day of Pentecost through the tongues of flame. Why? Because fire means awesome power. Everybody has a healthy respect of fire—or at least they ought to have it. Fire can destroy, it can refine, but it means power that needs to be under control if it is not to destroy. So, God often appeared as fire, as the God of power who can destroy but who is under his own control and who will refine those who are under his control.

So, Abram saw God standing between the carcass and God says, "I will now tell you the exact boundaries of the land that you will have. It will be the land from the river of Egypt to the river Euphrates." Unfortunately, many Jews today have got it all wrong. They think the river of Egypt is the Nile, but it is not. It is the Wadi el-Arish.

The Promised Land is a strip of green land down on the shores of the Mediterranean between that and the Arabian

Desert. The Wadi el-Arish is a valley that runs inland. It is still called that and it still means the River of Egypt because it was the last river before you went down into Egypt. It marked the end of this fertile strip. So, God said, "You'll have it down to there and up to the River Euphrates." In other words, it was that green strip which he promised. That and no more, and no less. The only time they ever had it in the days of the Bible was under King David when he got it. From the river of Egypt, the Wadi el-Arish, up to the River Euphrates, they have not had it since.

I taught some decades ago that modern Israel was too far west and too far south. They had the Sinai Peninsula, which God did not give to them. They did not have another part, which God did. One of the things that I said I expected to happen in the future at some time (I was not going to say when) was that Israel's boundaries would move north and east. They were not in the right place yet, although they had got a great deal of the land that God gave to Abraham that day. But God solemnly said, "That's the boundary, that's the land, and I have taken this solemn oath to give it to you." I am quite sure that, after that, Abraham went back into his tent, lay down on his mat, and fell fast asleep like a child. Because if you have ever had the experience of insomnia when you have worried about things, when you have been afraid of the future, and if you have really met God in the darkness and talked to him about it, and claimed his word and his promises, I will tell you this: you will go back to bed and you will sleep like a child. Prove it to yourself the next time that you are lying awake and you are worried. The God of Abraham and Isaac and Jacob is our God, he can still do it.

We are now going to look at chapter 16, the brief and tragic sequel to this high moment in Abram's life. When you preach right through the Bible you have got to tackle the difficult things – to look at the sordid as well as the beautiful; the sinful as well as the holy; the challenging as well as the comforting. This chapter is an awful contrast. After the high belief of chapter 15, chapter 16 introduces low unbelief. After the harmony and peace which came in 15, you get discord and strife in 16; it is a very sad chapter. But isn't the Bible an honest book? The Bible never presents to you the saints of old as stained-glass window people who never went wrong, but as real human beings.

By this time, ten years had passed and no son had come. The future looks as empty as ever for Abram, and Sarai is worried about it. She knows that his greatest desire is to have a son and she is frustrated, she cannot give him one. She now knows there is no hope (humanly speaking) of her ever doing this. She sees Abram worrying about this, year after year. She is worried for his sake, and she just cannot help him with this and she wonders what to do.

Now she comes up with an extraordinary solution— extraordinary to us, but not to them. Archaeologists digging in Ur of the Chaldees have discovered that it was a common practice there, if your wife could not give you a son, to take another woman, have a son, then bring him up as an heir. In fact, it is in the law called the Code of Hammurabi. Law number 144 says, "You may take a slave girl and have a son." Law number 146 says, "Then you can send the slave back to their slavery and you can keep the son as your own." In other words, it was ordinary practice, and into modern times we have had similar things going on in some royal families in some places. We have seen this happen where one queen has failed to produce a son and another woman is taken, where it is still the custom.

So, Sarah said, "Abram, you want a son more than anything else—I can't give you one. Here's my maid. Have one by her and we'll count it as our son and it will be your son. After all, God never said anything about me when he

promised you a son". Now, it all sounded logical, sensible.
It sounded like a speedy answer to the need, an answer to
prayer, in a sense. Abram may have thought, "Well, this is
what God probably meant, and so I'll do it."

The tragedy is that he never asked God but he listened
to his wife. I would want to say: Sarai is not your Lord.
However logical, however sensible her talk, it is as logical
and sensible as the talk of Eve to Adam, and of Delilah to
Samson. Abraham, you are the head of the house and the
Lord is your head and it is from him that you take your
orders. But Abram never asked God so the Bible does not
justify this act. Indeed, it is presented to us as an act of the
human flesh.

At this stage Abram was unequally yoked with Sarai. She
did not yet believe—there is not yet any sign of the faith
that will be in her later. This is the kind of situation some
Christians are in: they are married to someone who does not
believe. May I urge you, therefore, when your partner brings
you a sensible, logical plan to solve your problem, to ask the
Lord about it first before you accept it. It may or may not
be a good thing to do. Abram, why didn't you get on your
knees? Sarai is not a believer yet. Don't just take what she
says as the answer to your problem. Go to the Lord about it.
But he didn't and the whole plan backfired. This girl Hagar
was a part of his Egyptian past and within a very short time
Abram was in a triangle that has been known so many times
since, and we are all familiar with it.

Here is the girl coming in with something the wife cannot
give (like the work colleague who is more sympathetic to the
boss than his wife is). We have seen this happen so often that
it is almost commonplace. Here is Abram getting into this
situation and as soon as he was with Hagar she conceived.
Hagar said, "I can give Abram what his wife can't," and
here they were locked in this situation. The girl who ought

to have been looking up to her mistress now looked down on her and despised her for not being able to give her husband what she could give. It is a sad and a tragic story. God can bring people through it and out of it, but it started because something that sounded sensible was not taken to the Lord in prayer.

Now Sarah, like a frustrated, angry, jealous woman, came back to her husband and said, "It's all your fault. May the Lord do to you what she is doing to me. You caused her to have a baby and it's all you." Poor old Abraham, he got what he deserved. He should have understood his wife better. He tried to evade responsibility. He said, "It's your maid, it's your slave girl. You do what you want." Since Abram was the head of the house he should have grasped the responsibility; Abram should have taken the lead and shouldered this burden. Instead, he put it back on his wife.

Here they are arguing; the first real argument Abram and Sarai had had. They fell out, telling each other, "You shouldn't have done this to me," and so it goes on. It is a tragic situation, and Sarai, because she can't get Abram to do anything about it, turns her anger on to Hagar, who then runs away. It is so human and so real. Now it looked as if the problem was solved and I am sure Abram had thought when the girl ran away, "Well, that's got us out of that jam," but you do not escape from wrongdoing that easily.

The angel of the Lord was going to send the girl back. The angel of the Lord found the girl on her way home to Egypt. Think of this: here is a young slave who has been terribly wronged against but who has also done wrong. She is running away from it all and God meets her and says to her, "You must go back and face it. It must be put right there; you won't put it right by running back to Egypt." The angel deals so tenderly with her, he does not call her Abram's wife's slave, he says "maid of Sarai". He says, "God has heard all that has gone on." Do you realise that if you have an argument in your house, God hears every word? The angel says, "You're going to have a boy." An angel knew what sex the baby was going to be this early, because only the Lord knew. God sees as well as hears and the angel says, "Maid of Sarai, God has heard all those arguments, all those fights. So, when you get a little boy call him 'Ishmael' – God hears, God listens."

If the boss tears a strip off you tomorrow morning, just comfort yourself with the word "Ishmael". Whisper it to yourself under your breath. It will help to relieve your feelings no end. They may think you have found a new swear word, but you have not, you are just saying, "God heard that." God does hear. Above all, if you are tempted to speak harshly to somebody else, say "Ishmael" – God hears.

God says, "Now you must go back and submit. That's where your future belongs; you're going to have a little boy. He's going to be the head of a large tribe. An unusual boy, a bit of a wild boy. He's going to be on his own, he's going to be a loner, he's going to go against other people, but he's going to be a great multitude." Anyway, she came back with all the promises. She came back with a faith in a God who sees and hears. She called the well after the God who sees and she said, "Thou God seest me." I remember going into Sunday school and seeing a ghastly picture on the wall. Just a long frame with two big eyes and underneath the text in gothic lettering, "Thou God seest me." Have you seen that picture? I heard once of a Sunday school teacher who had to deal with a little girl who was very frightened of this picture and she said to the teacher, "I can't look at that wall. I don't like looking at that picture. Why are those eyes always staring at me wherever I am in the room?" The teacher said, "Because he loves you so much, he can't take his eyes off you." The phrase "Thou God seest me" was never meant to be a threat.

In this context, it was a comfort to this girl. It lifted her up. God had seen a girl in the middle of the desert all by herself, unhappy, lonely, and he had sent her back. God had said, "Where have you come from and where are you going?" She said, "Well, I've come from there," but she didn't know where she was going. She had no future and God put her somewhere she would be looked after.

So, at the end of the chapter, the baby is born, emphasising Abram's responsibility to bring it through – he brought the child into the world. So she bore Ishmael for Abram and he had to look after that boy for another fifteen years. He had to wait another fifteen years before he got his next son. I think we have something to learn from this socially here. So often it is the woman having the baby who has to carry the responsibility. Time and again in the Bible God puts the responsibility back on the man. He put that boy back in Abram's family and said, "Abram, you look after that boy until that boy is old enough to look after himself. He's your boy."

What was the real problem in chapter 16? That Abram lacked faith? Not really, because he still believed that he would have descendants. The one thing that Abram lacked was patience. He could not wait for God to answer his problem in God's time. When somebody came along with a shortcut (in the flesh) he accepted this instead of waiting by faith. Of course, we are even worse in a day of instant everything, and we want instant answers to prayers.

People come to me and say, "I've prayed for this and I've had no answer," and I say, "Well, when did you pray?" They say, "I prayed last Thursday and Friday." But, you see, God has his time. When God made the covenant with Abram, he was saying that it isn't *when* the thing comes, it is that you should be sure it is going to come. It may be four hundred years before this land belongs to your descendants but you must be sure of me and therefore know that it will come.

I do not know when Jesus Christ is coming back to earth, but I am sure that he is coming. Often the Lord keeps us waiting, sometimes until the last moment, because he wants us not to be sure of the thing but sure of him – sure of his word, sure of the proposition he has made. Abram's fault over Hagar was that he was rushing God; he was not waiting until God solved the problem. Fifteen years later, by a miracle, God gave him the little boy Isaac and the problem was solved.

READ GENESIS 17:1–18:15

Many years ago, I recall the publicity that was given to a marriage because the groom was ninety-six and the bride was ninety-two. This apparently was a record for the marriage registers of Britain so there was a great song and dance about it. They found themselves in newspaper headlines and they were visited by TV journalists. Now, I am going to talk about a much earlier marriage in which the man was ninety-nine, although the wife was only eighty-nine. But Abraham and Sarah got "married" at this extraordinary age. I don't mean that they married *each other* at this age, they were "married" to God at this age. Therefore, we shall have to stretch our imagination a little to understand what I am trying to convey. I am not trying to be gimmicky and I am not trying to give you a headline to get your interest. At the age of ninety-nine, *Abraham was married to God*. It came as the consummation and climax of a relationship that had been getting deeper and deeper, although it had had its ups and downs, and was now coming to the point where it was to be made everlasting, a permanent relationship based on mutual love and trust.

There are so many parallels between chapter 17 of Genesis and every wedding I have conducted, that I do not hesitate to call it a marriage. For example, whenever a ring is exchanged in a wedding service, some words like this are often used: that the ring is given as a token of the "vow and covenant" now made between the couple. But here in chapter 17, again and again God says, "the covenant made between you and me." This is the heart of it and so we are going to look at this "marriage".

The marriage which the media made so much of all those years ago was quite obviously going to be a marriage of partnership and most certainly not a marriage for parenthood; half the marriage was just not going to be fulfilled and could not be under the circumstances. Everybody understood that, although a few jokes were made to the contrary. But having said that, I am now going to focus on a marriage of two people, ninety-nine and eighty-nine, which *was* going to result in having children. It is a most extraordinary situation.

The result of these two getting married to God was that these two would have a child at that age. The very miracle of it ought to cause us to wonder. It is not the last miraculous birth in the Bible; there are at least eight that I have been able to find all the way through scripture, culminating in that divine moment where the Holy Ghost came upon a teenage girl called Mary, and said, "You are going to have a baby." She said, "Impossible—impossible." She was not even married and she did not know a man. The same miraculous power that caused Sarah to have a little boy was ultimately to enable Mary to have the boy, Jesus.

Let us get straight into the marriage itself. There are four features of every marriage, which are here in chapter 17. The first is this marriage, as with every other one, is based on a solemn, binding promise. The phrase, "I will," is the key phrase in this chapter. If you underline things in your Bible, get your pencil and underline "I will." You will be astonished how frequently it occurs. Some wag has said that the phrase, "I will," is the longest sentence in the English language. I think I understand what he means though I would not call it a sentence.

But what is the significance of the phrase, "I will"?

Why is it that at a certain, crucial stage in every wedding service—before you can go any further with it, before you can pronounce them man and wife, before you can sign the register, you must hear two little words from bride and groom, "I will"? It is the law that this is said, and there have to be witnesses that hear it said; they have to sign the register afterwards to confirm that it was said. What is the reason for these two little words? The reason is this: real love centres not in the mind, nor in the heart, but in the will. That is what it is saying and the tragedy is that so very few people today understand what real love is. Listen to the pop songs, analyse their definition of love, and you will find they are centring it at the wrong place. The pop song, "I Will Love You Forever Today", is such a typical example of the failure to centre love in the will.

Now, if I said to someone, "Wilt thou have this woman to be thy lawful wedded wife, for better, for worse, richer or for poorer, in sickness and in health, to love and to cherish till death us do part," and so on and the groom said, "Well I think I will," we could not proceed with the service. Or if he said, "Well, I really feel like it," we still could not proceed. Now there are some people who centre love and relationships in the mind. We talk about platonic friendships. There was a Scottish lad who said to his girl that he had not popped the question because he was making a list of her good points and he wanted twenty before he would ask her to marry him. He had only got fifteen thus far and her reply was, "You'd better hurry up because I'm making a list of your bad points and I've got to nineteen."

Now this kind of intellectual exercise, which some young people make the mistake of doing, illustrates why every marriage should be entered into soberly, thoughtfully, bearing in mind the purposes for which it is ordained. But if it is purely intellectual then, frankly, it is going to be a failure. That is too cold a marriage, but I think the opposite extreme is much more common today: a marriage that is purely built on romantic notions, of feelings—this notion that love is mainly centred in your feelings.

Well, of course, you feel wonderful and your heart goes speeding up every time you see her and especially on the marriage day when she appears in all her glory. Your heart is beating nineteen to the dozen. But is that all it is? Is it just centred in the feelings? Are you going to see the loving relationship as something that is only going to be feelings? If so, then there is no point in holding a wedding service and the young people are right who say, "We'll just live together as long as we feel like living together. As soon as we don't feel like it, we'll split." That is a notion of marriage that has crept right into our society.

But here in the little words "I will" the Bible is saying, God is saying, and in the marriage service we are saying, "It centres in the will." Whatever happens later to your thoughts and feelings, you have made a promise. I have heard people talk as if there is no virtue in staying together if your feelings have changed. On the contrary, you have said, "I will." You have said, "For better, for worse, I will. For richer or for poorer, I will," and that is a very solemn, binding promise. There will be wonderful feelings, there will be deep thoughts about each other and you cannot run life on one cylinder. You cannot just make it a bold, bare promise and leave it at that. There will be wonderful thoughts and feelings, but the centre of it is in the will and in a promise.

Thank God life is so—God is love and, therefore, God says, "I will." You may search the entire book and you will never hear God saying, "I feel like doing something." Have you noticed that? It is always, "I will." Nor does he ever talk of thinking of doing things, though he has thoughts which are higher than our thoughts. It is always "I will". This is the heart of a true relationship: people coming together and saying, "I'll be true to you; I promise. I will."

Now look at what God says: I will be your God, Abraham and your descendants. I'll look after your family. I will give you this land." "I will, I will, I will" – you count them up. In the first part of the conversation God says, "I will" seven times, which is the perfect number. Not content with the perfect number, he goes on to say it again on a number of other occasions later in the conversation—"I will". It is only because God says "I will" that we can depend on it. Isn't it wonderful to know that when we go to church God has said that he will meet us there? On a Sunday, there may be members of families who discuss whether they feel like going to church or not. There may be those who think about it and then have second thoughts about it. But whatever we feel about it or think about it, God does not say, "Well, I wonder if I feel like going to meet them at church this morning." He says, "I will be there in the midst".

Promise after promise in the scripture is based on the declaration "I will." This is what we mean by the word "covenant". It is something much deeper than a contract. It is something voluntarily entered into that is binding. A contract is something commercial; a contract is what you might have in a register office. But in a relationship of love, a covenant is freely entered into by one party towards the other and means: I will, whatever happens.

So we do not have to say, "I wonder if God feels like listening to our prayers this morning." Wouldn't it be terrible if we thought like that? There are some primitive religions in which people do feel that way. They are afraid of their god because they do not know how he will be that morning. Elijah said to the prophets of Baal, "Maybe your god has gone on holiday; shout a bit louder." Isn't it wonderful to have a God you can rely on? "I will," and it is an everlasting covenant. God never said, "'Till death us do part," because death does not part you from God. He said, "I will make an everlasting covenant with you." That is the first similarity between this chapter and a wedding.

The second is this: you change your names. This is something that traditionally happened at weddings. The bride agrees to sign her maiden name for the last time in the register and then she will never sign it that way again. At the first wedding I conducted, the bride was so eager to be "Mrs So-and-so" that she signed the certificate with her married name. I had to chase after them on the honeymoon and get it altered before I got into trouble with the registrar.

Wilfred Grenfell proposed to a lady on board a ship going across the Atlantic. She said, "Why, you don't even know my name." "Well," he said, "I was considering changing it anyway." That is how he met Lady Grenfell and she became the perfect partner to him. God changed the name Abram to Abraham and Sarai to Sarah. That was the "marriage ceremony".

The new names pointed to a new relationship, a whole new future that was opening out before them because now the names meant something much bigger than their former names. Abram means "father", but Abraham means "exalted father of many". Sarah means "mother of many, mother of nations". So you have this broadening out in the new name that is being given.

God himself chose to change *his* name and for the very first time in this chapter God says, "I am El Shaddai, God Almighty." That name has never appeared in the Bible before. It is as if God is saying, "This is going to be a double marriage. I'm going to give you a new name to call me and I will give you new names by which I will call you. You are Abraham, you are Sarah and I am El Shaddai, God Almighty. You can pray to God Almighty now".

Thirdly, a visible token was given of the marriage. Now there comes the delightful point in a wedding where a ring is exchanged. It is a visible sign of the relationship. In the case of marriage it is, of course, to symbolise everlasting surrounding. You are surrounding your love with an everlasting symbol—a ring has no end. It is a visible token. It almost says to people, "Keep off now, this person belongs to someone else." The visible token that God gave in this marriage was something even more profound. It was circumcision, a thing that we do not understand too well now because it is not so widespread in our society. If it is done, it is usually for hygienic or physical reasons. It was a widespread sign or usage in the ancient world, but primarily as a symbol of puberty, of becoming a man. It has persisted into the modern era in some societies or cultures. In the case of Abraham it is a symbol given of that "marriage" – that these are children of this marriage and that God will not only be faithful to the ones he has married, but to their descendants. He has taken on the responsibility for the whole family.

I spent some time thinking about why God should choose such an extraordinary visible token of the marriage. I came to these conclusions. First of all, it is indelible and permanent. It could not be disguised. Secondly, it was on the organ of reproduction, which in a very deep way, spoke of the continuation of God's "marriage" down the line. Thirdly, it was, of course, a sign that would not be displayed publicly, but would be kept private and hidden. Therefore, it was a sign that would be primarily between the people and God rather than one that would be displayed openly.

It was a very painful sign. I want to return to that at the end of this chapter, but I'll just leave it there for the moment. It later became such a symbol of belonging to God that Jews were called "The Circumcision" and the Philistines, for example, were called "The Uncircumcision". It became a very clear demarcating line, although, interestingly enough, of course, the Arabs have kept up this symbol as a sign of manhood, and observed it much later in life, to this very day. They have kept it in a fleshly way from Abraham, but the Jews have kept it in the way that Abraham meant.

So there was a binding promise, and this was not just binding on the bridegroom. The bride was told, "Walk before me and be blameless." That was the equivalent of a command to love, honour and obey in God's marriage. The phrase, "Walk before me", meant stay where I can see you; don't have any secrets from me. Secondly, there was the changed name. Thirdly, there is the visible token and fourthly, there is potential parenthood.

Now we live in a day in which two purposes of marriage are being separated and in some cases, separated too widely. In a traditional church marriage service, the minister begins by affirming the purposes for which matrimony is ordained, which include both partnership and parenthood. Children ought to be brought up in the fear and knowledge of the Lord.

Now there are a number of things that have caused people today to separate parenthood and partnership. Contraception is, of course, one of the most obvious. I am not now saying what is right and wrong about this. It is a matter for deep Christian thought and discussion. But what it does make possible is the complete separation of these two purposes. Abortion is yet another thing. There are a number of other things that are now becoming an accepted part of our society which separate those two purposes of marriage for selfish purposes. No marriage is complete, or a godly marriage, if the two go into it with the declared intention of deliberately avoiding parenthood so that they can enjoy the partnership more.

In this marriage that God brought together – himself

marrying Abraham and Sarah – God made it quite clear from the beginning that the purpose was not only partnership. "I will be your God and you will be my people." The purpose was also parenthood in a literal way. "Abraham, the result of this covenant is going to be that you will have a son," and Abraham burst out laughing. I think the Bible is so honest about the reactions of people. It begins this solemn chapter by saying that Abraham fell on his face and it now says he burst out laughing. It was now thirteen years since he had had Ishmael by a slave girl, but the idea that Sarah and he could have a child seemed ludicrous and he burst out laughing. He was going to be given a reminder of that foolish laughter for the rest of his life because God said, "You will have a son and you'd better call him Joke." That is what God was saying, "You'd better call him Laughter, Amusement." The Hebrew word covers all this. It covers joking, laughing, mocking, being amused, being cynical, anything ludicrous. God said, "Call him that and you can live with that name for the rest of your life. You laughed at me and I was being perfectly serious." So there were potential offspring.

Now let me go a little further and I am being quite direct because the Bible is direct. Sometimes a couple fall in love but one of them already has a child, sometimes an illegitimate child, and the other partner is faced with a question: "What is to be my attitude to the child that already exists?" This was a problem here because Abraham had already had a child, wrongly, not by God's will, and over thirteen years he had become fond of the boy. In fact, he asked God to regard this boy as the fruit of this marriage instead of a new son. He said, "Lord, let Ishmael live before you; let Ishmael be our boy. I've got this boy already. Will you, as it were, regard him as your son?" God said a lovely thing. God said, "For your sake, I will bless that boy and help that boy and he'll be a father of many princes" – but the covenant was to be established with Isaac, the heir of the promise, son of Abraham and Sarah. So it turned out. It is a most unusual marriage—here is a couple too old to have children, but who have already got a boy, coming to God, being married to God and God is saying: I'll look after the boy you've got, but I'm going to enable you to have one boy yourselves who will be mine.

There is from this marriage, right through to the account of Joseph and Mary, a scarlet thread of God's purpose. God will not have man giving him plans. God will not have our circumstances overruling what he intends to do. So right the way through to the story of Joseph and Mary—that delicate story in which Joseph wanted to divorce his betrothed Mary—God, in a lovely way, takes hold of a human situation that seems impossible and brings his purpose out of it. Ever since, people have felt that God was guiding them to help in this kind of situation. Christians have been in the forefront in helping to take such situations and bring God's purpose out of them and redeem them.

Now let us look briefly at chapter 18, which we might call the kitchen and the dining room. It is a very much more domestic chapter. Just as the high moment of the wedding and the solemn vows is followed by the washing up, so you have almost a coming down to earth. You have got hospitality: meals being prepared, Sarah rushing around the kitchen, visitors arriving unexpectedly, all the paraphernalia of ordinary married life. We come down to earth and yet not down to earth. Here we have a visit from three people to Abraham and Sarah. They have settled down in their married life, in their tent, and Sarah is obviously a good cook and here they are. Three people approach. Now I can only speak in terms of awe and wonder because I do not understand what was happening here. Of these three, all of them were supernatural visitors from another world and not human beings. They were not *three* angels—the Bible makes this quite clear in the following chapter where we learn that two of them were angels and the third was the Lord himself in human form.

Do not ever imagine that the first time God visited the earth in human form was from Bethlehem onwards. There are a number of previous occasions on which he did this. The Lord himself did not just appear as a human, but he ate a meal as a human being right here. Once again, there is a scarlet thread from this passage right through to the supreme moment when he was born as a human being. But here he is, visiting the earth as a human being, sitting down and eating a meal—a very holy moment.

If ever you have read anything about Bedouin hospitality in the Middle East or if ever you have had the privilege of experiencing it, as I have occasionally, you will discover that this is so true of Bedouin hospitality. They will literally give you their last bit of food and stand and watch you eat it, if that is all they have got. They will talk about the lavish food they bring out in the same kind of understated way —as Abraham does in v. 5. He says, "While I fetch a morsel of bread," and he comes back with curds, milk, a calf, kneaded fine meal, and cakes. This was a "morsel" of bread. This is just how the Arabs talk today: "Let me give you a little meal," and three hours later you sit down to a piece of the desert groaning with food. It goes on and on. Here is typical Middle Eastern hospitality.

There is, perhaps, a profound lesson here for all of us. We are told in the New Testament to be given to hospitality. Here is a couple giving their very best to a chance visitor who comes at an awkward time. And it was an awkward time; it was high noon, which is siesta hour, when nobody goes visiting, yet out comes the very best. Abraham himself stands and waits, and sees that they get enough to eat. It is a lovely picture of a home thrown open to anybody who comes.

The New Testament says, "Be given to hospitality, for some have entertained angels unaware." That could happen to you. How would you feel if you got to heaven and met an angel and they said, "I once came to your house and you told me it was an awkward time, or you made it clear that it was, or you just shrugged me off?"

So the Lord and two angels came two thousand years before Christ in human form came to the Earth. They visited Abraham in his tent and said, "You'll have a baby next spring." Abraham had already accepted this. Whether he told his wife and she had not believed him or whether he had not told her yet, I don't know, but Sarah was listening and her ears were pricking up, possibly because she heard her name being mentioned. Then she heard. Me, have a boy? She literally creased out from behind the tent and they heard her laughing and they heard her giggles behind the tent. She thought it was ludicrous. They said, "You laughed." Immediately she replied, "No, I didn't." They said, "You did." Isaac: laughter. Of course, he became a happy boy and a joy to his parents' hearts, but the very name would be a reminder that they laughed at God. Now comes that phrase which is one of the greatest texts in the Bible, repeated eight times in the Old and the New Testament by Jeremiah, by Zechariah; it is there when the Holy Ghost comes upon Mary and she conceives. You will find this text right the way through the Bible with slight variations in words: "Is anything too hard for the Lord?" Is anything impossible to the Lord? Sarah was faced with this. "You laughed simply because you don't believe that God can do anything."

Of course, some of the things that God does and promises to do, and says he is going to do, seem to us incredible: to think that God is going to make a new heaven and a new earth, to think that God is going to give each one of us a new body, to think that God is going to transform everything and make it new — I find that incredible. People make jokes about heaven and hell, the furniture of the one place and the temperature of the other, because it seems ludicrous to them. But God says, "You laughed. Is anything too hard for the Lord?"

Let us finish our study with this: the theme that God marries human beings in covenants runs right through the Bible. The prophets thundered against Israel: you are an unfaithful wife to God in going after other gods. ("Baal" meant "husband".)

In the New Testament, Jesus said, "I've come to establish a new covenant in my blood" – this was to be a new marriage. Paul, writing to some Christians says: "I have betrothed you to Christ."

Christians look forward to the marriage, the consummation of the relationship and the new name that will be given in heaven. We look forward to the second coming of Christ, to the marriage supper of the Lamb, to the wedding. From heaven he came and sought her to be his holy bride. Like Abraham, and as the sons of Abraham through faith, we are to enter into a consummated covenant and be married forever to Jesus Christ.

READ GENESIS 18:16–19 end

Sodom and Gomorrah are probably the best-known towns in history. The only trace that archeologists have been able to find is the corner of a graveyard to the south of the Dead Sea. Otherwise, every trace of these communities has been obliterated from the face of the earth. Yet in living memory a Hollywood film appeared on the circuits called *Sodom and Gomorrah*, proving that after four thousand years the human race has not learned its lesson, and that we still hanker after those things which caused the extinction of these great cities. The Dead Sea is part of the crack in the earth's surface stretching from Mount Hermon right down through the Red Sea, which is part of the crack, right through Ethiopia into Africa, the Great Rift Valley. It is the biggest crack there has ever been—thousands of miles long.

The lowest point of the crack is the Dead Sea. Sodom was at the lowest point on the earth's surface, the furthest from heaven you can get. It was not only the lowest geographically, it was the lowest city morally. It seems that down in that steamy, humid hot area around the Dead Sea men sank to lower depths than anywhere else on earth. Sodom and Gomorrah, and two other towns at the south of the Dead Sea, shared this depravity. So much so that the word "sodomy" appears in the Oxford English Dictionary today and is now a word spelled with a small "s", and describes perversions which are unmentionable.

This is the city that Lot was gradually drawn into. He

did not rush into this with one fell swoop. This was not one great sudden step into evil; it was a gradual drift, which is how most of us become entangled. We glide into these situations rather than step into them deliberately. It began when he looked into the valley and thought that it looked a nice place to live, a place of security, and so he went down into the valley. He still lived in a tent like his uncle Abraham but he moved that tent nearer and nearer to the city, and then began to look at the houses there which appeared a good deal more comfortable than his tent outside it, so he moved in. By the time we read this chapter he had become the magistrate in the city of Sodom. He sat in the gate, which means he was an elder trying the crimes of the city. So Lot, who in God's sight was a righteous man—the Bible makes it quite clear that in God's sight he was basically a good man — became entangled in the city until such point that he did not know right from wrong and was confused even in his own conscience.

What disaster overtook these towns? Archeology cannot tell us. The Dead Sea, as you probably know, is drying up. Maybe that part of the Dead Sea, which covers this area will go and we may well discover traces of Sodom and Gomorrah when that happens. So far we only have the record of the Bible for what happened. But since the region itself abounds in petroleum, bitumen, sulphur and salt, there is absolutely no scientific reason for not believing the account that we have in the Bible for the destruction of these cities.

I would give the title to chapter 18 "Abraham and God's Justice". To chapter 19 I would give the title, "Lot and God's Mercy". Here is the perfect balance of scripture. Just as you never find a nettle without a dock leaf nearby to rub into the sting, you never find in scripture the mention of God's judgment and justice without somewhere near his mercy being offered to people. This is the pattern, a divine balance in the truth. It is so easy for us to go to one or the other extreme, for example by concentrating on God's justice, for which some preachers have dangled people over the pit the whole time. It is also easy to go to the other extreme, and so emphasise God's mercy that people think God is an indulgent old grandfather who would never hurt a fly. The truth is that he is both just and merciful — perfectly balanced.

We come then to Abraham and God's justice. The Lord and two angels have visited Abraham in bodily form. The two angels have gone off towards Sodom on an errand of judgment, and the Lord stays with Abraham. Should he let Abraham think that the destruction of Sodom is a purely natural disaster or should he tell him that it is in fact a miraculous act of judgment? Should he leave Abraham thinking for the rest of his life that the people of Sodom have perished by chance in the kind of natural disaster that occurs around the world, or should he say it happened because they were morally degraded?

We have an insight into God's mind at this point. If he keeps it quiet and does not tell Abraham that this is a judgment, then people are more likely to bless themselves by Abraham, because if they do not know that he has been connected in any way with the curse of God on Sodom then they are more likely to bless themselves by him. Whereas, if God makes it known that Lot, Abraham's nephew, is involved in this then people will say, "Don't bless yourself by Abraham, you might have the curse of God on you, not his blessing." In other words, when people realise that God curses as well as blesses, that he punishes as well as pardons, they tend to keep away from him. They would not come to Abraham for blessing if they knew that he was connected with this. But God showed him that this was a judgment and he was able to pass on to his descendants the warning and so to help them. God tells him so that he can pass the story on and nobody can be left without warning of what happens when these things go on unhindered. So he says: "Abraham, the outcry against this city is great." Now where did that outcry come from? Was it just to God the outcry of the evil in it, that it stank in his nostrils, as God puts it elsewhere? Was it the outcry of angels patrolling the earth and reporting back to heaven on what they had seen, as angels do report back?

I would conjecture and it is only speculation, that the outcry against Sodom came from the hearts of parents and brothers and sisters who had seen their relatives sucked into the whirlpool of vice in that city. These were big cities attracting young people away from their country homes and sucking them down into this vortex of sin. I think the outcry that was coming up to God was the outcry of parents crying out against a city that was doing this to their children, as parents are crying out today for exactly the same reason. God says the outcry has reached him, the cry against this city has reached him, and he is going to take a thorough look at it to see if it really is as bad as people say. Now that is the outcry against the city.

One of the most lovely passages in the whole Bible is: "an outcry for the city". There are men crying against this city, but there is somebody who is going to cry for it and say, "There is a little bit of good in it." These are the two cries that are going to come to God – the prosecution and the defence. Abraham, in the first recorded intercessory prayer in the Bible, shows us how to pray for people in trouble. It is a bold prayer, it is a frank prayer, a persistent prayer, a humble prayer, a believing prayer—it is all that prayer should be. It is talking to God in reality about real things.

So Abraham says: Lord, I want to speak to you. Lord, you are the judge of all the earth. Even a judge of a little bit of the earth has to distinguish between the righteous and the wicked. He must not lump people together and condemn them all together. Even an earthly judge has to do that. Lord, you're the judge of all the earth, surely you must do right. Will you destroy the righteous with the wicked? Will you lump them all together? Is there not something in that city that you can see that's good?

It is a wonderful prayer and it is wrung from the heart of a man appealing to justice. He is not asking for mercy, he is not asking for favours, he is asking for simple justice. So he says, "Lord, if there are fifty righteous in that city it would not be just, would it, to lump them all together and destroy them all?" God says, "No, it wouldn't and I won't do it."

Abraham goes further: "But Lord, if there are forty-five . . . . " Forty, thirty, twenty, ten — down he comes in his numbers all the way. Do you see what he is doing? He is not sure enough that God will be fair. He is frank enough to say so, but is it not true that time and time again all of us are tempted to think that God is not fair? In the very questions we ask, such as "Why did God allow this? Why should God do that?", we are all subject to the human temptation of thinking that God is not just. But Abraham is hanging on to the fact that God is just. Even if there are ten, it would be unjust, wouldn't it? And God says, "Even if there are ten...." In other words, God is showing his patience with a man who is showing his persistence, and this is real prayer. A man who is persistent will find that God is patient.

So, God is letting Abraham know that he does not need to worry and does not need to reduce all these figures. The answer is the same the whole way – God is just. He does not do anything unfair and he never will. He is the judge of all the earth and we can trust him as the judge. He will do what is right. So Abraham leaves the Lord and the prayer is over. You see that the city, even the wicked, would have benefitted from the presence of the righteous. Far from the righteous suffering at the presence of the wicked, the wicked would have benefitted because of the presence of the righteous. Indeed, this is still true. There are people living comfortable, secure lives in England who never give a thought to God, and yet it is to the presence of Christian people in England that they owe their security, and that they owe so much that they enjoy in this land. They enjoy the presence of the righteous, the salt of the earth, without realising it.

We now turn to the side of the story which I could call "Lot and God's mercy". Even the first sentence of chapter nineteen is full of meaning. The thing that convinces me that God wrote every word of the Bible and that every word is true is precisely that every word has meaning and every word counts. There are no wasted words in all these three quarters of a million words. Take the first sentence of chapter 19, "The two angels came to Sodom in the evening." When they came to Abraham up on the hills they came at high noon in the blaze of day, because a good man can stand in the sunshine, he has got nothing to hide. They came in the blaze of day. That is when Abraham did things, in the day, and he wisely slept in the night. But in Sodom they stayed in bed in the day and the day began at night. At dusk they came out onto the streets.

This is the difference between good and evil. Men love darkness rather than the light because their works are evil. So, when Abraham was going to bed in his tent, the nightclubs of Sodom were opening – and it has always been that way. You can judge a city's morals by whether it is more alive during the day or during the night. So, they came to Sodom in the evening, and for the rest of this chapter you get a sense of blackness, of darkness, physical and moral, whereas, in the previous chapter you were up on the hills in high noon. The contrast is striking, with just a little phrase, "in the evening".

They found Lot sitting in the gate—the judge in this city, the magistrate responsible for law and order. He is still a righteous man, but we are told in the New Testament in 2 Peter 2:7–8 that "Lot was vexed and tormented in his righteous spirit by the lawless deeds which he had to witness." Can you imagine what it was like living in Sodom if you had a spark of decency in your heart?

Now vv. 1–11 describe the most horrible event, and I want, in a sense, to hurry over it. I want you to notice how anxious Lot was to get them off the streets before darkness came. He said, "Come, stay in my house quickly. Come into my house and rise up early and get on your way." As much as to say: I'm sure you're just passing through and I don't want you to stay here and see what I have to see. He tried to get them off the streets and they said, "No, we will stay on the street. We have been sent by God to see what goes on in this city. We are going to stay on the streets." That is where the evil was done in Sodom at night, on the streets. If you want to see something like Sodom you walk through Piccadilly Circus at midnight on Saturday. Lot said, "No, come on in," and they were persuaded to go in.

Now comes the suggestion that has given the name "sodomy" to the Oxford English Dictionary. All the men of the city—all, young and old all perverted, came and shouted through the door the filthy suggestion that Lot should bring his visitors out so that they might have homosexual intercourse with them. In other words, like most perverts, they needed variety, and here were some new people. That was what they shouted through the closed door, and that is what has given the name of that town to our language. It is the first mention of homosexuality in the Bible, and it is always treated as a sin and not as a disease.

One of the things of our time, which we are battling against, is that crime is now regarded as a disease, not a sin

– that sinners are to be treated as patients and not responsible human beings. I believe the Bible indicates very clearly that in all of us, because of our fallen human nature, there are tendencies – in some these are greater than in others, varying from personality to personality. Some teenagers go through such a period of tendency, and have crushes on teachers or someone else of their own sex. The sin comes in giving way to such tendencies and exploiting them and developing them.

If this is only disease and something that cannot be helped then why should it be that it is so prevalent in major films dealing with this subject and providing it for entertainment? If it is just a disease and something people cannot help, why should we display things that people cannot help? But we exploit and foster it, which gives the whole game away. That is all I am going to say about this. But if you read Romans 1, you will find the same position is taken up in the New Testament. This is not a disease which people cannot help, it is a tendency of fallen human nature to which we must not give way.

Lot now pleads with the people at his door and he calls it a wicked act. Here is their own magistrate, their own judge, their own Justice of the Peace saying, "This is wicked. Men, do not do so wickedly to strangers. Don't drag them down with you." He is almost pleading with them. He knows them perfectly well, and their own judge is saying, "It's wicked," but then in a sad moment—showing that even his own moral conscience has been perverted by living in that place—he says, "Here are my unmarried daughters; you can do to them what you want." In other words, "Rape isn't nearly so bad, so you have them." It is an incredible thing, and yet it shows that the environment in which you live can twist your moral insights, to the degree you can think that you are choosing the lesser of two evils.

Where the scene would have ended, but for the

supernatural intervention of those angels, I do not know, but the angels mercifully "dazzled" – that is the literal word – the sight and blinded temporarily the people of that city. Now the angels had seen enough. They had seen all the people, to the last man, and there were not even ten righteous in this city. In fact, there was only one, and a few of his relatives whom he had been able to influence.

So the angels said to Lot: this city is going to go; the landlord is going to eject the bad tenants from Earth, and you must get out quickly – and anybody you can influence for good and anybody you can save, bring out with you. So Lot turned to his sons-in-law. Now they were not yet married to his daughters, they were betrothed, but betrothal was so serious that they were called sons-in-law in those days. He turned to these two young men who were to marry his daughters and he said, "This city is going to be destroyed, you must come out of it with me." They said, "You must be joking." Typical young men in a situation like this. There used to be a gentleman who attended the church of which I was the pastor, who walked around Piccadilly Circus bearing a banner saying that the end of the world will come. I am quite sure that then, as now, there were many young men who took precisely the same attitude as the sons-in-law of Lot. I am not suggesting here whether or not this is the best way to tell people. I am illustrating the attitude of the sons-in-law to any suggestion that there is a danger of judgment to come and that a city can be destroyed by God—so they laughed and there are those who still laugh and are heedless of the warnings that preachers give, and Christians give, and the Word of God gives. These are people who think that their town or city is going to last forever, that the world will always be here, that God will never judge, that God is not that kind of God. There are people who still joke about such serious things. Even Lot himself lingered, terribly undecided.

In the mercy of the Lord, the angels got Lot by the hand and said, "Even if you're going to linger, we're not going to let you, come on," and began to pull Lot and his two daughters and his wife out of that terrible place. It says, "God could not destroy it while Lot was in it." Even one righteous man in that city prevented Sodom from being destroyed. Which is why in the New Testament we are told that when Jesus comes again he will have to take all the righteous out of the world before he can destroy it, and "one shall be taken and the other left". That is why he will have to do that, because he could not destroy a world with one righteous person in it. It would be unjust.

Now Lot is given an urgent plea: flee for your life, that's what's at stake; don't look back, there must be no lingering doubts, no stopping near the city. You must go to the hills, back to the life that you left when you came here. Go back to Abraham. Go back to your tent. You are better in a tent on the hills than in a luxury mansion in this city. But Lot had lived in a city too long to consider going back to a tent. He said, "Lord, I can't face the hills. I can't face going back to that." And the Lord in his wonderful mercy said, "Well, alright Lot. I am determined to get you out. If you won't go to the hills, where will you go?" Lot said, "Well, there's a little city over there, halfway up the hill. Can I go there?" God in his mercy said, "Well, yes. If you'll get out of this city you can go there." So Lot went to the city of Zoar. It was a wonderful concession that God made that day; it was a favour. Lot came to Sodom, a wealthy man with flocks, herds, and servants. He left it a pauper, without a penny in his pocket, and he went to Zoar. Brimstone, fire and all the rest of the substances of that evil, foul region, which kill all vegetation, blew up and showered down upon that city. You can see the traces of it all today. You can go to a place called Sdom where now they dredge potash from the shores of the

Dead Sea. And you can look out over the wilderness—that is all that is left of a civilisation that went wrong.

Lot's wife looked back—quite clearly she was reluctant to go. Quite clearly she did not keep up with Lot, who obeyed the Lord literally and fled. He reached Zoar before she did, but, as soon as Lot reached Zoar, Sodom's end began, and she looked back. Why? Was she feeling pity for those in Sodom? Was she regretting the friendships that she was leaving behind, evil though they had been? What was it? There is no need to postulate a kind of miraculous transformation of Lot's wife, such as religious films have tried to do with trick photography. The word means, quite literally: she was engulfed in a heap of salt. The phrase is almost, as I sometimes joke with my children, "Do you want to see me do a trick? Then I'll turn into a garage," and that is literally what it means. I am afraid this is one case where we have imagined things that obviously are not implied, that she suddenly became crystallised salt. It is true, the Arab guides will still show you a pillar, a large pillar forty feet high the shape of a fleeing woman, which is one of those things like the cross on the back of a donkey, which by a strange coincidence reminds us of those days.

But quite clearly, the Hebrew language implies that because she hesitated she was caught in the eruption, and all that you could see where she had been standing was a heap of rock salt. Centuries later, Jesus himself was to say, "Remember Lot's wife." Don't look back. Don't have regrets about leaving, get out of it and be what God wants you to be.

Meanwhile Abraham was at his tent door up on the hills breathing the pure air of the Judean country, but he stood before the Lord and looked down from those hills, and I can see it so clearly (and if you go there, you can see so clearly) from those hills. You look right down into the valley, you can see it in the distance, you can see the Dead Sea sparkling down, but he could not see it. All he could see was smoke.

He did not know at that time that Lot had got out, but it says that God remembered Abraham and brought Lot out. I wish we could finish the story there, but we cannot. There is an unfortunate sequel, and it carries its own lesson for everybody who has been redeemed from sin. Here is the lesson: Lot went to Zoar with his two daughters and God had said, "You can go there," and Lot was now being called to live by faith in God, to get back into the way of God that he walked with his uncle, Abraham. He was to believe that God would look after him, that God would build up a new life for him, and that God would be his Father. But it says that Lot began to fear, and instead of faith fear began to dominate his actions. Fear of what? The Bible does not say, but I think I can tell you. You must simply accept this as my understanding and if you feel that there is another reason you can have yours.

I think he began to be afraid of people, of what they would say, of what they might do, of whether they would say, "Well, don't let your young men go out with those two girls, they've been in Sodom." I think they began to fear talk, and they should not have done because God had sent them to Zoar, and he was going to look after them. They would have been better off still back in the hills with Abraham, but God had made that concession, and he told them to go to Zoar.

The result was that Lot withdrew his daughters from normal social intercourse and they went and hid in a cave. The very thing those three people needed was to get back into normal healthy society, but Lot shut them away in a cave. That was the worst thing he could have done and there they were—these people who had lived in a luxury house in Sodom were now in a dark, cold, uncomfortable hole in the earth. The result was that his daughters went wrong. Of course, you could hardly blame them, they had been brought up in Sodom. They had no idea what was right and what was wrong – except that they knew that their father would not approve of what they thought of doing. There was that spark of conscience there—that they felt they could not do what they had decided to do unless they got him drunk so that he did not know what was going on. So, they both got him drunk and committed incest with him and they both had children.

One had Moab, and the Moabites forever afterwards were a thorn in the flesh of the people of God. It was from the Moabites that Israel learned one of the most perverted sexual practices that crept in and spoiled them. The other girl had a boy, the father of the Ammonites. From the Ammonites and from an Ammonite called Molech the people of Israel learned the cruellest religious practice in the world, namely sacrificing live children to gods. The evil that men do lives after them.

If only Lot had not feared men but had trusted God instead. If only after he had been saved from all this he had let God put his life straight and stayed in normal, healthy society, unafraid of men because God was his God, then this tragic sequel would never have occurred.

I finish by saying two more things. Jesus believed this whole series of tragic events to be absolutely true, and so do I. He mentioned them time and time again. When he was speaking of his own second coming he said, "As in the days of Noah, they ate and drank and married, so shall it be in the days of the Son of Man." He also said, "As in the days of Lot, so shall it be in the days of the coming of the Son of Man." It is very interesting that the prophet Ezekiel said that Sodom's downfall began with pride, fullness of bread, and abundance of ease.

In other words, the sexual perversion came as the result of affluence and leisure, because people did not know what to do with their money and their leisure and had to find something new and exciting to do. Can't you see the parallel to our society? Pride, fullness of bread, and abundance of ease? And Jesus said, "As it was in the days of Lot so shall it be in the days of the coming of the Son of Man." It was then that he uttered the memorable phrase, "Remember Lot's wife."

There must be no lingering, there must be no hesitation — you can either choose to belong to Christ or to the world, you cannot hesitate between both. We are living in days when we are rightly looking for the coming of the Son of Man. Every generation does, but there are things that have happened in our lifetime that make us, I think, look even more for this great event – as it was in the days of Lot.

The final thing with which I will close this chapter, is also the most important. It would be tragically easy for us to condemn Sodom and go away patting ourselves on the back for our respectable lives. "Oh, we've never had anything to do with anything like that" — how easy. But let me tell you now something else which Jesus said about Sodom. He once said about Capernaum, that lovely little seaside town on the shores of Galilee: "Woe unto you Capernaum, it will be more tolerable for Sodom on the Day of Judgment than for you, Capernaum."

Why did he say that? Because Capernaum had done something far worse than Sodom. Do you know what Capernaum had done? They had rejected Jesus. You may never have been involved in what the world would call dirt. You may never have been in the Sunday papers, but to reject Jesus is far, far worse. The other thing Jesus once said was this. He called his disciples together, seventy of them. Then he sent them out two by two and he said, "Go into every town in my name. Go and tell them, 'The kingdom of God is coming.' If they receive you that's wonderful, but if they reject you, shake the dust off your feet. It will be more tolerable for Sodom in the Day of Judgment than for those cities."

In other words, not just rejecting Christ, but rejecting Christians is more serious than the sin of Sodom. Therefore, let us get away from Hollywood and the news of the world's definition of sin, and let us get back to Jesus' definition of sin. He says the worst sin of all is to reject a Christian who has come to tell you about the kingdom of God. On the Day of Judgment, which we must all face – and you notice that even the people of Sodom will be there that day – the people of Sodom will find the judgment, the day of Judgment, easier to bear than those who have rejected Christians. This is our Lord's last word, lest we think that sexual perversion is the worst sin, as most people seem to do, and lest we forget that the worse sin of all is unbelief.

READ GENESIS 20–21

One of the things that convinces me that the Bible is true is its absolute honesty about people. In this book, we have events as they really happened and a true picture of people as they really were, "warts and all" as Oliver Cromwell said of his portrait. In this passage we have a kind of sandwich and the jam in the middle of the sandwich is very sweet. It is the story of Isaac and the birth of this boy, when humanly speaking it was impossible. But alas, this sweet part of the story is sandwiched between two unhappy and unsavoury events.

On the one hand Abraham is lying and getting his wife into trouble again, and on the other hand, immediately afterwards, a quarrel between Ishmael and Isaac results in Hagar and Ishmael being cast out into the wilderness. Here we see the honesty of the Bible. If this were fiction, no writer would dare to sandwich the climax of the story between two such unhappy events. But this is life, and this is truth. Abraham is presented not as a plaster saint but as a real man who could fall into sin.

We start, then, with this extraordinary story, which is almost a carbon copy of something that happened twenty-five years earlier in Egypt. Abraham lies about his wife and says, "She is my sister," which was half true and, like other half-true lies, more damaging than a full lie. He goes through exactly the same motions. Therefore, some clever scholars have tried to tell us that this story is simply a duplicate of the other, and has got misplaced in the Bible, which sounds like a very clever idea. I would just say to those scholars who say this kind of thing: you wait till you are an old man and see whether your early temptations come creeping back.

I have spoken to men in their later years, and they have sometimes confessed to me that temptations they thought they had left behind twenty years previously have a way of coming back in old age, and becoming a real battle. Abraham is now ninety-nine years of age, and he has not committed this sin for twenty-five years. The reason why he has not done so is very simple: he has not been in the same circumstances for twenty-five years. Just because we are in different circumstances and an old temptation no longer troubles us does not mean we are finished with it. You and I will not be safe from the devil until we are in our graves. "Let him who thinks he stands take heed, lest he fall." Now Abraham is nearer to Egypt than he has ever been before. He has gone to Gerar, which is on the way down to Egypt. Again, the same old fears come, he is afraid of being killed so that his wife will be taken. Now she is in her eighties and there is a slight problem here: that a king should want a lady in her eighties for his harem is outstanding and unusual, to say the least, and has raised many questions in people's minds.

Well, let me explain it. Sarah had discovered how to keep her beauty. The Bible tells us the secret. We are told that from the very beginning Sarah was a very beautiful woman. Alas, nowadays we confuse glamour with beauty. Glamour you cannot keep, no woman can keep it however much she tries. She will soon be described as mutton dressed up as lamb if she tries to keep glamour. But the Bible tells every woman that she can keep her beauty or can develop beauty. The Bible has quite a lot to say about this.

Funnily enough, the hint or clue comes from the only apostle who was married, as far as we know – Simon Peter. In one of his letters in the New Testament he talks of Sarah,

Rebecca and Rachel, and says of these wives that they kept their beauty not by using jewellery or elaborate hair-dos or fine clothes, but they kept it because they had a meek and gentle spirit, were submissive to their husbands and loved the Lord. There is the secret of beauty. And the person who said, "Every person over forty is responsible for their face" was uttering a profound truth. Sarah kept her beauty, so much that even though she was now in her later years a king saw her and felt that she would be a good companion. That is a remarkable tribute to this lovely lady.

Now, let us go back to Abraham. The real failure again was so simple: that he went by common sense instead of faith. He said, "There will be no fear of God in this place, so I can't take God into my thinking. I must scheme to protect myself in some other way," and when faith goes, fear comes. Faith and fear are incompatible – you are either afraid or you trust, but you can never do both. So faith went, fear came and lies followed, and one lie led to another and caused trouble to come to many people. What I want to declare first is this: no matter how long you have walked with the Lord, if the spirit gets weak, the flesh reasserts itself. If the new life in God is neglected, the old life outside of God will come back. The flesh and the spirit are both there until you die, and if the Spirit is not leading you, the flesh will. It is one or the other, and it can never be both. Let us learn this from Abraham.

Now let us look at this story through another pair of eyes. Let us look at it through Abimelech's eyes. I feel sorry for Abimelech; my sympathies go out to him. He seems a decent fellow, he seems a good, honest pagan, if you will forgive the expression. The Philistines later were to cause so much trouble to Israel, but this king seems a decent enough man. He presents us with the question, which I am often asked and which I often ask myself: "How is it that some really good pagans show up the people of God in their attitudes and behaviour?" Sometimes those who do not acknowledge God and do not acknowledge Christ behave in a generous and fair and good way, where the people of God do not. Abimelech presents this problem because, of the two people in this chapter, he stands head and shoulders above Abraham in the way he behaves.

Let us look at this problem: Abimelech is warned by God in a dream. God would have to speak to him that way because in a dream you are prepared to believe anything. This is why God often chooses dreams to speak to people, because when you are dreaming you don't stop and say, "Well, that can't be true, that can't happen." You believe in miracles in your dreams, you believe in anything. So, in a dream God speaks to this man and says: "Abimelech, you're a dead man if you keep this woman."

Now Abimelech straightaway says quite rightly, "Lord, I didn't know she was someone's wife. I'm innocent, the integrity of my heart, the innocence of my life, surely you won't punish the innocent." And God said, "No I won't because you haven't sinned yet, and I have stopped you sinning before you did," which tells me that God can control pagans, and he does. It is marvellous to have a God who can not only control his people but can control others who do not acknowledge him, and overrule circumstances and turn their minds and hearts and stop them doing and saying things that are wrong. It is wonderful when God does this.

But Abimelech was right and so God said, "Well, Abraham will pray for you if you ask him." Now the thing that startles me in this chapter is this: God is still the God of Abraham and not of Abimelech. However good and honest and upright this pagan is, God is the God of Abraham because he is the believer. Even though morally Abraham is below Abimelech in this instance, God still says that it is Abraham's prayers he listens to. This is something we must grasp and understand if we are going to understand God's ways with people. Once we have become believers and once we are righteous in God's sight, it is our prayers that God listens to. He ties himself to believers even though they fall, rather than to the good, honest pagan.

This is because he is a God of grace and because no pagan and nobody can be good enough for God. Once he has set his seal on a believer he stands by that believer, even when the believer falls. He says to Abimelech: "He may have lied to you, but he is my prophet and he speaks for me. He may have deceived you, but he can still pray for you." He is saying, "Abimelech, even though he has done this bad thing, he is still my prophet and therefore you must ask him to pray for you."

Now you can say what you like about the morals of that, but this is the principle on which God has worked all through history. Once he chose the Jews he stuck by them, even when they failed to stand by him. Once he chooses Christians he stands by them, even though they fail him. It is still their prayers that are going to help the honest pagan. So, Abimelech accepts this, good man that he is. He asks Abraham to pray, he gives Abraham gifts and he says, "Let's straighten the whole thing out." I am quite sure that Abraham was even more embarrassed to be asked for his prayer than he was to be discovered in the lie. Can you imagine? A believer having lied to a pagan and the pagan coming and saying, "Would you please pray for me?" The humiliation of it would cure Abraham on the spot. Now let us look at this through another pair of eyes. Let us look at this through Sarah's eyes.

She had been told to lie and she did lie. But she had been told to lie by her husband, who was her authority and her leader. Therefore, not only had he made her lie, he said, "This is what you must say." But also, he had played upon her feelings and motives by saying, "This is the kindness you must do to me." Playing on her feminine compassion he had caused her to lie to cover himself and to save himself. It was a despicable thing to have done. But he did it and it has been done before and since.

Abimelech was concerned with this woman's reputation. So he publicly vindicated her and declared her to be innocent in the sight of all. He said, "It is your vindication in the eyes of all who are with you and before everyone, you are righted." In other words, let it be known that you lied because this man had a hold over you, and he was making you protect him by appealing wrongly to your motives. That is the vindication of Sarah. I still have not finished with this chapter. There are others from whose perspective I want to look at the story.

I have looked at it through Abraham's eyes and, incidentally, he arranged this lie with Sarah before he left Ur of the Chaldees. This was something that came from his distant past, popping up again after many years. I have looked at it through the eyes of Abimelech, that good pagan whom God restrained. I have looked at it through the eyes of Sarah, who was at last vindicated in the sight of all. Let me now look at it through the eyes of another being who is not mentioned in the chapter, but who was responsible for it: Satan.

Why do I say he was responsible for it? For two reasons: this evil being Satan was gloating over this, first because Satan loves to see a saint of God fall after many years of walking with the Lord. Because in a moment he can undo so much, that is why we must never, never lower our guard however old we are in the faith, however experienced we are. Again, one has known time and time again of men and women who have walked with the Lord for many years and then Satan has made them fall. It has undone so much of the good that they had done. But there is something more. Satan was gloating over Abraham falling, but he was also gloating over the fact that he had got Sarah into a pagan king's harem. Why should he gloat over that? For the simple reason that this is just at the very time when God said, "Next spring I will visit you and you will have a son." That son Isaac was to be the chosen line going down through two thousand years until Jesus was born, and Satan did not want Jesus born and he would do anything to stop that line going on. Satan knew perfectly well that in a king's harem Sarah could not have a child – she was too old. Satan tried to stop the chosen line of David, the chosen line of Jesus, getting any further than Sarah. He was foiled, but can you see why he did this at this stage after twenty-five years? He got Abraham and Sarah away from each other because God had said, "I'm going to bring you together, and you will conceive and have a son."

Now let us look at it through God's eyes. He is mentioned more than any other person. The impression I get from this chapter is that it does not matter what men do, it does not even matter what Satan does – if God has said he will do something, he will do it. His power is such that you cannot thwart or frustrate his will and God had said, "Sarah, you're going to have a baby boy." So, God saw that that purpose was fulfilled. He did it by rendering infertile all the women in that palace, which stopped effectively any procreation at that time.

Now this may seem a strange thing to do, but let us say straight away, it is not too hard for the Lord to do this, given that people in the twentieth century were able to discover pills that do this. Almighty God can also do this, maybe even in the same physical way, by adjusting the hormones. Whatever method he used, God rendered them infertile for that period, and he effectively stopped what was going on in that king's palace.

This is God's power, and it is against the backcloth of rendering those women infertile that the miracle of rendering Sarah fertile is seen in its true perspective. It is against the word "barren" that the word "conceived" becomes a miracle. Sarah was barren, Rebecca was barren, Rachel was barren, Hannah was barren, Elizabeth was barren yet John the Baptist was born. All this leads right through the ages to that wonderful moment when the Virgin Mary conceived. It is God's power both to destroy and create, to prevent life and to give it, to render infertile and to make fertile.

Therefore, this chapter 20 and its last verse ("For the Lord had closed all the wombs of the house of Abimelech because of Sarah") highlights the next verse in the next chapter, which tells us that he visited Sarah as he had said. We now turn to this lovely story.

I want to take one little phrase from the New Testament: "In the fullness of time". God is never in a hurry, God can wait twenty-five years in a person's life before doing for them what he said. The trouble is, we are desperately in a hurry. Around Christmas, for instance we hear that there are so many shopping days till Christmas, and we tear around like ants in an ant heap at that moment. At such times the main high street provides a stark contrast with the quiet, waiting of God when the fullness of time had come. He had waited twenty-five years for Isaac to be born. God was and is in no hurry.

Philip Brooks, a great preacher, once said, "The trouble is that I'm in a hurry and God isn't." That is a very profound remark, and I am sure you will have found it to be true. In the first verse I love the phrase, "The Lord visited Sarah as he had said, and the Lord did to Sarah as he had promised." You will find people who let you down. You will meet people who promise one thing and fail to keep that promise, but you will never be able to say that about God. He said, "I promise you Sarah," and he did it – the utter reliability of God's Word.

Why do you think I preach from the Bible and no other book? There are plenty of other helpful books to read. Why do I stick to this book? Because it is the only book you can absolutely rely on – it contains the promises of God. If he says a thing, it will happen. Therefore, my defence is the truth, and this enables me to preach confidently because I am absolutely convinced that everything God says he will do he will do. This is the case even with specific details. For instance, he said, "I will visit you next spring," and he came next spring. Furthermore, he said it will be a boy and only in the last few years have human beings discovered a way of telling the sex before a baby is born, and then only for a few months before they are born, and certainly not before they are conceived, yet God says, "You're going to have a boy." So, this prediction came true. It was of course a miracle, as much a miracle as the infertility had been in the household of Abimelech.

Now the name of this boy, which God had given took on a new meaning. He had been called Laughter, Joke. Just as we call girls Joy, hoping that they will be happy little girls. He was called Laughter because Sarah and Abraham had said to God, "You must be joking," when God had said they were going to have a son in their old age. But now they have got a different kind of laughter: Sarah is bubbling over. You go into a maternity ward in any hospital and look at the face of a mother who has just delivered a child. Laughter – this is a different kind of laughter. It is not joking at impossibilities, it is laughing for sheer joy.

There are plenty of people making jokes about religion these days. It has become fashionable, and that is one kind of laughter. I would rather have the laughter of sheer joy – the laughter of knowing it is true, the laughter of knowing that heaven does exist, the laughter of seeing it – that is the laughter that is pure, holy and wholesome as opposed to the cheap jesting and jokes about things that God has promised to fulfil. Isaac became Laughter.

As we read this passage we can't help thinking about Christmas, can we? Here is a boy child promised years before he was born, born miraculously because humanly speaking he could never have come, and we think of another child. This amazing parallel between Isaac and Jesus will be continued. We will come to one of the loveliest chapters in Genesis, the offering of Isaac – the only begotten and only beloved son of the father carrying the wood, which was to be the means of his own execution up the hill. Can't you see this? This is what we mean when we say Isaac is a *type* of Jesus. We mean that if you look at Isaac you can see Jesus – if you look at him, the way he was born, if you look at the sacrifice that he nearly became, you can see Jesus foreshadowed, pictured, in a life centuries before Jesus came. We will return to that thrilling and lovely theme.

Let me now come to the last part of this chapter's study. Alas, I have got to come down into the valley again from the mountaintop. The birth of this boy brought conflict, disturbance and danger to this little family. He was an unmixed delight to his parents. They laughed over him; they played with this little boy, and for three years all seemed to be going well. But there was already another boy in the household and that boy was jealous of the new baby. This is not unknown. The other boy was now in his early teens, and as he saw this baby supplanting him, becoming the favourite of Abraham, he began to hate this boy. When the baby was three and weaned, Abraham held a great feast, a third birthday and Sarah saw a horrible thing.

It says here that she saw the son of Hagar the Egyptian playing with her son Isaac. Other versions of the Bible use the word "mocking". The New Testament uses the word "persecuting". Actually, the word in the Hebrew is "Isaacing". She saw Ishmael "Isaac-ing" her son Isaac. You will remember what "Isaac" means. It can mean holy laughter or it can mean mockery. It can mean malicious jesting, it can mean teasing or it can mean persecuting. When she looked over she saw the elder son, this teenage boy, mocking Isaac, pushing him around. She realised that there was danger in the family circle and that this child of the slave woman could easily kill her boy.

Like any mother anxious to protect her baby, she went straight to her husband and she said, "We must get rid of that slave girl and her boy, quickly." Abraham, as a father in those circumstances, the actual father of the slave girl's boy, was unhappy about it and did not know what to do. He rightly asked God about it, and God said that the time had come for the two boys to live separately. He was grown up now – you must let him go away with his mother. So, the woman and the boy went away. We know how God looked after them in the wilderness. They went down to Egypt, her home. He got a wife there, he became a hunter and God looked after that boy and his need of water in the wilderness.

I want to finish like this—these two boys, Ishmael and Isaac, represent the deepest division of the human race. There is a fundamental gulf or rift between them, which gets wider and wider and deeper until the biggest difference in the human race is between the Ishmaels and the Isaacs. They are the same two groups as our Lord calls the sheep and the goats in the Day of Judgment. These two boys represent two entirely different kinds of people, and there is a line going right through congregations, right through towns, right through countries, dividing everybody into Ishmaels or Isaacs. Let me explain.

What is the division between these two boys? It is, of course, the division between Israeli and Arab, and that is a bad enough division. But that is not the deepest gulf in the human race. There is the difference between Jew and Gentile, but that is not the deepest division within the human race. It is basically the division between those who are born of the flesh and those who are born of the Spirit. There is no deeper division than that—it cuts the human race right into two. Everybody is either an Ishmael, born of the flesh, or an Isaac, born of the Spirit. Furthermore, we can take this into the realm of religion, because, in fact, the New Testament does.

This is illustrated in one short passage from the New Testament, this time from Paul's writings. It is written that Abraham had two sons, one from his slave wife and one from his freeborn wife. There was nothing unusual about the birth of the slave wife's baby, but the baby of the freeborn wife was born only after God had especially promised he would come. Now this true story is an illustration of God's two ways of helping people. One way was by giving them his laws to obey. He did this on Mount Sinai when he gave the Ten Commandments to Moses.

Mount Sinai, by the way, is called Mount Hagar by the Arabs, and in my illustration Abraham's slave wife, Hagar, represents Jerusalem, the mother city of the Jews, the centre of that system of trying to please God by trying to obey the commandments. The Jews who follow that system are her slave children. But our mother city is the heavenly Jerusalem, and she is not a slave to Jewish laws. That is what Isaiah meant when he prophesied, "Now you can rejoice, O childless woman, you can shout with joy, though you never before had a child. For I am going to give you many children, more children than the slave wife has."

You and I, dear brothers, are among the children that God promised, just as Isaac was. So, we who are born of the Holy Spirit are persecuted now by those who want us to keep the Jewish laws just as Isaac, the child of promise, was persecuted by Ishmael, the slave wife's son. But the scriptures say that God told Abraham to send away the slave wife and her son, for the slave wife's son could not inherit Abraham's home and lands along with the free woman's son. Dear brothers, we are not slave children obligated to the Jewish laws, but children of the free woman, acceptable to God because of faith.

Let me put it in simple language: all the Ishmaels of this world who are here because they have been born of the flesh will try to inherit the kingdom of God by keeping God's laws, by trying to be good, by trying to be kind, by trying to be helpful, and they will all fail because such a way is slavery. All those who are Isaacs, who have been born again of the Spirit, will inherit because of faith and are free even from the law in the sight of God—that is the difference. So, you see, we are reading about ourselves when we read the story of Ishmael and Isaac.

Everyone in a church is either an Isaac, a son of Abraham by faith, free in our religion from the law, or we are an Ishmael, a child of the flesh, just trying to do good to get to heaven—you cannot be both. I will summarise this passage; in the story of Abimelech, we saw how in Abraham flesh dominated his spirit. In the story of the birth of Isaac, we saw how the spirit dominated the flesh in Sarah. In the story of Ishmael we see that flesh and Spirit cannot go on living together in the same house, any more than they can go on living together in your heart. It must be one or the other. You either live the life of Ishmael or you live the life of Isaac. As Jesus said to Nicodemus, "That which is born of the flesh is flesh, and that which is born of the Spirit is Spirit."

READ GENESIS 22

Outside the Jaffa Gate on the west side of the city of
Jerusalem and just down the hill a little, at the head of the
Valley of Hinnom, or Gehenna, there has been built a little
colony of artists' shops and studios. Three of us were walking
down this little arcade many years ago and we went into a
shop right at the bottom because in the window there was
the most beautiful photograph. It showed the wilderness
of Sinai and superimposed on the wilderness was clearly a
photograph of a sculpture of Moses with his hands uplifted
in prayer, supported on either side by Aaron and Hur – it
was a lovely photograph.

I barged into the shop and asked the little man there,
"Where could I get a copy of that photograph? That's a
wonderful photomontage." I was looking into the face of a
little man in a little chair—the face was that of Solzhenitsyn,
almost exactly, if you can imagine it. Clearly, he was a cripple
for there were two crutches behind him, and he was seated
at a little workbench. At first, he would hardly talk, and so
one looked around and noticed that behind him were some
of the most exquisite little silver sculptures with figures,
maybe an inch and a quarter high, of Old Testament scenes.

Then one noticed that the bench at which he sat was
covered with tiny fragments of silver and a little blowlamp
and a magnifying glass some six inches across, suspended
on a kind of angle-poise stand. Then after a bit he looked
up and said, "Tell me the story of the photograph in the

window." So I told him the story. "Yes," he said, "that's right." He said, "You know, as long as Moses' hands were in the air we were winning, but as soon as they went down we were losing," and he described it as if he had been present: "we", not "they".

Then for about twenty minutes he put me through a Bible examination, and I got the first question wrong. He said, "Do you love the Bible?" I said, "We wouldn't be here if we didn't." He said, "I don't like talking to tourists, I don't like having any dealings with tourists," and we knew that because shortly afterwards some American tourists came into the shop and he just closed like a clam; he just wouldn't talk. But he put me through it.

The first question he asked me was this: "How old was Isaac when Abraham offered him on Mount Moriah?" I was very annoyed because I had the right answer in my notes at home and I had forgotten. I have since looked up my notes and I had it right, but I said at the time, "About twelve." Shall I tell you the answer? He was in his thirties. You check up your Bible. So he put me through my paces for twenty minutes.

Then he said, "Do you like my works?" We began to look at them and there was one that really caught my eye. There were maybe forty or fifty most beautiful pieces of work. I said, "Yes, but I love that one most of all. Dare I ask how much it is?" He replied, "You're in too much of a hurry." So I humbled myself again and waited. He said, "Watch how I make them." Then he began to work with little pieces of silver.

I noticed then that one hand was not very free and, in fact, he put a strap around his hand and moved it with his body. He said, "I'm an ugly little man." He said, "I lost this leg in the 1967 War. My shoulder has three bullets in it from the Yom Kippur War. I was a geologist travelling around this land, now I have to sit here. So I've had to teach myself a new trade. I tried painting; I taught myself painting. Then I taught myself woodcarving." But he said, "As soon as I began to work with silver I knew I'd found what I could do. So, I sit here making little silver things. Now watch me."

I watched him with his face now and again grimacing with pain as he moved that arm to create the little silver things. So we talked on. He kept plying me with questions or closing up when a tourist came in, and then, perhaps after fifty minutes, he asked, "Which one are you really interested in?" I said, "The one of Abraham and Isaac. The piece of rock on which they stand, is that from Mount Moriah?"

He answered, "I am an artist, where else?" He had another one of Moses before Pharaoh on a little block of marble, which he had obtained from an Italian firm which had imported it from Egypt especially for him so that it was real. I looked at that and here was a little figure of Abraham with a knife upraised, a full-grown man Isaac lying on the rock, and away up an angel with arms outstretched saying, "Stop! Stop!"

Something else excited me as I looked at the block of stone from Mount Moriah—he had put Isaac on the second highest peak. The highest peak is Golgotha, Calvary, and he had left the highest peak empty. When you face the sculpture, you see on the left-hand side the highest peak, where there is a cave below the rock. I just fell in love with that. So I said, "Well, I don't think I have the courage, but dare I ask how much you would let that go for?" He named a figure and I said, "Well, thank you so much for letting me look at it," and I turned to go. Then a strange expression crossed his face.

He told us later that in fact it caused him great pain when someone couldn't afford one of his works. So he looked again and he came down to way below half the price. Then he spent, I suppose, twenty or twenty-five minutes wrapping it up – lovingly, carefully, putting it in a box with little tissue paper, and there was pain as he put it away. Then he handed it to me and said, "Remember, that is not yours; it is always mine." Abraham and Isaac in the mountain of the Lord – "it shall be provided".

To talk about this event concerning Abraham and Isaac we have got to go four thousand years back in history so that it seems like yesterday. We have got to go to approximately 2,000 BC for this event which occurred as long before Christ as we live after Christ. We have got to go to the southernmost border of the Promised Land. I recall looking over the rolling barley field south of the Judean hills to the town of Beersheba with its seven wells, and the story began there. It began when life was good for Abraham.

There, in Beersheba, Abraham had much to praise God for. Twenty-five years of God's blessing. He had got the son he wanted, the promise of the future. He was getting on well with his neighbours; he had come to an agreement with Abimelech. Everything was fine and you would have thought that now, surely, God would leave him to enjoy the fruits of his faith in his old age. It was the time for settling down, the time for enjoying life; the time for retirement. God took Abraham at that point for the biggest test of his whole life, the biggest proof of his faith there had ever been.

This chapter represents the very peak of Abraham's career, the very climax of his life, indeed of the book of Genesis. Immediately afterwards, the story of Abraham trails off and disappears like a river in the desert. This is the watershed and everything was building up to this supreme test. Altogether, Abraham was given fourteen promises by God, and the last one was given in this story. No man ever received so many promises from God as Abraham and no god ever kept them like Yahweh. So that was the scene and it is intriguing that the chapter begins after these things.

After all the blessings, the trials, the experiences, after he had got settled in a lovely place where there was plenty of water, where he was at peace with his neighbours, then Abraham was called to do something. I want you to get very clearly the difference between testing and tempting; this is vital. God tests his saints; he never tempts them. The New Testament gives you the Word of God that God tempts no man – but he does *test* you. The difference between a test and a temptation is this: when you are tested it is to bring out the good in you, but when you are tempted it is to bring out the bad in you. The one who tests you is trying to get you to succeed; one who tempts you is trying to get you to fail. God never tempted Abraham but he did test him, and God will never tempt you. He may abandon you to be tempted—that is the meaning of the phrase "Lead us not into temptation", but it does not say "Don't tempt us" because God never tempts us. He leaves that to others and sometimes he leaves us to those others to teach us a lesson. But he never tempts us himself; he tests us to prove us, to refine us, to make us better, to help us to succeed, to make us stronger than we were before.

So after these things God tested Abraham – and what a test. "Abraham, Abraham" – twice by name. God usually calls you twice just to make sure you get the message. "Samuel, Samuel." "Saul, Saul." "Abraham, Abraham." "Here am I" is the response of a servant who is ready for anything. But when you say to the Lord, "Here am I," you just don't know what he is going to say next. It is a most dangerous phrase to use.

"Abraham, Abraham." "Here am I." "Isaiah, Isaiah." "Here am I, send me." "Go and tell this people." "Here am I." "What are your orders?" In others words, "At your service" – that is the meaning of "Here am I." Now comes the test of Abraham's faith, his hope and his love, and these are the three greatest things you can possess. Everything else you leave behind. Even the gifts of the Spirit you will leave behind when you go to glory but there are three things that abide, that will go on, that will dwell with you where you go. You can take them with you; you can pack these in your bags now and know that they can be sent as luggage in advance: faith, hope, love.

First of all, God was going to test Abraham's faith. The proof that you trust a person is that you do what they tell you. The proof that you trust is that you obey. Trust and obey – those are the two sides of faith. If you really trust someone you will do something that seems incredible, that seems against all common sense, that seems to cut right across your natural desires. If you really trust someone you will do it, and Abraham's faith was going to be tested.

Notice that his obedience was immediate: he rose up early in the morning. Notice that his obedience was unquestioning, though it was an incredible thing he was asked to do. Notice that his obedience was practical: he got wood and an ass and he got ready. Notice that his obedience was sustained: after three days he was still keeping it up and seeing it right through. Notice that his obedience was complete: he was to offer Isaac up as a burnt offering, and that was the one offering that had to be offered entirely to God. A wave offering or a meal offering was shared with the worshipper, but in the case of a burnt offering every bit of it had to go— that was obedience and he came through with flying colours.

It is no wonder that everywhere in the New Testament, Abraham is upheld as the perfect example of a man who trusted God so much that he would do anything he was told— that was his faith. The second thing that was tested was his hope, and Abraham's hope for the future was centred not in his bank balance, not in his business, but in his boy. Apart from that boy he had no hope. I have often wondered why the long genealogies are in scripture but every time I study one I find out why. In Genesis 11 there is a long genealogy and I know it describes the chosen line, but there is a deeper reason for it than that. Have you noticed that it goes "begat, begat, begat"? All this begetting was going on all the time and suddenly Sarah was barren and all the begetting changes to barren and it looks as if the whole thing has stopped. Abraham's greatest disappointment was that his wife had no son. This meant that there was no hope for the future; the line would die out with Abraham. So, they had ancestry but no progeny and it was at that point that God stepped in and gave him a son.

Now I know that Sarah thought she had better ideas than God and she persuaded Abraham to have a son by the slave girl and Ishmael was born. It is a tragedy that ever happened, in a sense. Though Abraham was fond of Ishmael, Ishmael had to go, and the whole political situation in the Middle East between Arab and Israeli goes back to those two boys – for the Arabs are descended from Ishmael and the Jews are descended from Isaac.

During one of my early visits to the Holy Land there was trouble . Twenty minutes after we went through Hebron we sensed the tension and knew that something was going to happen. Twenty minutes after we left it was closed down to tourists and nobody else was allowed in that day. We missed trouble after trouble. We were out of Jerusalem the day that there were killings in David's street, just around the corner from our hospice. We heard the wailing at night. All those troubles. Once we drove a bus through the minefields on the Golan Heights down a road and we found ourselves among the tank traps and the minefields on the Golan Heights. Why this deadly enmity? They are cousins. It goes back to this; it has lasted four thousand years. So, Abraham's hopes were centred on one boy: Isaac. However, God challenged that hope: "Where does your hope lie – in God or in Isaac? Are you willing to let that hope go?" That was a sore test – he had only got one boy and he didn't expect any more, not from Sarah. What a test of his hope.

Now Abraham went through with it because his hope was in God, not in Isaac. Because he hoped. Remember that in the Bible the word "hope" means not to wish but to be absolutely certain. His hope was this: just as Isaac had been born supernaturally late in his mother's life, long past the childbearing age of a woman, so Abraham hoped in God – that God would give Isaac back supernaturally. He believed in the resurrection, and that is why he said to the two young men when they left them, "I and the lad are going further, we will both come back to you."

He expressed his hope in God by saying, "We'll both come back." He was not trying to fool them; he was not disguising from Isaac and the young men what he was going to do. He hoped in God and that hope was an anchor to his soul within the veil. Even if he killed his son Isaac, Abraham believed in the resurrection and you can find all that in Hebrews 11 where it is perfectly described, "We will come back to you."

Abraham's faith was tested and he passed top of the class; his hope was tested and he came out A1. But what about his love? You see, he had been fond of Ishmael but he loved Isaac as a father loves an only son. Notice the three tests: the test to his faith was, "Sacrifice your son"; the test to his hope was, "Sacrifice your only son"; the sacrifice to his love was, "Sacrifice your son, your only son, whom you love." I want you to pause for a moment and ask yourself what your most precious possession in life is, whether it is a thing or a person or whatever. What is your most precious treasure? Then that is how Abraham felt about Isaac. God implicitly asks, "Would you be willing to give that up?"

You see, the problem is that we come to love the gifts

more than the Giver; we come to love the creatures and the creation more than the Creator, and that is idolatry. You don't know whether God is first in your life until he puts his finger on that which you love the most. "Hear O Israel, the Lord our God, the Lord is one. You shall have no other gods besides me." In other words, God will have only one place in your life and that is first place. If you feel that God is not in your life, one of the first questions you can ask is this: has he slipped to second place in my personal charts?

Do you know why I think God loved Abraham for this? I will tell you why—because God saw his own image in Abraham. That is why God made man: that he might reflect the divine image. God waited so long to see this; it was lost when Adam took that fruit from Eve, but when God looked at Abraham, God saw his own reflection. He saw a father and God is a Father. He saw a father with an only son, and God is a Father with an only Son. He saw a father prepared to sacrifice his only son, and God is a Father prepared to sacrifice his only Son.

God tests your faith too. Which brings me to the second part of this study. So far, we have considered the obedience of Abraham, and we will now consider the offering of Isaac. From now on we turn our thoughts away from the father to the son, and we see in the son a kind of picture. Some scholars call it a "type". I am not terribly struck by that word. In its original meaning it meant a "model" or "foreshadowing" – something that was not the real thing but was like the real thing. Certainly, when we look at Isaac we see a type, we see a model, we see a foreshadowing; we cannot help but see it. When the father puts the wood on Isaac's back, we see a picture of Jesus going out bearing his own cross to the place of execution. The picture becomes so clear that it does not take a clever preacher to point it out.

Some have seen in the three days of their journey from

Beersheba to Mount Moriah the three years of ministry during which Jesus walked with his Father through that same land. Maybe that is pushing it a bit, and I am not going to stress it, but one thing is certain: the narrative slows down as they get nearer and nearer to Mount Moriah. More and more details come in, and the four Gospels are the same. Rushing through the first two and a half years of the ministry of Jesus they begin to slow up, until finally they go through months, weeks, days, hours. Like an express train slowing to a halt at a station, the Gospels do it; this chapter does it. It seems as if the whole narrative slows down to that terrible point where they meet at the peak of Mount Moriah.

This is the only passage in the whole of the Old Testament that hints that God demands a human sacrifice. I read a commentator who said the following of this passage: "This passage proves that the God of the Jews disapproves of human sacrifice and does not want it." I tell you, the truth is exactly the opposite. This passage is the proof that the God of the Jews wants a human sacrifice. All it proves is that Isaac was not good enough, but it points to the need of God for a human sacrifice. After all, animals can never atone for human sin. Sinful human beings can never atone for sinful human beings, but God needs a human sacrifice.

Religions that have sacrificed sinful human beings are regarded with horror in the Old Testament. I have walked down into that Valley of Hinnom, and right down in that deep dark valley I thought of the days when they sacrificed babies to Molech, to the god of the skies, and God disapproved of that. Not because he does not demand human sacrifice, but because there was no human sacrifice adequate in the days of the Old Testament. Therefore, human lives would be wasted and animal lives were allowed to take their place.

There are three things to say at this point. First of all, Isaac was sacrificed on an altar. For three days they wandered through the hills of southern Judea until they came to a mount, a dome of rock, over which there is now another dome. They walked alone for the last part of the journey, father and son together, as Jesus in Gethsemane was left alone with his Father. I want you to notice that there is no place in this story for the mother. Sarah did not take any part, nor is there any place for Mary in the redemption which Jesus wrought for us. It was a transaction between father and son alone. It was the father who raised the knife; it was the father who had the fire, and fire and knife have always been symbols of death, judgment, execution.

It was the father who laid it on the son, it was the father who raised the knife. We need to understand that when Jesus died on a cross it was not first of all Pilate who put him there, or Annas and Caiphas, nor Herod or any of the others who took part in that, nor the soldiers who drove the nails in – it was the Father who put him on that cross. In this we sense, in Isaac's feelings at this point, just a hint of the strange dereliction that Jesus himself felt: feeling that his own Father had turned against him. Can you imagine Isaac's feelings, his meek submission to his father? Remember, he was in his thirties as Jesus was; remember that Abraham was an old man and that Isaac could have overcome him easily. Remember all that, and then you see him lying down allowing himself to be bound on that rock. Yes, Isaac is a lovely picture of Jesus.

There is, however, one difference, and that is an angel stopped it, but no angel stopped Calvary. That is the big difference and it is here that the parallel breaks down, and though Jesus cried, "Eloi, Eloi, Lama Sabachthani, My God, My God..." no angel put his hands out and said, "Stop, stop!" But an angel did with Isaac. Why? There are many things I have noted here. One is because God wanted Abraham not Isaac; God wanted a living heart not a dead one, and he knew he had got that. Another is that Isaac was not adequate as a sacrifice, as we shall see later. Another is that the test had been passed and now it could be stopped. So an angel stepped in.

I want you to notice that at this point in the story, just at this point, the word "God" changes to the word "LORD". We read, "The angel of the LORD". If you remember, Psalm 22 begins, "My God, My God," the situation of dereliction, but the relief came and the word changes to "LORD". Well, here it is happening again. "God" is changed to "LORD". The God who seems to demand becomes the Lord who saves. Now Isaac changes. You see, the parallel has not only broken down, it has been switched around. Now Isaac becomes a type, a foreshadowing, a model not of Christ but of the Christian — one whose life is saved by the sacrifice of another. The whole picture turns right around and there is more truth coming through now, and we must switch tracks, we must change our minds. We look at Isaac now not to see Jesus but to see ourselves. For when the angel said, "Stop," Abraham turned around and he saw a ram, not a lamb.

I wish the New Testament would be consistent in translation. When we say, "Lamb," we think of a little cuddly, woolly, white thing, that you see roaming the fields. That is not the word used in scripture, the word is always "ram". It must be a ram, grown, in its prime. Not a little cuddly lamb, but a strong ram with horns. Jesus at thirty-three was not a lamb, he was a ram. He was strong; he was in his prime. Abraham turned around and saw a ram, not a lamb, with its head caught in the thicket.

We saw thickets as we walked down from the Mount of Beatitudes through the fields to Capernaum. During that marvellous walk, we picked up about fifty different kinds of wild flower about a half mile walk from the Mount of Beatitudes down to the shore at Capernaum. But we also saw thistles; I brought one back with me, pressed. Those thistles in Palestine are the worst there are, and the thorns are the worst there are. Thorns so dangerous that we had to be careful not to be pricked; they are medically dangerous; they carry all kinds of things.

He turned around and he saw a ram with its head in thorns. The ram had its head caught in that. Can you imagine Isaac's relief when that ram was offered up instead of him? Again, if you have not seen in the cross that it was God the Father raising the knife against his Son Jesus, and again, if you have not seen in the cross a ram with its head caught in the thorns dying in your place, you have not seen the cross. You do not understand it. For we are now seeing the cross through something that happened two thousand years before. Its head was caught in the thicket, so it was offered up instead.

What was God saying? Do you notice by the way that Abraham had to turn around to see the ram? You always have to turn around to see the ram. "Turn around" is the same as the word "repent". You always have to repent to see the ram that can be offered in your place. You need to turn right around and face in a new direction, then you see the ram and you know that there is a substitute for yourself in death. What was God saying? God was saying, firstly: I don't want Isaac; he's not good enough. Secondly, he is saying, "I do need sacrifice." Thirdly, he is saying: "I will provide a sacrifice." Isn't it glorious? Whatever God requires from you, he will give to you. Think that through: he never asks for anything from you that he has not first given to you. Fourthly, he is saying: I will provide in this place – and the ram was there.

But there was more to the phrase than that. The phrase "Yahweh Jireh" means two things. It means either "The Lord sees" or "The Lord provides" or it means both. "In the Mount of the Lord it shall be seen, in the Mount of the Lord it shall be provided," says the book of Genesis. "To this day the mountain is called Yahweh Jireh for in this mountain the Lord's provision will be seen." We traced Mount Moriah up through the Muslim quarter of the city, out of the wall where you can clearly see the ridge, cut across the moat that has been artificially cut to the top of Mount Moriah, the place of the cranium, the place of the skull just by the bus station outside Jerusalem. It is all one mount. The temple is built on the lower peak and the top peak was empty until in the Mount of the Lord it was provided.

There is something even more wonderful. It does not say, "The Lord will himself provide," it says, "The Lord will provide himself a sacrifice." Isn't that interesting? The ram was not the fulfilment, the ram was only a partial fulfilment because it is the Lord who "will provide himself a sacrifice." For centuries, the Jews who called that mountain Jehovah Jireh missed that meaning and they still do. "The Lord will provide himself a sacrifice." Oh, the truth of Holy scripture leaves you breathless.

So, Isaac was restored, doubly precious now. Because Abraham had passed the test he was rewarded, not because he merited it but because God loves to reward obedience. God swore, and when God swears he really does swear. He made a promise and he made an oath. He made the last of fourteen promises. He repeated three that he had already made and added a fourth new one, and thus set his seal on all fourteen promises. But he not only made a promise, he made an oath.

Now whenever you swear you always swear by something that is more powerful than you are, of which you are afraid. You are saying to someone, "I swear by that so that you can trust my word because that greater power could strike me if I don't keep it." So, you swear by that which is greater than yourself, you swear by heaven, even by hell. When people want to swear so that others can trust their word, in a court of law they take the Bible in their hands and say, "I swear by Almighty God". In other words, "May God strike me dead if I don't tell the truth." Do you know who God swears by when he swears? He swears by himself, and God said, "By God I'll keep this promise to you. By myself I have sworn."

Blessing – I will bless you. Multiplying, I will multiply you. All the nations of the earth shall be blessed through you. Now those three had all been given before the last one, the fourteenth: your seed shall possess the gate of your enemies. That one is still waiting to be fulfilled, but God will keep it.

I have summed up these promises, this oath, this wonderful double promise of God in three headings: the kingdom, the power, and the glory. First of all, he says: I will give you a kingdom. Your descendants will be as many as the stars of the sky or the grains of sand of the seashore. It has been pointed out that in Abraham's day that seems a crazy statement because they could only see about six hundred stars with the naked eye on a normal night. With very clear perception they might have been able to see up to six thousand but that would be as many as they could see. Now, six thousand grains of sand is a handful and yet here is God saying to Abraham: I'll make them as many as the stars and the sand. Only God knew that both are numberless.

Now our radio telescopes have revealed that there are as many stars in the sky as grains of sand on the seashore. That has come true and is coming true, for there have been millions of physical descendants of this man Abraham – remember six million of them died in World War II. One of our most sobering experiences was to visit the museum of the Holocaust in silence. But there are billions of others who have become sons of Abraham by faith. One of them is writing this now. There are hundreds of millions of people in the world today who profess to believe in Jesus Christ.

Only God knows the exact number of those who mean it, but they are sons of Abraham if they do.

"The kingdom will be yours and the power. You will possess the gate of your enemies." Again, there have been two fulfilments. There is a spiritual fulfilment—the true sons of Abraham have the victory. "In all these things we are more than conquerors. I am persuaded that neither death nor life, nor angels nor principalities, nor powers, nor things present nor things to come, nor height nor depth, nor any other creature shall be able to separate us from the love of God which is in Christ Jesus." But I believe there is a physical victory yet to come. When we stood on the Hill of Megiddo and viewed the Vale of Esdraelon and knew we were standing on Armageddon, we knew we were looking at not only the cockpit of the Middle East, as far as the past goes, we were looking at the future too. We knew that the Lord, strong in battle, the Lord of hosts, will give his people victory.

"The kingdom, the power, and the glory, all the nations of the earth will be blessed through you." Do you know this is already true in a remarkable way? In every sphere of life in which man engages you will find Jews near the top of it, exerting an influence out of all proportion to their numbers. Whether it is art, music, science, philosophy or commerce— every one of us is benefiting now from this people out of all proportion to their numbers. I think of the late Arthur Rubenstein at eighty-nine having confessed his faith in Jesus as Messiah, nearly blind, playing with technical perfection. I also recall looking at the architecture of the synagogue in the children's kibbutz Yemin Orde, named after Orde Wingate, called the "friend of Israel".

I remember seeing an ironic, sarcastic sculpture of Einstein in bronze, a pedestal four feet high, and on the pedestal was the planet Earth about a foot in diameter with the continents in brass and the seas in bronze, and piled on top a heap of cogwheels and stretching up at forty-five degrees a lattice work girder about two feet long, and written on it $E=MC^2$, and on the top of the girder, two grasping, greedy hands encircling a little moon, and on top of the moon a brass replica of the stars and stripes—what a sarcastic sculpture! It just spoke of man's grasping that which he does not have, but the formula that made it possible came from a Jew: Einstein.

You do not know what you owe to this people. All nations have been blessed wonderfully. One of the reasons Hitler hated them was that three quarters of professors in Germany before World War II were Jewish, and over half the banking in Germany was in Jewish hands, the Rothschild family. Oh yes, we have already been blessed in physical ways but if their rejection brought blessing to us Gentiles, what will their acceptance mean? Can you imagine? God has a future for this people. Read Romans 9 – 11, it is written there so clearly. They were cut off so that we might be grafted into their roots.

Whenever I have travelled to Israel with a group, we have just wanted to share with Jews and we have invariably received lovely opportunities. We have been able to say, "Look, it's your scriptures we believe, it's your Messiah, your promises, your land, your everything. We owe it under God to you." "In you shall all the nations be blessed," and one day the glory of the nations will be brought into the New Jerusalem. On an early trip many decades ago, we saw the cultural mix in Israel, and saw how architecture and music, folklore from all over the world were gathering in Jerusalem, we looked forward to the day when they will bless others spiritually as they have blessed us in almost every other way.

The end of the chapter seems a bit of an anti-climax, doesn't it? They went back to Beersheba and Abraham got a letter from his brother, a few hundred miles away in what is now Syria, a place called Haran, northeast of Damascus.

The letter was just full of gossipy family news about babies born and marriages taking place. Is it an anti-climax? Oh no, because in that letter and the list of names of babies that had been born, up there in Haran is the name of a little girl, Rebekah. The beginning of the very next chapter says "Sarah died." We are now reading the family tree of our Lord Jesus, HaMashiach, *Yeshua HaMashiach*.

Abraham, after this supreme test was given in a gossipy family letter the news about some girls and boys being born up at Haran. He said, "Isaac, I'm going to get you a wife from up there. You'll marry one of your cousins." Rebekah, a very beautiful girl, was found and they married, and Jacob was born and named "Israel". When I turn to the New Testament, I find that almost every writer lifts up this man Abraham as an example of faith, and says that the true sons of Abraham are those who share his faith.

You can read in Matthew and Luke how John the Baptist came and he said, "Don't you call yourself sons of Abraham. God is able to make these stones into sons of Abraham." In John chapter 8 you can read about the time when Jesus came teaching and the Jews said to him, "We are sons of Abraham," and Jesus said: "You are nothing of the kind. Your father is the devil. Before Abraham was, I AM." They said, "You're not even fifty years old, how do you know Abraham?"

Before Abraham was, I AM. If you turn to the book of Acts you will find that Peter and Stephen both preach about Abraham.

Turn to Paul's letters and read Romans 4; it is a wonderful chapter, and it is all about Abraham. Turn to Galatians 3 and the same man is upheld. Turn to Hebrews and you will find him mentioned in chapters 6 and 11. Turn to the letter of James, and James, who was a practical man, said, "Do you want to know what faith is? Then I'll tell you: when

Abraham offered up Isaac, that was faith

So this man goes down in history as the father of those who believe. You are his son or you are his daughter if you share his faith. What was his faith? I tell you in a sentence: he trusted God sufficiently to entrust God with his most precious treasure—that was his faith. If you entrust God with your most precious treasure, even if for you it would mean losing that treasure for a time, then you are a child of Abraham.

READ GENESIS 23:1–24:27

We are very near the end of Abraham's story. Chapter 22 was the climax, and 23–25 finish off the story in a beautiful, quiet way. But Abraham, to the very last ditch, had to be a man of faith – had to believe in the future. There were two promises that God had made to him, as you may remember. One was to give him the land of Canaan forever. The other promise was to give him descendants, and Abraham really had not received either yet.

Take the promise about the land: he was living in it but he did not own a square inch. He was what is still called in Arabian countries a *gur*, which means a stranger, a sojourner – moving around, grazing his crops, but never owning it. We would call such people gypsies or travellers today. Just as the gypsies in England roam about in their caravans, owning no property, with no title deeds to any part of England, Abraham was a gypsy still. He was in the land which God had given to him and he didn't possess any of it.

The second promise was about descendants. He had one son, no grandsons, and the son though an adult, was not married. In chapters 23–24 we see the beginning of the practical fulfilment of the two promises. First of all, he comes to own a field with a cave and some trees. Second, he lives to see two grandsons. He died happy because he saw those two things. We come to chapter 23. He got these two things by losing Sarah and by finding Rebekah. In chapter 23 he lost Sarah; in chapter 24 he found Rebekah.

At the beginning of chapter 23 there is a simple statement: "Sarah died." That is a statement that you could write over every person's life sooner or later. The Bible is an honest book and it looks the facts squarely in the face. One of the facts that we must face very squarely today is that some day that will be said of us. You will hear: "John David Pawson died." And others will hear the same said about you. Funnily enough, this is a taboo subject today. However, it is only right and proper that we should address it.

Philip II of Macedon, the great king who founded the city of Philippi, had a slave who was paid, or ordered, to wake him up every morning, and after he had got him fully awake he was to say to him, "Philip, remember you must die." Every morning in life the great king awoke to the words, "Remember you must die. There will be a day when you won't wake up." A great philosopher used to sleep with a human skull by his bedside. Today that would be regarded as morbid; he would be sent to a psychiatrist. But he was a very sensible philosopher and he kept it there as a reminder.

We live in a society that is on the run from the fact of death. It cannot face it, because it does not like it and therefore, the word "died" is not even used when someone has died. Instead, we hear phrases like "passed away", "passed over", "passed on", to avoid the terrible word. But the Bible, being an honest book, says "Sarah died". It really did happen. It was not something to hide or run away from, it was the biggest fact of life. She had lived a long and useful life for 127 years, but she still died.

On the law of statistical averages during a decade, a fifth of a church's members will die and we should live with this fact. We should not run from it, we should not become morbid about it, we should not panic about it, but we should recognise that this is life, and in the midst of life we are in death.

Now I want to consider this death from three angles.
First of all, I want to look at Sarah, then I want to look at
Abraham, then I want to look at this man Ephron and his
part in the funeral arrangements. First of all, Sarah: 127 is a
wonderful age. I once said to a dear old lady, who was then
just into her nineties, "Now, for your hundredth birthday
I'll come see you, wherever I am." I have only made that
promise once. I have learned the hard way not to make rash
promises. But, several years later she sent a letter to me:
"I'm expecting you on November 7th," and I had to travel
three hundred miles to keep that promise to go and see her.
A couple of years after that I got a letter to say she had died
at 102 and she is now with the Lord in glory.

Looking back over Sarah's life in this wonderful book the
Bible, we get a picture of a very human woman—a woman
who was physically attractive until very late in life, but more
than that, a woman who had weaknesses and strengths. There
is an accurate picture here. Her weakness was that she was
a jealous woman, and because of this she had trouble with
that young girl Hagar who came to live in the house. We
know too that she was a woman who found it difficult to
believe God's promises, and found it easy to laugh about
them. But she was a good wife and a good mother. She was
faithful to Abraham; she went with him wherever he went;
she journeyed at a great age; she lived in a tent, she became
a gypsy for Abraham's sake.

She was a good mother—she had a real problem: she had
to adapt herself at the age of ninety to looking after a little
baby. I want to let that sink in. My parents as grandparents
just loved our children for two and a half days and then they
began to escape into another room. It is not easy when you
are elderly to cope with noisy little children running about,
but Sarah coped.

Abraham was a man of God, a man of faith, who believed

in the resurrection from the dead – how does he react? Traditionally in Britain it was considered the right behaviour to keep a stiff upper lip, to show no tears, not to mourn, not to wear black, not to show in any way that you were sorry, but to hide your grief – that was considered decent behaviour. However, there was a time before when that was not considered the way, and the detached approach does not align with the biblical position. We are told in the next sentence that Abraham went in to mourn and to weep. Here is a man of God, a man of faith, a man who believes that God can raise the dead, and he goes in to weep and we are told that he does so. The saints of God are not stoics; they are not tough, hard people who cannot shed a tear. The saints of God are real, human people and they naturally feel sorrow.

But let us go further. Do you know what the shortest verse in the Bible is? It is only two words: "Jesus wept." It refers to his reaction at the grave of Lazarus. So, he understands. But the next verse says that Abraham rose up and set about doing things. In other words, his grief was not overwhelming. He wept and got over it; he sorrowed and got on with it. This is the combination that you find in the saints of God – I have found it again and again.

A pastor whom I knew suffered bereavement with the death of his wife and on the following Sunday he was taking his morning service – that is a saint of God; that is what a man of God does. He was lost, he has wept, and now he has risen up to work. I had the great privilege of sharing with him the blessing that he had in a passing that was free from fear and that faced the future calmly and beautifully. His wife had known everything and prepared for everything, even choosing the hymns for her funeral that would take place the following Wednesday. This was like Abraham, and this is the saints of God through the ages. They weep, they sorrow, and then they get up, and they get on with whatever needs to be done. In Abraham's case, he had to act as his own undertaker. There was nobody to help him, nobody to do anything, he got up to do what needed to be done. This great man of God just got on with his work after he had mourned in sorrow for his beloved wife.

The third person who comes into the picture is Ephron. This lovely character is a pagan, a Hittite, but a man who respects Abraham deeply, and who feels for him in this moment. He wants to help him because Abraham literally has nowhere to bury his wife. Now, if you have ever been to the Holy Land you will know that there is no depth to the soil there; you can't bury a person downwards, you must find a cave, a sepulchre in the rock, and there are many caves in the limestone of the Holy Land.

Abraham rose up and went to the Hittites and said, "I don't live here; I don't belong here; I've no land here. Would you sell me a piece of land? Could you let me have a sepulchre?" Ephron said yes; in fact, they all said Abraham could use any of theirs, but do you notice they said it in such a way that it was clear they did not want him to buy it. They did not like the idea of this traveller buying a cave.

It is at this point, in the middle of Abraham making funeral arrangements, that God blessed him with his first piece of property in the Holy Land. Isn't it amazing how God fulfils his purpose? Abraham would never have guessed this. Never would he have thought that the funeral of his wife would bring the fulfilment of the promise. But he said to Ephron — and here we have a delightful picture of the courtesies of the Middle East and I can see Arabs saying all this as they bargain to buy and sell – "What is four hundred shekels between you and me?" That is the way of fixing the price. You say, "What is that between you and me?" It is all done with little hot drinks and tremendous courtesy, and you just hint at the price and you work around it like this. It is so true

297

to life. So Ephron finally sells the piece of land.

If you go to Hebron today you can enter a mosque and you can go down into a kind of crypt and look down through some openings in the floor. You can see below some catafalques, six of them: Abraham, Isaac, Jacob, and their three wives. I don't know if they are actually buried under there in the cave under that mosque, which has been a church, a mosque and I don't know what else in its time. But somewhere near that point, because Hebron is an authentic site, lie Abraham, Isaac, and Jacob.

Four thousand years have passed since then, but as I stood in Hebron and looked down at those catafalques I said, "They are not there, they are alive." God is not the God of the dead he is the God of the living. He is the God of Abraham, Isaac, and Jacob. They are not dead, and neither is any believer. They are alive as God is alive. So there they lay in Hebron.

The point I want to make is this: it was through death that Abraham first got a bit of the Promised Land. It was through what men would have said was the end of everything that he saw the beginning of everything, and it is the same with us. One of the things that the pastor's wife I mentioned earlier, talked with me about before her death was this. She said, "I want more of the Lord. Can you tell me how I can have more of him?" She has got more of him now in a way maybe she had not expected, just like this. But she got her prayer answered through death. I recall the hymn with the the following line: "When I tread the verge of Jordan, bid my anxious fears subside; death of death's and hell's destruction, land me safe on Canaan's side."

We now turn to Genesis 24:1–27. All the world loves a story and all the world loves a love story, and this is one of the most romantic love stories in the Bible. Not only will people die during this year, people will fall in love and get married, and have children. Life goes on, one generation goes, and the new one comes. The Bible moves on with generation after generation. All the time the message is this: "Lord, you have been our dwelling place in all generations." God is always the same; people come and go.

In spite of the fact that I said it is a romantic story, there is not one teenager who would like to find their wife this way! The idea that the father should set out to find a husband and say, "Here she is," or "Here he is" would be anathema to this generation. They would say, "What have you got to do with it?" Far from asking for hands in marriage nowadays they just say, "This is him," or "This is her." The pendulum has swung right from one extreme to the other. But let us look at this romantic story, even though it is an usual one. It led to a wonderful, successful marriage, which I would have thought is finally the main test because the proof of the pudding is in the eating. It is not how you found your wife or husband that matters, it is whether you got the right one that is important. So, look at this romance. Again, we will look at it from three points of view: Abraham's, the servant's, and, finally, Rebekah's.

Abraham is now old; physically his condition is declining, spiritually his condition is improving. It says, "He was advanced in years and the Lord blessed him in all things." Isn't that terrific? Here is a man who as he gets older has an increasing desire that the next generation will know his blessing. He is concerned that his children and grandchildren should have the kind of relationship with God he has had. Isn't it wonderful when old people have that concern for the young? In one church where I ministered there was a widow in her seventies who always dressed in black, and was not the sort of person that you would have thought young people would look at twice. Yet to her little room there used to go a steady stream of teenagers, one after the other. They were not doing it because they were trying to do her good and "look after the old fogies". They were doing it because she helped them, because she was concerned that they should know the blessing she had experienced, and because she wanted to guide them. It is wonderful when you meet that kind of bridge over the generation gap – an older person who is concerned to guide and to help younger people – and Abraham is similarly concerned that Isaac should find the right wife and that he should be blessed.

What part can parents play today? Well, don't try and play the matchmaker. But parents can play a great part. First of all, in being the kind of parents to whom children will come for a bit of advice. I can think of nothing more wonderful in a sense at the human level than the kind of parent-child relationship in which the child will come and say, "How do you like her?" "How do you like him?" But, secondly, I address this now to Christian parents: you can do everything you can to make sure that your children meet as many other Christian young people as possible. That is terribly important because it is tough on young Christians. Their field is far more limited, it is bound to be, and this is especially so for girls. Therefore, Christian parents can do a great deal to see that their children and teenagers have as wide a Christian social life as possible. That means something much wider than the local church. Sometimes somebody finds within the local church a life partner and every church has couples within it who came to meet because they sang together, or worked in the Sunday school together. Happy are you if you found your partner that way, but the chances of many young people finding their partner within the local fellowship are slim.

Abraham sent his servant out to look for someone a long way off. One of the things parents can do is to throw their home open and invite lots of young people in from all over the place and have them to stay. Parents can still, even in this age, do quite a lot. But Abraham was living in a day when it was not considered strange for the parents to do even more. After all, parents have been around more corners in life than their youngsters have, and they know better, having lived a married life, what kind of person makes a better partner, and Abraham sent his servant off to look for Isaac's wife.

First of all, he said, "It must be among the people that God has chosen," and this is one thing that one wants to write in gold letters up on a wall. If a church were purely for young people, I would put the text "marry in the Lord" up on the wall. Following that direction would avoid the heartache, tension and strain that is caused when one partner is a Christian and the other is not, when one belongs to the people God has chosen and the other does not.

It works out for a time, it certainly works out during the courtship because naturally they both come together to church. The Christian can be deceived that the other is interested in the church rather than in them. It may even work out for a short time during the early part of marriage, or it may not. Many wives have told me their husbands stopped going to church the first Sunday after they married. Usually the non-Christian partner will stop going when the baby comes and there is an excuse for one to stay at home.

"Don't take a wife for Isaac from the people of the land here." They would not understand what kind of a young man he was, what his background was, what his faith was, what his God is like. "You go and find someone from my people." This goes right through to the New Testament. Hard though it is to say it, it may well be better for a person not to marry and to know the blessing of God all their life than to marry someone who could not share it. I say that advisedly, realising all the difficulties, but if you are going to marry a child of the devil you will have problems with your father-in-law your whole married life.

Not only has it to be one of the right people, but it must be someone who is willing to live in the right place. Now here you have Isaac facing the future, having to live where God wants him to live, and he must have a wife who will not say, "Well, I'm not moving from my folks. I'm going to live in this place and you must just live with me." Isaac needs a wife, as every man of God needs a wife, who will say, "Where you go, I will go, and your God will be my God."

Next, the servant set off to find the right person who would be willing to go to the right place, if necessary to leave home, kindred, country, and go and live where God wanted. I think of missionaries and I think of missionaries' wives. When she marries him she has to be willing to go and live with him where God put him. That will be part of her willingness to be a wife of a man of God.

So the servant set off with Abraham saying: this is what he needs. At this point, may I just underline the seriousness of the oath he made him swear: he made the servant put his hand right between his legs, in his most private part, the organ of reproduction, from which Isaac had come, and said, "Now swear there that you will find the right wife for my son." It was a very solemn and binding and private oath, and off the servant went to fulfil it.

Now, let us look at the servant. What a lovely character: loyal, obedient, humble, full of faith, he set off to do what he had to do. Nowadays the very word "servant" has become like a swear word in our society. Who would like to be called someone's servant today? The very word is dropping out of our language because we don't like the idea that we are subservient to anybody else. We will work jolly hard for our own interests but to be someone's servant, to look after their business, their property, to look after everything for them and ask for no reward save the opportunity to serve, that is a rare quality today and here it is in this man.

He is not given a name in this chapter but I think it was Eliezer who is mentioned in chapter 15 where we are told that Eliezer, Abraham's servant, would have inherited all Abraham's property unless Abraham had a son. Can you imagine a man who was going to inherit all the property, continuing happily as a servant when the son was born and he knew he would not get it? Eliezer was the faithful, loyal servant, and he went on looking after the property of Abraham even though he was not now going to get it, and was going to see it go to another. I have met people like this in my lifetime, people who have served others faithfully, and what lovely characters they have. They have not had the property they might have had; they have not had the financial rewards. They have served and they have just quietly been a servant to someone else. Now let us look at what he did. We have a wonderful example here of a servant who knew how to get guidance. I think in my pastoral counselling I have discovered this: more people come to me to ask how to get guidance than any other question. Many problems come to a pastor, but this is number one. "How do I know God's guidance? How do I know God's will? How do I know what he wants me to do, where he wants me to go, what job he wants me to have, what person he wants me to marry, whether he wants me to marry at all?" Here is a man who knew how to get guidance. Let us see how he got it.

First of all, he prayed about it. He was a man of prayer. He went to God for his guidance, and he said, "Oh God, give me success, show me." But, secondly, he was a man who went looking for the guidance. Now, this is the right combination. Some people sit down and do nothing but pray for guidance and expect a telegram down the chimney or something. Other people don't pray at all and set off and try to manage their own lives. The right combination is to pray and then go looking.

In other words, ask, "God, show me your way," and then to get on and look at the possibilities, to explore this avenue of employment, that job, and that career, or whatever it may be. Not to sit at home by the fireside as some of our Victorian ladies were apparently supposed to do and pray for a man to come walking through the door, but to go out and mix and make plenty of friends and ask God to guide you as you go.

Surely this is the right combination: prayer and action; prayer and looking. These two go together in true guidance. The man who sat down and prayed for rain because his house was on fire had not understood that action must go with prayer as prayer must go with action. So, the servant prayed and then he went off looking and that is what we should do. If you want guidance about a job, pray and go looking. If you want guidance about partners or friendships, pray and go looking—that is what you should do.

That is a general prayer and he prayed for success but I want to underline that this man was seeking guidance for someone else. I can only say that every single case I have ever been asked about involved the person seeking guidance for themselves. This guidance came for someone else, and maybe we would get to know how God guides much more if we sought guidance for other people. If we said, "Lord, would you show me what will help them," then I think we would begin to get on God's wavelength. The trouble is we are so concerned about guidance because we want to know what we have got to do, what we are going to do, and what our future is. But this dear saint of God said, "God, I want to know Isaac's future. Will you guide me?" Unselfish motives through and through.

But then he asked for a particular sign. Now, we have got to be careful here – "putting out the fleece," we call it. People are always saying, "Well, Lord, if such and such a thing happens by next Thursday then I'll do such and such."

It is terribly easy to do this. One young man came to me and he said, "I told the Lord that if my young lady got in touch with me tomorrow that that would mean she was the right one for me, and she did." Now, of course, that young lady got in touch with him most days and he was giving a ninety to ten chance to God. It was not a fair sign at all; it was a loaded sign. The fleece was already three-quarters wet before he put it out. We have got to be very careful in laying out fleeces and telling God what signs we want.

The sign that this man asked for was not a miraculous, spectacular sign, it was not an arbitrary sign, it was a sign that would reveal the qualities that were needed in a good wife. Therefore, it was a sensible sign to ask for. The sign he asked for was that the woman he asked to give him a drink at the well would not only give him a drink, but would in outflowing kindness and courtesy, do something that she need not do even by the rules of normal decency, and water his camels too. In other words, he is saying in effect: "Lord, show me a girl who is kind, generous, helpful, and outgoing to strangers." That is the kind of sign to ask for if you are looking for a partner. In other words, use common sense and ask God for the kind of sign that will tell you what you need to know about yourself, about someone else, about the job, about the situation. It is asking God for a revelation that will help you to be more sure that this is right.

That is the second part of guidance. The general prayer is "Give me success and show me," and the particular guidance is "Here is the kind of thing I'm looking for, will you show whether this is in the situation or not?"

The other thing I want to say about the servant is that when he got the answer he did not forget to pray and say "Thank you." He worshipped the Lord, and in a most beautiful prayer of thanks he thought of God first, Abraham second, and himself last.

"Oh God, I worship you for doing this. Thank you for helping my master Abraham, and as for me, you led me." Is there anything more thrilling than being led by the Lord? Is there anything more exciting than having made a decision to know that it was God's decision not yours, that you are where God wants you to be, that you are living with the person God wanted you to live with. Isn't that exciting? So exciting, and so the servant came back to worship God.

Now what about Rebekah? She had everything: good looks, kindness, character — the lot. She had a beauty that was not just glamour and not just good looks because it lasted all her life, like Sarah. She had a beauty that was due to character, a beauty that came out. The world might not have called it glamour, although others took notice of her, but it was the beauty within. She was a girl in a thousand and she was not married. She was being kept for Isaac. It is much better to wait for Mr Right. Was she of Abraham's people? Yes, she was. Was she willing to come and be a wife to someone she had never met, never seen, believing that God had ordained it? Well, we go on with the next instalment of this romance.

We have looked at these two chapters. We have looked at death and a generation going to be with the Lord, and we have looked at love, marriage, and a new generation being born. As we move through the years, and the generations come and go, when we have all gone, if the Lord has not come first, there will be our children and our grandchildren. I pray that they will be worshipping the same God, marrying and having children, and serving the Lord faithfully to their dying day.

GENESIS 24:28–25 end

I want to show you the three levels, at least, at which you can read the Bible. Some people read it quite superficially. I came across a volume in a bookshop some time ago which said, "The Bible designed to be read as literature." Well, it wasn't designed by God for that purpose, but man did in that volume. Some people do read it as an interesting ancient book, and that is all. I would call this the level of human interest. It is a way of reading the Bible simply as a personal story of real lives.

The second level is to read it at the devotional level, which means to read it not just for human interest but for good examples, and to ask what lessons you may learn from the people who lived so long ago.

Thirdly, there is a deeper, theological level, and looking for divine patterns. Human interest, that's very shallow and you don't learn much by reading it that way. Good example, you will learn a lot that way. Divine pattern – you learn most that way.

Now look at this story. If you approach it purely from the human interest aspect there is really not a great deal to see on the surface. You have to read between the lines to get it. You have got to imagine things that are not told us. You've got to get the feelings. For example, look at Rebekah. Can you imagine her feelings, setting off? Supposing you are an unmarried young lady with good looks and character. You set off to Marks and Spencer's one morning, and you meet a man outside the shop who tells you he's been searching for you and come a very long way to find you to take you to be a wife to someone you have never met. I would imagine that your feelings would hardly be calm as you made your way back home afterwards and told your family about it.

Rebekah must have been terribly excited, disturbed, even frightened by the whole thing. She arrived home dripping with jewellery given to her by this strange man. In fact, if she had been properly brought up she might have been told never to accept such things. However, those were simpler, less sophisticated days when life was more straightforward. She appears as a girl of courage too, because she decided to accept this man's words at their face value and to go, and to marry an unknown man, because she believed she was led by the Lord. But it required courage to go into a strange land without anybody but her dear old nurse Deborah, who was to become a faithful family retainer for the next two generations.

Or look at Laban from the point of view of human interest. I get the message very clearly that Laban was impressed with that jewellery. Did you notice that, reading between the lines? Her father must have been dead, her brother is there. Laban sees all this jewellery, and it is obvious that this impresses him so deeply that he has no more reservations. In fact, he did fairly well out of it as we read later. Laban obviously had an eye to an opportunity, again reading between the lines.

Or take Isaac, the least interesting of the three patriarchs, Abraham, Isaac and Jacob. Isaac is a kind of colourless character. It is not so much what he does, as what is done to him that makes him interesting. He is a quiet man, meditating in the field. Have you got the picture? A typical child of elderly parents and I have noticed that when a child is born to parents who are too old to play with that child, the child tends to be a quiet and meditative kind of child. This is the human interest in Isaac, and I could spend a lot of time looking into that more deeply. But at this level of human interest there is really not much in the story for you.

And why should you be interested in people who lived four thousand years ago?

I am going to move on to the next deeper level of this story. You see, if you just read the Bible through and only look at the human interest, it is not a book that you would read again. After all, you have read it once and you know it, and you may have heard it in Sunday school. You probably won't read it again as an adult if that was all you saw then. But now think about reading it with a deeper point of view, the devotional level at which you look for a good example. In this story I find three things that stick out a mile about these three people: Laban, Rebekah and Isaac.

The first is this: they all three acknowledge the Lord. Quite freely in their conversation, without forcing it, without being pious, they talk about the Lord. Every one and a half inches in my Bible, the Lord is mentioned by one of these three. It is so natural — they just come together and say: the Lord did this; the Lord has blessed me; the Lord has led me. This is how God's people talk. They do it naturally, not saying, "It's about time I mentioned the Lord again. I've done at least one and a half inches of conversation and I ought to bring him in again." I just point that out because it is so regular. People just say "the Lord" as they might talk about Mrs Jones or Mr Smith, it is natural to them. "The Lord did this, and I did that...." He is acknowledged.

More than that, they all three submitted to the Lord's control. Instead of making their own decisions as to where they lived, who they married, all three of them not only acknowledged the Lord in their conversation, they submitted to him and allowed him to do with them what he wished. Perhaps the most marvellous example is Rebekah, deciding to go within twenty-four hours of meeting this strange man, deciding to go, because she said, "The Lord is in it, I must go." The third lesson is that they were all blessed by the

Lord because of this; the word "blessing" comes in again and again in this chapter. Did you notice it? The two key words are "Lord" and "blessed". The servant was blessed, Laban was blessed, Rebekah was blessed, Isaac was blessed. Now do you get the message?

When you read the Bible at this level, the message becomes absolutely clear. Acknowledge the Lord, allow him to control your life, and you will be blessed. But there are far too many people trying to get number three without numbers one and two, and you can't do it. I would rather go into the future, unknown as it is, knowing that God was going to bless it than anything else in the world. Wouldn't you? But you cannot know that unless you have numbers one and two in your life. How can God bless a person if they do not now acknowledge him and do not let him make the decisions? How can God bless a person who never mentions him, never talks about him, never thinks about him and decides their own career, their own home, their own marriage, everything themselves? How can he bless? Here is the message.

We get much more out of the Bible by reading it at the deeper level, but now let me go to a deeper level still. We look into this story not only for human interest, which doesn't really yield a great deal. We look into it for good example, which tells us a great deal. We look into it for divine patterns. What do I mean by that? I mean that when God operates, he operates in a certain pattern. Once you have got the pattern you can learn things at a very deep level. We have already seen that Isaac is a pattern of Jesus. The Bible would say he is a "type" of Jesus, a pattern. When we saw the beloved son of Abraham carrying the wood which was to be the means of his own death up the very hill, which we later knew as Calvary, we see a pattern in Isaac – of Jesus. At that level, when we read the story of the offering of Isaac, we saw the cross. We saw the pattern of a beloved father ready to give a beloved son in death as a sacrifice, and we saw the pattern which God operated on when he sent Jesus. Now I want to carry that further. If in Isaac you see the divine pattern of Jesus, in Rebekah you can see the divine pattern of the Church, because just as Rebekah was brought to be the bride for Isaac, the Church is to be the holy Bride for Jesus.

Now if we follow through this divine pattern, we are going to learn tremendous things from this chapter. We see a father, Abraham, who gives us a pattern of God, sending someone to find a bride – in whom we see the pattern of the Church – for his son Isaac, in whom we see the pattern of Jesus. We ask, therefore, of whom is the servant the pattern? The answer is two-fold. First, the Holy Spirit. It is the Holy Spirit himself who has come into the world to capture a Bride for Christ, and without the Holy Spirit Christ would have no Bride at all. There would be no Church. But that is not the end of the pattern, for the Holy Spirit chooses, since he has no body of his own, to inhabit our bodies, which become his temple.

Therefore, secondly, every Christian reading my words here is the servant Eleazar – sent by God the Father out into the world to find a Bride for Jesus, the Son. When young people from the church that I used to pastor went out at night into the pubs, coffee bars and youth clubs of Guildford looking for people for Christ, they were fulfilling the divine pattern of Eleazar in Genesis 24. They were seeking a Bride for the Saviour – that is the whole point of evangelism. As soon as you see this, then this chapter becomes your evangelistic handbook for your task in this twenty-first century.

First of all I point out, for example, that you must not just sit and pray. You have got to go and look. This is a very simple lesson, which we fail to learn because so often our evangelism says, "Come to our meetings, come to our services, come to our church," but Abraham said to Eleazer, "You go and look." Pray, yes, but go too.

The second lesson we shall need to learn is that we must be guided to the right people. We must ask the Holy Spirit, "Lead me to someone today. Lead me to the person who needs me out of the crowds I'll meet."

A minister made a New Year's resolution to speak to somebody, a stranger, about Christ every day. Shortly after January 10th, which is when New Year's resolutions begin to slip, he was sitting in his study at ten o'clock at night, and he suddenly realised he hadn't kept his resolution that day. What should he do? Due to the time, the streets were empty. Well, he said, "Lord, I'm going out to keep it." And out he went into the streets, and there was a policeman on his beat. Little did that policeman know what was coming. But the minister, determined to keep his resolution, went up to this policeman and said, "You'll think I'm crazy, but I've just got to talk to you." He did and discovered that the policeman was carrying a heavy spiritual burden and was just longing for someone to talk about it with him. Now as Abraham said to his servant, "An angel will go ahead of you and prepare the person for you to come and meet and talk to," so when we go out in the name of Christ we must claim the angels.

To believe that an angel could go into the youth centre before us, to believe that an angel could go into your neighbour's home and prepare the heart of your neighbor—do you see the divine pattern emerging? I want you to notice how tactful and how delicately the servant spoke to Rebekah. He didn't rush up to her and say, "I'm looking for a wife for Isaac, will you come?" Just as we are not called to rush straight up to someone and say, "Are you saved?" But Eleazar tactfully, delicately, lovingly opened a conversation, and opened it by asking for a favour from the person he was talking to.

There is a method of evangelism which we neglect. Christ used it with a woman at the well of Samaria. He said, "Will you give me a drink?" Sometimes the very best thing you could do to open a conversation would be to ask for a favour from someone else. Have you ever tried it? It creates an open door. So, we can learn a lot from there and there is more to be said but I want to finish the story of Abraham in chapter 25. Crucially though, once you have seen the divine pattern it becomes clear that here is the pattern for our task in the twenty-first century. God the Father has told us his servants in the Holy Spirit to go and look for a Bride for his Son, Jesus. As we reach out in 2019 and beyond, that is what we are doing – preparing for a wedding.

Two final words about this. One is the constant spiritual telegrams Eleazar sent to heaven. All the time, he keeps praying and, above all, when he has found the girl he comes back to bless the Lord. There is no greater thrill for any Christian than to lead someone else to Christ. I pray that every Christian may know that thrill this year. I want you to know the joy. When you do, come back and bless the Lord and say, "Lord, you did it, I didn't."

The other thing about Eleazar is this: the pride and the joy with which he came back all the way to Isaac with the bride whom he had won. There will come a day when you leave your possessions behind, your money behind, your house behind, your career behind. There is one thing I would love you to have in that day and it is to look around the faces of the Bride of Christ and see the faces of people whom you brought into it. That is the greatest wealth that you could have in heaven, to know that as you look around, part of the Bride you brought to Jesus, the Bridegroom.

Incidentally, do you notice that he did not stop with finding her or getting a decision? He took her all the way to the marriage. It is not enough in our task of evangelism to go out and be content with somebody deciding for Christ. That is the beginning of your work, not the end. The rest is the long journey, which may be a very long and exhausting one of staying with them until they are with Christ, of leading them, of watching over them, and of taking care of them for his sake. Often that is the harder task in evangelism, and since many young people are prepared to try anything once it can be too easy to get decisions for Christ that are shallow and superficial. The harder task is to take them from that decision, however simple it has been, and deepen their relationship and walk with them, helping them to see that they get right through to the full glory that Jesus has for them.

Chapter 25 concerns this spiritual giant, Abraham. I have asked myself what made Abraham the great man that he was and have come to this conclusion: it was the fact that out of the three things that help us to be on the straight and narrow he had only one. We have examples from the past, fellowship in the present, and promises in the future. He had no examples in the past, no fellowship in the present; he only had the future. He had no Bible to read, and you have a Bible. He had no fellowship of a church that inspired him, but you have. He only had the future, and therefore he had to live by faith. When I realised this, I found I was ashamed of myself. I have got a Bible, I have got the encouragement of meeting for fellowship every week and seeing saints of God. Do I have as much faith as Abraham had in the future? Am I as sure as he was of things that I can't see? I have certainly got so much more opportunity.

This chapter sees a kind of population explosion. From one man, Abraham, came eight children and fourteen grandchildren. Let's look at Abraham himself first, vv. 1–11. We know that he had one child by Hagar, Ishmael. He should not have had that child, but he did. We know that he had one child by his own wife Sarah, Isaac. But now in this chapter we learn that he had six others by a wife called Keturah. It rather looks as if she wasn't a wife, she was a concubine. I know it looks as if he married her after Sarah's death, but in fact that is not implied by the Hebrew. Since she is called a concubine it is quite clear that he had her before Sarah died. So he had one child by Hagar, six by Keturah, and one by Sarah simultaneously. We are told that he had deliberately to send the other children away when Isaac came along.

Here we are left with one of the problems of Abraham's life: he was a polygamist; he had more than one wife. Many people have raised this as a criticism of this great man. Now I notice that though we are told he had more than one wife at the same time, this is neither commended nor condemned by God at this stage. Since God doesn't make a comment on it I think we are wiser not to either. Having said that, it becomes quite clear that God's blessing would only go through the one son that God had intended Abraham to have. Therefore, Abraham himself recognised this and gave all that he had to Isaac, who was the heir. He was not unfair to the concubines, he gave them gifts, but at least he recognised that God's blessing was going to follow the pattern of one wife.

I remind you that although God intended at the very beginning one man to marry one woman, this was very soon forgotten by men. Lamech was the first to have two wives and, therefore, by Abraham's day it is highly unlikely that he would have known of this. Not until Moses came along was monogamy declared clearly in writing to be God's will. I am not trying to excuse Abraham, but I think it very doubtful that he knew that this was God's will. God makes it quite clear that it would be through the child that he intended him to have that his blessing would go on.

"Abraham died full of years." I think that is a lovely expression. It does not just mean an old man, it means it was time well spent. I heard of a man of whom it was said, "He was dead at fifty and buried at seventy." Do you know what I mean by that? He wasn't full of years. He'd had fifty full years and twenty empty ones. Some people have seventy empty years, but to live a life that is full of years is a wonderful thing. Whether it be short or long, it is important that it should be full and that every moment should be spent well. "Then he was gathered to his people" – that means, quite simply, that people survive death. It does not mean that he was buried in the same grave, because he was not gathered to his people, he was buried with Sarah – only two of them were buried in Machpelah. He was not even taken back to his country, Chaldea, to be buried, yet he was gathered to his people. The thing I want to tell you now, which may be a great comfort to you, is this: when you leave your relatives on earth you can join your relatives in glory. You may leave some behind, but you are gathered to your people in the Lord and that is a wonderful comfort.

Abraham joined those who had gone ahead in the Lord. People don't cease to be when they die. The Bible is clear that we go on beyond death. The body doesn't survive death, but the real person does. That is an assumption that lies behind the whole teaching of scripture. That does not mean that everybody's future is good. It can mean the opposite, but it does mean that everybody has a future beyond the grave.

At the funeral, two sons came together who had not seen each other in years. There is something very human about that. At the funeral the relatives gathered. Some families never get together except for funerals – is that not a pity? But here were these two who came together, and they saw each other. Two brothers, and they lived miles apart. They were at the grave of Abraham but Abraham was not dead. God is not the God of the dead, he is the God of the living. Abraham lived, in fact, to see Jacob and Esau reach their fifteenth birthdays – he saw his grandsons.

But Abraham lived to see Jesus born at Bethlehem, because Jesus once said, "Abraham saw my day and was glad," and that was two thousand years later. Abraham saw him born, because Abraham is alive. It is this sense of the living. We have got to the end of Abraham's story on earth, but it is not the end of Abraham. He is mentioned again and again through the rest of the Bible over the next two thousand years as a living man, and this is the Christian hope for the future. I know that some have died, but they are not dead, they are alive in the Lord. They are just the other half of the Church – the Church Triumphant, as we are the Church Militant.

Now we have a paragraph on Ishmael – twelve sons by an unnamed Egyptian wife. Ishmael lived separately from his brother Isaac, and his twelve sons lived separately from each other. But the thing I want you to notice about Ishmael and his sons is this: there is nothing whatever in their story for you. There is not a single thing from vv. 12–18 that is of any help to you whatever today – except in a negative way, that there is nothing in their lives worth noting. They married, they had children, they built villages, they settled down, they had a job and they died, and that is all you can say about them. That is all you can say about godless people in the world today. They are born, they marry, they have children and they die. There is nothing in their life worth noting. There is nothing that inspires the next generation. What a waste of a human life to live like that, so that all that people can say is, "Born on such and such a date, died on such and such a date." That is all they can put on their stone. What a thing if there is nothing more in your life than that. But that is what it is to be a son of Ishmael, to be born of the flesh and not born of the Spirit. There are lives that are like roundabouts: you get on, you have a great time while you are going around, and you get off where you got on, and you have lost your money. That is life without God – meaningless, hopeless, empty, purposeless. If you lost all your money tomorrow, how much would you be worth? If you knew that you were going to die tomorrow, how would you feel about the life you have lived? Worthwhile, useful, fruitful? You can do more of lasting value in a few years with God than you can do in decades without him.

So we leave Ishmael, just history—there is no mention of God in this section. Why did God put it into the Bible? The answer is very simple: just as a brief warning that life without God is nothing – you are just born, and then eventually you die, like an animal. There is nothing else to record. You may have built a village. You may have had a career, you may have had children, but there is still nothing to record, nothing in God's sight that is of value.

But now we turn to Isaac. Abraham lived to see his grandsons born to Isaac. I can imagine Abraham with Jacob and Esau on his two knees. Can't you see that? Did you ever realise that Abraham knew them both? Perhaps you didn't, because Abraham's death is mentioned before their birth, but if you work out the dates, you will find that he saw them when they were fifteen years old. But Isaac had to wait twenty years for his children.

Every letter he had from Ishmael would have said, "We've got another son." There was that Egyptian wife, who seemed as fertile as anybody, and there was Isaac waiting, as the years came and went—twenty years with not a sign. They had begun to give up hope, and in fact they probably had. But remember that Isaac knew that he had been born in a special way and that his mother had been like this. So Isaac prayed, "God, you did it for my mother, you can do it for my wife."

This is how faith goes down the generations – when things come hard to your children, praise God. It is when things come easier to your children than to you that you can't pass your faith on. It was when things came easier to me than to my parents that I found it difficult to trust God. The tragedy is that we live in a generation where things have come easy, and young people are paid to do things that formerly they had to work to do. Thank God when he makes things difficult for your children because it will drive them to the God you had to go to. Isaac had a problem here – it did not come easily. So he needed to pray: Lord, you did it for that generation, do it in this generation.

Faith goes on from generation to generation as each new generation says, "Lord, you did it for our fathers, do it again." This is the basis of prayer for revival. You may feel that in England it doesn't look as if there is going to be a spiritual revival. Humanly speaking it doesn't. But God did do it in the 1850s and he did it in the 1900s. Like Isaac, we could pray, "Lord, you did it then; you haven't changed. Do it again." Isaac said, "Lord, do it again," and God did it again and gave him full measure – twins. That was the answer.

We read that Rebekah was worried because they were struggling within her, and she thought there was something terribly wrong. She said, "Why do I live? There is something wrong." Then God said, "There's nothing wrong. They are twins and they are going to be two nations and the older will serve the younger." That is the opposite of the human way of thinking. It is always the other way around in human circles. God has a way of turning our values upside down: the last shall be first; the younger shall be older. God's knowledge of the future comes out.

We need not spend a lot of time on the story of the birth and the development of Jacob and Esau. Suffice to say that they were not identical twins. That comes out very clearly; one red and hairy; the other—it doesn't tell us what he was like physically, but what he was like emotionally and mentally, quiet. These two boys were so different. Esau: adventurous, hunter, tough, out-of-doors type, a father's boy. Jacob: mother's boy. He is just the opposite to Esau.

Isn't it strange how out of the same stable you can get two horses so different running the race? Here we have Jacob and Esau, so different from each other. My wife and I look at our three children and we think, "How different they are in temperament." The point I want to make is this: of these two grandsons of Abraham, which would the world choose and which would God choose to have a blessed life? It is quite clear that every time the world has sympathy with Esau, this tough hunter out in the fields, this big hairy ginger-haired man. This man goes out and gets it, the man who lives a man's life with his father, that's the man the world admires — but God hated Esau and loved Jacob.

Why? There is a very simple reason. First of all, Jacob had a determination to possess things, which once it was directed towards God would make him. He was grasping things from the day of his birth. He was holding on to Esau when he was born, and he was holding on to Esau's birthright when he matured. But there would come a day when he would hold on to God and be as determined to hang on to God and get a blessing from God as he was determined to get everything else in life. There was a determination in Jacob to get what he wanted, and once you apply that to God you are made.

The second thing in Jacob that God loved was this: Jacob was a man who lived for the future rather than the present. Whereas Esau was a man only with an eye to the present opportunity — he was an existentialist. He would have said: It is the now that matters; it is the thrill of today that matters, not the promise of tomorrow which may never come. "Pie in the sky when you die," Esau could have said mockingly to Jacob. But Jacob wanted a birthright then. Esau in the Bible is described as a profane man – a man who is so profane that he grasps a plate of soup now rather than some vague blessing in the future. He is the kind of man who says, "I'm not interested in heaven, I'm only interested in my pay packet this week. I want a good time now."

That is Esau, and God hated Esau and he loved Jacob.

Jacob with all his faults, with all his flabbiness, with all his weak points, which are all there, was yet a man who would say: I'm going to see to the future, and I'm going to grasp it with every opportunity I have. So, he made a takeover bid for Esau's birthright and he got it. Many descendants of Jacob have been involved in takeover bids ever since. But when that is directed to God instead of just to money or to business, then that quality makes a man supreme. This is, in a sense, the height and the depth of the whole nation of Israel named after Jacob. When they give their gifts they go right to the head of the tree. They are at the top of almost every profession. You name it, you will find a Jew at the head of it.

But when that quality is devoted to God and a Jew says of God, "This one thing I do," as Saint Paul did, my, what can happen then. All that determination, that living for the future, which is inherent in them, makes them men of God. So Abraham died full of years and of old age. He lived to see two grandsons. At first sight one of them looked like a real man who would be able to continue the line, but God said that it was the second one, the younger one, who was going to keep the blessing and who would go on living as he had lived.

There would come a day when Jacob himself wrestled with God and said, "God, I'm finished with the other things I've grasped. I want you now, and I'm going to hang on to you until you bless me." And God said, "I bless you and I give you another name. I'm going to call you Israel, and from now on you'll be the father of the nation." The God of Abraham, and of Isaac and of Jacob is the God we worship today.

ABOUT
DAVID
PAWSON

A speaker and author with uncompromising faithfulness to the Holy Scriptures, David brings clarity and a message of urgency to Christians to uncover hidden treasures in God's Word.

Born in England in 1930, David began his career with a degree in Agriculture from Durham University. When God intervened and called him to become a Minister, he completed an MA in Theology at Cambridge University and served as a Chaplain in the Royal Air Force for three years. He moved on to pastor several churches, including the Millmead Centre in Guildford, which became a model for many UK church leaders. In 1979, the Lord led him into an international ministry. His current itinerant ministry is predominantly to church leaders. David and his wife Enid currently reside in the county of Hampshire in the UK.

Over the years, he has written a large number of books, booklets, and daily reading notes. His extensive and very accessible overviews of the books of the Bible have been published and recorded in *Unlocking the Bible*. Millions of copies of his teachings have been distributed in more than 120 countries, providing a solid biblical foundation.

He is reputed to be the "most influential Western preacher in China" through the broadcast of his best-selling *Unlocking the Bible* series into every Chinese province by Good TV. In the UK, David's teachings are often broadcast on Revelation TV.

Countless believers worldwide have also benefited from his generous decision in 2011 to make available his extensive audio video teaching library free of charge at **www.davidpawson.org** and we have recently uploaded all of David's video to a dedicated channel on **www.youtube.com**

TAKE A LOOK AT YOUTUBE
www.youtube.com/user/DavidPawsonMinistry

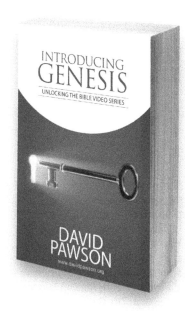

ALSO AVAILABLE

INTRODUCING GENESIS

IN THE
UNLOCKING THE BIBLE VIDEO SERIES

ISBN 978-1-911173-80-9

This book, following the *Unlocking the Bible* series of video talks by David Pawson, provides a concise, foundational introduction to the whole of Genesis, in which key points about major characters are explained, revealing crucial links with the New Testament – above all in the person of Jesus.

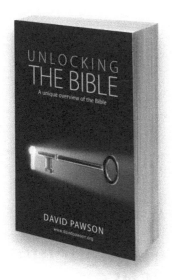

UNLOCKING THE BIBLE

A unique overview of both the Old and New Testaments, from internationally acclaimed evangelical speaker and author David Pawson. *Unlocking the Bible* opens up the Word of God in a fresh and powerful way. Avoiding the small detail of verse by verse studies, it sets out the epic story of God and his people in Israel. The culture, historical background and people are introduced and the teaching applied to the modern world. Eight volumes have been brought into one compact and easy to use guide to cover both the Old and New Testaments in one massive omnibus edition. *The Old Testament: The Maker's Instructions* (The five books of law); *A Land and A Kingdom* (Joshua, Judges, Ruth, 1&2 Samuel, 1&2 Kings); *Poems of Worship and Wisdom* (Psalms, Song of Solomon, Proverbs, Ecclesiastes, Job); *Decline and Fall of an Empire* (Isaiah, Jeremiah and other prophets); *The Struggle to Survive* (Chronicles and prophets of exile); *The New Testament: The Hinge of History* (Mathew, Mark, Luke, John and Acts); *The Thirteenth Apostle* (Paul and his letters); *Through Suffering to Glory* (Hebrews, the letters of James, Peter and Jude, the Book of Revelation). Already an international bestseller.

OTHER LANGUAGES

Unlocking the Bible is available in book, video and audio formats and has been translated into other languages.

WATCH DAVID'S INTRO
www.davidpawson.com/utbintro

WATCH
www.davidpawson.com/utbwatch

LISTEN
www.davidpawson.com/utblisten

PURCHASE THE BOOK
www.davidpawson.com/utbbuybook

PURCHASE THE EBOOK
www.davidpawson.com/utbbuykindle

PURCHASE THE DVD
www.davidpawson.com/utbbuydvd

PURCHASE USB
FLASH DRIVE INCLUDING:
- ALL VIDEO (MP4)
- ALL AUDIO TRACKS (MP3)
- CHARTS (PDF)

www.davidpawson.com/buyusb

THE EXPLAINING SERIES
BIBLICAL TRUTH SIMPLY EXPLAINED

If you have been blessed reading this book, we have more books available in David's Explaining Series. Please register to download for free by visiting **www.explainingbiblicaltruth.global**

Other booklets in the *Explaining* series include:
The Amazing Story of Jesus
The Resurrection: *The Heart of Christianity*
Studying the Bible
Being Anointed and Filled with the Holy Spirit
New Testament Baptism
How to study a book of the Bible: Jude
The Key Steps to Becoming a Christian
What the Bible says about Money
What the Bible says about Work
Grace – *Undeserved Favour, Irresistible Force or Unconditional Forgiveness?*
Eternally secure? – *What the Bible says about being saved*
De-Greecing the Church – The impact of Greek thinking on Christian beliefs
Three texts often taken out of context: *Expounding the truth and exposing error*
The Trinity
The Truth about Christmas

They will also be available to purchase as print copies from:
Amazon or **www.thebookdepository.com**

OTHER TEACHINGS
BY DAVID PAWSON

For the most up to date list of David's Books
go to: **www.davidpawsonbooks.com**

To purchase David's Teachings
go to: **www.davidpawson.com**

Printed in December 2021
by Rotomail Italia S.p.A., Vignate (MI) - Italy